Praise for OUR DOGS, OURSELVES

"If you love dogs, and even talk to them, you're going to rejoice at this entertaining and enlightening book."

—*BookPage*

"History, facts, and data are woven along with entertaining personal anecdotes and asides, allowing Horowitz's findings to be delivered in an appealing, accessible way that readers, especially dog lovers, will savor and absorb."

—*Shelf Awareness*

"Fans of Horowitz's earlier book will recognize the incredibly effective way she writes about dogs, adroitly mixing her own personal experiences, whether happy or heartbreaking, with broader questions about the bond at the heart of her book."

—*The Christian Science Monitor*

"Though grounded in extensive academic research, Horowitz's book speaks to a broad audience through personal anecdotes and relatable prose."

—*Library Journal*

"Altogether fascinating."

—*Brain Pickings*

"For a wide-ranging exploration of the human-dog relationship, including its perils and pitfalls, pick up *Our Dogs, Ourselves*.... [It] will make you see canine companions in new ways."

—*Science News*

"Alexandra Horowitz's masterful and witty biography of two intertwined species fully captures the profundity, joy, and absurdity of our bonds with our closest animal companions. *Our Dogs, Ourselves* is a treat for dog lovers, but also essential reading for anyone interested in our relationship with nature, and what that says about us."

—Ed Yong, bestselling author of *I Contain Multitudes*

"In *Our Dogs, Ourselves*, Alexandra Horowitz has achieved the rare and admirable feat of combining hard scientific information with a storyteller's gift of detail and depth, a gossip columnist's gift for eavesdropping, and a philosopher's work of making us face the difficult aspects of our love of dogs—all the time reinforcing the rightness of our choice to love them."

—Mary Gordon

ALSO BY ALEXANDRA HOROWITZ

Inside of a Dog:
What Dogs See, Smell, and Know

On Looking

Being a Dog:
Following the Dog into a World of Smell

OUR DOGS, OURSELVES

THE STORY OF A SINGULAR BOND

ALEXANDRA HOROWITZ

SCRIBNER

New York   London   Toronto   Sydney   New Delhi

Scribner
An Imprint of Simon & Schuster, Inc.
1230 Avenue of the Americas
New York, NY 10020

First Scribner trade paperback edition August 2020

SCRIBNER and design are registered trademarks of The Gale Group, Inc.,
used under license by Simon & Schuster, Inc., the publisher of this work.

For information about special discounts for bulk purchases,
please contact Simon & Schuster Special Sales at 1-866-506-1949
or business@simonandschuster.com.

The Simon & Schuster Speakers Bureau can bring authors to your live event.
For more information or to book an event, contact the Simon & Schuster Speakers Bureau
at 1-866-248-3049 or visit our website at www.simonspeakers.com.

Interior design by Erich Hobbing

Manufactured in the United States of America

1   3   5   7   9   10   8   6   4   2

Library of Congress Cataloging-in-Publication Data

Names: Horowitz, Alexandra, author.
Title: Our dogs, ourselves : the story of a singular bond / Alexandra Horowitz.
Description: New York : Scribner, 2019. | Includes bibliographical references.
Identifiers: LCCN 2019017043| ISBN 9781501175008 (hardcover) |
ISBN 9781501175015 (paperback) | ISBN 9781501175022 (ebook)
Subjects: LCSH: Dogs. | Human-animal relationships. | Dog owners.
Classification: LCC SF426 .H64 2019 | DDC 636.7—dc23
LC record available at https://lccn.loc.gov/2019017043

ISBN 978-1-5011-7500-8
ISBN 978-1-5011-7501-5 (pbk)
ISBN 978-1-5011-7502-2 (ebook)

For all the dogs who have been,
are now, and are yet to be

Contents

For the curious reader: Happily, dogs pop up everywhere in this book—including at each chapter's beginning and in the margins. If you see a dog in the margin, follow that dog (if you're so inclined): the subject at hand is discussed more fully in that dog's chapter.

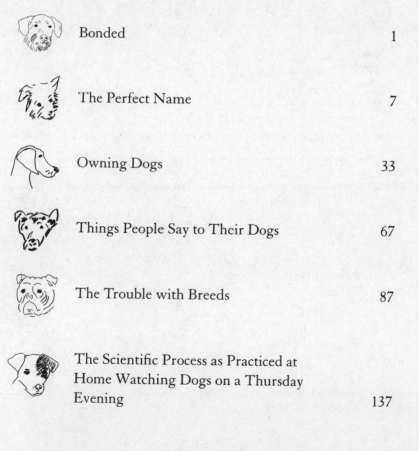

CONTENTS

Bonded

Once a dog has your heart, you are stuck: there is no undoing it. Scientists, ever unromantic, call it the "dog-human bond." "Bond" captures not just the tight connection, but also the reciprocity; not just the mutuality, but also the affection. We love dogs and (we assume) are loved by them. We keep dogs but are also kept by them.

We could call it the human-dog bond, but then we'd have our priorities wrong. The dog figures largely in the short-hand used to encapsulate the unique, symbiotic relationship between us and our pups. Most everything that the dog does serves to strengthen the connection: both effusive greetings and hopelessly bad behavior. The writing of E. B. White, who lived with over a dozen dogs through his life—many known to the readers of his pieces in the *New Yorker*—exemplified the humanity that the bond allows us to grant to dogs. When Americans heard that Russia was going to send a dog into space, White reasoned he knew why: "The little moon is incomplete without a dog to bay at it."

Or, it may just be assumed that if we're going to the moon, we'll want to bring our constant companions with us. They have been by our sides for thousands of years before we dreamed of traveling into space—before not just rockets, but every technological step that produced them, from metalworking to motor making. Before we were living in cities—before any of the recognizable elements of contemporary civilization were in place—we were living alongside dogs.

When early humans unconsciously made the decision to begin domesticating the wolves around them, they changed the course of the species' development. And, too, when each person makes the decision to breed, buy, or rescue a dog, we enter into a relationship that will change us. It changes the course of our days: dogs need to be walked, fed, attended to. It changes the course of our lives: dogs weave their way into our psyches with their steady presence by our sides. It has changed the course of *Homo sapiens*.

The story of dogs and humans has even led, in the twenty-first century, to the appearance of humans who research dog cognition. This is where I come in: my job is observing and studying dogs. Not petting; not playing with; not just looking fondly at. It comes as a great disappointment to those who apply to work with me in the Dog Cognition Lab that we do not keep puppies nor do we even touch puppies as part of our work.* In fact, when we run behavioral experiments—asking

---

* And it *is* disappointing: it takes great self-restraint for me not to effuse over a dog who's come to meet me, even if I must only refrain for a short time.

questions like whether dogs can sniff out a small difference in food, or whether they prefer one odor over another—any people in the room with the dog have to make themselves completely boring to the dogs. This means: no talking to, cooing over, calling, or responding to a dog; no sharing adoring gazes with or tickling under the chin of the dog. Sometimes we wear sunglasses in their presence or turn our backs should a dog look to us for any reason. In other words, in the experimental room with dogs we fall somewhere between acting like trees and acting inexcusably rude.

We are not aloof; it's just hard enough to see what's happening without being part of what's happening. Since the tools animal-behavior researchers use—eyes—are those we use for other means, it can be hard to tune them to see the behavior in front of us, rather than what we expect to see.

That said, humans are natural animal observers. Historically, we had to be. To elude predators, or to hunt prey, our hominid ancestors had to watch what animals were doing, to notice the appearance of something new moving in the grass or trees: it affected them. Their skill at watching was the difference between getting dinner and being dinner. Hence my job turns evolution's job on its head: I'm not looking for the newest element of a scene. Instead, I aim to look at that which we mostly ignore—that with which we're most familiar—and to see it again in a new way.

I study dogs because I'm interested in dogs—not just for what dogs can tell us about humans. Still, every aspect of looking closely at dog behavior has a human component. We look at our dogs—looking back at us waggingly—and wonder about ancient humans who met their first proto-dogs. We ask the questions of dog mind that we do because of our interest in the workings of our own minds. We examine how dogs react to us—so differently than other species do. We wonder what effect living with dogs has on our society, salutary or damaging. We gaze into dogs' eyes and want to know who dogs see when they gaze back. Our lifestyle with dogs and our science of dogs both reflect human interests.

While considering dogs scientifically, I have become more and more alert to the culture of dogdom. Dogs come to our lab with their owners, and though we are often only looking at the behavior of the quadrupedal member of that pair, the dog-owner relationship is the elephant in the room. As someone who has always lived with dogs, it is the very culture that I am immersed in; but I began to see it more clearly from the perspective of an outsider, wearing my scientist's hat. The ways we acquire, name, train, raise, treat, talk to, and see our dogs deserve more attention. Dogs can slip from being bonded to us to being bound by us. Much of what we accept as the way to live with dogs is odd, surprising, revelatory, even disturbing—and contradictory.

In fact, the dog's place in society is steeped in contradiction. We sense their animalism (feeding them bones, taking them outside to pee), yet enforce an ersatz humanness (dressing them in raincoats, celebrating their birthdays). To maintain the look of a breed, we cut their ears (to look more like wild canids), but squash their faces (to look more like primates). We speak of their gender yet regulate their sex life.

Dogs have the legal status of property, but we endow them with agency: they want, they choose, they demand, they insist. They are objects, to the law, but they share our homes—and often our sofas and beds. They are family, but they are owned; they are treasured, yet they are regularly abandoned. We name one, yet euthanize millions of nameless others.

We celebrate their individuality but breed them for sameness. In developing fantastical breeds, we are destroying the species: we've made short-nosed dogs who cannot breathe properly; small-headed dogs who have too little room for their brains; giant dogs who cannot bear their own weight.

They have become familiar, but in so being they are obscured. They have stopped being viewed for who they are. We talk to them, but we do not listen; we see them, but we do not see.

This state of affairs should startle us. Our interest in dogs is *as dogs*: as animals; as non-humans. They are friendly, tail-wagging ambassadors for the animal world that we increasingly distance ourselves from. As our gaze turns ever-more toward technology we have stopped simply being in the world—a world peopled by animals. Animals on your property, in your city? *Nuisance*. Animals you haven't invited into your house? *Pests*. Those who you have? *Family members*, but also *owned property*. Part of what we love about the dogs who occupy the exalted, final position is that they are unlike the rest of our family. There is something of the Other behind those wide-open eyes; someone unexplained, unexplainable; a reminder of our animal selves. And yet today we seem to be doing all we can to eliminate the animalness from dogs just as we are walking the human race out of the natural world, tethered to our phones, visiting our friends via screens (not in person), reading screens (not books), visiting places on screens (not on foot).

I find myself reflecting on the animals we live with—and on how they reflect upon us. I walk down the sidewalk with my dog Finnegan and catch a fractured image of us in the polished marble of the building we're passing. Finn lightly prances perfectly in step with my long stride. We are part of the same shadow in the stone, appended in motion and space by more than the leash that allegedly holds us together. We are dog-human. And the magic is in that hyphen between us.

The explanation for how that hyphen got squeezed between us is to be found in the myriad ways that dogs tell us about ourselves, personally and societally. As a dog researcher, and as a person who loves and lives with dogs, I aim to explore what my science tells us about dogs, about animals, and about ourselves. And, beyond the science, how human foibles and the laws of our culture reveal and restrict the dog-human bond.

How do we live with dogs now? How should we live with dogs tomorrow?

The Perfect Name

As we sit in the waiting room of the veterinary emergency center, a young doctor comes out in scrubs, his eyes fixed on the clipboard in his hand. "Um." The heads of the waiting room waiters lift, awaiting his next move. He pauses, puzzling at the paper in front of him. After a beat: "Brussel sprout?"

A young couple scoop up their miniature husky—who bears little resemblance to brassica—and follow him down the hall.

Our black one's named Finnegan. Oh, and also Finnegan Begin-again, Sweetie, Goofball, Puppy. I've called him Mr. Nose, Mr. Wet Nose, Mr. Sniffy-Pants, Mr. Licky. He's been christened Mouse, Snuffle, Kiddo, and Cutie-pie anew each day. Plus he's Finn.

We humans are namers. A child stares and points; we name the thing pointed at. *Doggy!*, I hear nearly daily when passing parents and toddlers on the sidewalk with my dogs. (*Kid!*, I once in a while say to my pups in response.)

No animal names itself, but we name animals—we *love* naming animals. Simply spotting a newly discovered species, minutely different than another nearby species, is occasion for a christening. By convention, the discoverer of a new species is given Latin naming rights: often, this is the occasion of much silliness. So there is a beetle *Anelipsistus americanus* ("helpless American"), a box jellyfish *Tamoya ohboya* (so named for the sound one might make upon being stung by one), a trapdoor spider *Aname aragog*, and a fungus *Spongiforma squarepantsii*. Misunderstandings and unintended consequences also obtain on such namings. The Madagascan tree-dwelling lemur called indri was so named by the Frenchman who heard the Malagasy call out "indry!" when they spotted it: he mistakenly thought they were naming it, when they were in fact calling "behold!" or "there he is!"* Likewise, the familiar bird native to the Canary Islands might be put out to learn that the name of the island is thought to come from the classical Latin *canāria*, of or relating to dogs.

Such sorting and specifying is not without merit: a species name helps us begin to see the animals behind it; to notice their differences; to consider their lives. But often we end right there, with the species name. A new bird alights on the bird feeder and we ask its name, satisfied when we've pinned it: *scarlet tanager*. On a safari, there are checklists—the "Big Five"—of the animals that one might see. Spot an elephant, rhino, hippo, giraffe, or lion, and it is captured, collected. We

---

* The Malagasy name is *babakoto*.

can pull "I saw an African elephant" out of our pocket for years to come. Oh, we might go beyond the name and find out the flash-card facts of the animal's biology: life span, weight, gestation time, diet. But the animals soon move on and so, for the most part, do we.

Too often names are used as substitutes for understanding: to see the animals but not have to bother to use anything but our eyes.

Still, I am a fan of naming. Not by profession: science frowns on giving animals names. That is to say, *species* naming is fine, but naming of individuals is not. My fields of study—animal behavior and cognitive science—are interesting in this regard, as they are based in observing or experimenting with animals. In particular, animals are most commonly studied not as individuals, but as representatives, ambassadors to their kind. Each "specimen" stands for all members of the species group: each macaque monkey is seen as a prototypic monkey whose behavior can tell us something about all other monkeys.

Having an individual name would work against this. Naming is personalizing: if, among the animals with genus name *Macaque*, each has his own given name, each is his own *person*. In the development of the field of ethology, though, what was seen as the "troublesome effects" of actual differences between individual animals on studying the species' behavior led to a change. Where a single animal's slightly unusual behavior—migrating late, lingering with a dead relative, capturing but not killing prey—was once seen as "statistical noise," the field came to acknowledge the importance of these differences, and began to try to track individual animals. But not by naming; by numbering, by marking—telling individuals apart via marks such as putting a collar on a tiger, tattooing a monkey, dyeing a bird's feathers, tagging a seal, clipping a series of toes off frogs or toads, or cutting a distinctive notch in the ear of a mouse.* Jane Goodall, against approved scholarly practice, did name the chimpanzees she observed, and named them fabulously: David Greybeard, Fifi, Flint, Frodo, Goliath, Passion. It is safe to say that the field of ethology was not immediately prepared to embrace a woman studying a chimp she called Fifi. Goodall has said she named them out of naïveté, not being aware that in scholarly research, animals—even chimpanzees, whose genetic code is in the greatest part indistinguishable from that of humans—were not supposed to have the personalities that may seem to come with a name. "I had no idea," she wrote, "that it would have been more appropriate—once I got to know him or her—to assign each of the chimpanzees a number rather than a name."

Since the time of Goodall's ethological work, research has come to take it as given that animals have personalities—and researchers have even studied personality, in subjects from chimps to pigs to cats. Individual naming abounds, but only on the Q.T., not in publications. We can see this beginning even with the formative Russian psychologist Ivan Pavlov in the early twentieth century, who studied the dog because of "its great intellectual development" and the species' implicit "understanding and compliance" even when being experimented on or vivisected.† Pavlov named his best performing

---

* These methods, most of which are still used, come with problems of their own: the individual animal so collared, tattooed, dyed, tagged, clipped, or notched often behaves differently because of it. Marks have been seen to disrupt normal feeding, territory securing, or migratory behavior, and some mothers reject tagged young. Researchers now work to decrease problems, including damage from the stress of handling and short-term consequences from anesthesia, or, in the long term, the energetic cost of dealing with the increased weight of the mark (considerable for, say, a young bird), which can be fatal.

† As contrasted to cats, which he thought "such impatient, loud, malicious animals." Clever cats.

dog Druzhok—"little friend" or "buddy" in Russian—and experimented on Druzhok for three years. These experiments included separating Druzhok's esophagus from his stomach and inserting an "isolated sac" for consumed food, in order to examine his secretions at the sight of food. Every surgery was done without anesthesia, which Pavlov thought blunted normal behavior and thus should be avoided. Though Pavlov conceded that, by virtue of their sensitivity and closeness to humans, a dog is "almost a participant" in the experiment on himself, Druzhok, like the others, became critically ill and died directly as a result of Pavlov's surgeries, pokings, and proddings.

The field of psychology owes much to Pavlov's discoveries. It doesn't, however, know Druzhok, who remained unidentified in public view. Druzhok was not named or acknowledged in Pavlov's 1927 book, *Conditioned Reflexes*, which relates many of his experimental findings. Readers can find mention of "the animal," "the dog," "this dog," "the excitable dog," dogs No. 1, 2, and 3, even "our dogs." But no little friend.

In contemporary neuroscience labs studying primates, the animals are also named, privately. Often, as anthropologist Lesley Sharp has shown, monkeys in a study are named in a fanciful, affecting way—after the princesses from Disney movies, or after Greek gods. Some are named half inspirationally, half ironically—as the primates in one laboratory named after Nobel Prize–winning scientists. Pet names are also used: "Spartacus" may also be "Jamie's monkey," or, because he's a finger biter, "Ratfink." Though it is usually a bioengineer or supervising postdoc who gets to name the subjects, even the head of a lab, the Principal Investigator, will use the name—within the lab. "You're never allowed to use the name of a monkey in a public forum, or in a publication," Sharp says, noting that, nonetheless, it's not unusual for labs to have memorials for the animals who they eventually have used up and killed, in the form of plaques or memory gardens.

But what of the dogs? I hear you asking me. There are countless dogs in neuroscience, psychology, and medical studies who live their lives in labs. The dogs may have names to the lab workers, but in publications they are identified only by sex, age, or breed (often "beagle"). But not in my lab. My own Dog Cognition Lab studies a topic that would not have been even a twinkle in Pavlov's grandson's eye—but that counts on the same cooperativeness and subject complaisance that Pavlov counted on. I don't keep dogs: my subjects live with their owners, and only meet me for the purposes of doing a study. They are all owned, and they are all named. In studies at our lab—which sometimes take place at a doggie day care or training gym after hours, the owner's home, or a local park—we call the dogs by their names. Certainly one can reasonably infer that these dogs also understand their names. By six months of age, human infants can recognize speech sounds enough to start to disentangle their names from the other words that are spoken around them. They are still very much pre-verbal, and cognitively not as advanced as most dogs. For a dog, a name, said repeatedly over days and weeks, becomes the sound that lets your dog know that you are talking to her. They know.

In many of the dog-cognition publications, the dogs' names make it in. It's the only animal research I know of where this regularly occurs.* Indeed, some reviewers—the other scientists who anonymously read a submitted paper for a jour-

---

* We now know that named animals might out-perform unnamed animals: in one study, farms that named cows yielded 258 liters more milk per lactation period than farms where they didn't call cows by name—presumably because of the positive effect of being treated with respect.

nal and give recommendations on its acceptance, revision, or rejection—call for names to be added, if they're absent. And it is in this way that we know that subjects in Vienna, Austria, participating in a study on dogs' ability to follow an owner pointing to food were named Akira, Archimedes, Nanook, and Schnackerl. Max, Missy, Luca, and Lily were there; good dogs named French, Cash, and Sky. In Germany, researchers asked Alischa, Arco, and Aslan to complete a visual perspective-taking task, testing their ability to sneak a bit of forbidden food when a barrier blocks a person from seeing them. Lotte, Lucy, Luna, and Lupo completed this one. In England, Ashka, Arffer, Iggy, and Ozzie. Pippa, Poppy, Whilma, Zippy.

In 2013, our lab in New York City recruited participants to take on the serious business of trying to sniff out which of two covered plates contained a larger quantity of hot dogs. I don't want to tell you who could do it, but I'm just saying: we could nearly make a complete alphabet of hot-dog sniffers ready to turn professional: A.J., Biffy, Charlie, Daisy, Ella, Frankie, Gus, Horatio, Jack (and Jackson), Lucy (times three), Merlot, Olive (and two Olivers and an Olivia), Pebbles, Rex, Shane, Teddy (and Theo and Theodore), Wyatt, Xero, and Zoey.* In that same year, it should be known, three of the dogs' names (Madison, Mia, and Olivia) were among the most popular (human) baby names in the metropolis.

Of course all the dogs have names. "Without names," one of my academic colleagues has said of dogs, "they're not persons." By contrast, non-pet dogs, kept for other purposes,

---

* And Allie, Amber, Anouk, Asia, Bailey, Batman, Clyde, Dakota, Dipper, Duffy, Ellis, Fern, Fina, Frankie, Grayson, Harris, Hennrey, Henry, Hudson, Jake, other Jake, Joey, Leila, Madison, Maebe, Maggie, Marlow, two Mias, Mojo, Monty, Mugsy, Porter, Rex, River, Sadie Alexandra, Scooter, Shakey, Shelby, Stitch Casbar, Walter, Webster, Wilbur, and Wilson: you are not forgotten.

may not be called by names. Racing greyhounds have formal, fancy names in the programs which are rarely used; in racing they are but a number on their flank, as muzzles are strapped on their faces. Few dogs in our society will be named "Dog"; "Mister Dog," maybe. "Dog" is the name of a species; to name the one who you invite into your home is to personalize the dog. And one of the first things we do—one of the first steps in adding a member of your family—is to name them.

• • •

Like bringing a baby home, a new dog, whether a wobble-headed, wiggly puppy or a wide-eyed re-homed adult, obliges that you adopt new habits. Unlike bringing a baby home, these habits include adjusting where you can safely leave a partly eaten sandwich, and rising early to step outside for toileting. From the first day you take the pup out, you will find that not only have you added a family member, you have added a strange attracting device to your person. For taking a puppy outside on a walk is the social equivalent of carrying a tray of warm brownies and wearing a "Please help me, I made too many delicious brownies" sign around your neck: you are no longer alone on the sidewalk. A person walking a dog is approachable, susceptible to engagement, and, research suggests, considered more attractive than a person without. Many a (human) friendship has been forged via talking to the dog at the end of someone's leash—whether the talker has a dog themselves or not.

 "What's her name?" is the most common query to a dog owner, right up there with *"how old is she?"* and *"what's his breed?"* No answer will truly get to the heart of anything remotely important about the dog, for the purpose of the interaction. But the name does seem to be a signifier of

something. It bespeaks of the namer, certainly. And it may enable further dog-mediated conversation, if I elaborate: *"It's really Finnegan Begin-again the Third . . ."*

But rarely, in the US at least, does the dog's name have to do with how I feel about the stranger on the street. Not so in parts of Africa. The Baatombu of Benin, in western Africa, give their dogs particular names so as to indirectly communicate with their neighbors. Dogs can be given proverbial names—taken from familiar proverbs—as a strategy to perform what are called "face-threatening acts" to another person in the community. Among the Baatombu, it is shameful to confront another person to his face, but it is not uncommon to have a dispute with the behavior of another person. Should a dog owner feel that his neighbor owes him payment for a service, he may give his puppy a name that is the beginning of a proverb meaning "When goodness is overdue, the idiot has forgotten." Then, when the neighbor owing the payment comes by, "the master may spot the neighbor at whom the name is directed, and purposefully call his dog just at that moment"—thereby speaking to and chastising his neighbor, without ever needing to look at or address him. A dog named "Ya duura," called slyly when the neighbor comes into sight, warns "What you have sown." In both cases, any open confrontation is avoided; but the person chastised—via the dog—is now publicly accused, and must face whatever reprehensible wrong they have performed. At times, the person addressed via the puppy may then themselves go and get ahold of a new puppy—and give her a name by way of response. Conceivably, many puppies could be taken in and named for a particularly contentious dispute.

This proverbial naming strategy is an open secret, sufficiently so that if the village's local "elderly men, sitting under the palaver tree" hear that a new puppy has been named, "it will become the subject of their talk." Among other African tribes, dog names are used specifically to enable a person of inferior status to stand up to a superior—something they cannot do directly. Unlike encounters on the streets of Manhattan, the dog is used so that the people do not have to speak to each other.

I begin to imagine the proverbial names that could be wielded in my daily encounters with some of the 1.6 million inhabitants of this small northeastern island where I live. Just today I could have found use for the old proverb, "The elevator is not for your exclusive personal use," had I given my dog that name instead of "Upton." Last night, a dog named "He who plays music loudly after midnight may be loudly awakened by his neighbors early the next morning" would have prevented any vengeful Rachmaninoff playing at dawn.

• • •

If popularity serves as a recommendation, you should definitely name your dog Max or Bella. For these have been among the top dog names for the last several years running in my neck of the woods. Should you want to go further afield, there's advice aplenty. I have been asked about tips for naming dogs for just about as long as I've been studying dogs. It's one place that some would like certainty: surely there must be a name that will make the dog perfect—perfectly sweet, polite, obedient. What to name your dog has not verily been a subject of *science*, per se—and I hope it never will be. Species naming is scientific; your dog's name should be your affair (perhaps with the input of your dog). This is not to say that professed dog experts haven't weighed in on the matter. The name should be short, one veterinarian suggests. Others extol non-human names. It should be distinct from other words you might want to give meaning to, like "sit" and "walk" (rarely does one meet a dog named Mitt or Smitt, Chalk or Squawk). Should end with an *O*. End with an *A*. Definitely, absolutely end with an *E* or *Y*. Eventually, even I sallied forth with some ostensive professional wisdom: simply reminding people that they'd better pick a name they are happy saying many, many times.

These instructions are perfectly sensible and fine, but unnecessary in the extreme. Still, such advice has evidently been readily given out since at least the time of Xenophon, in 400 BCE, who counseled "short names" that can be shouted out. That he finds the names "Spigot," "Bubbler," and "Audacious" acceptable should go into our consideration of his recommmendations.* I wish I'd met the dogs thereby named "Topsy-Turvy," "Much Ado," and "Gladsome." Alexander the Great named his dog Peritas (meaning January), and named a conquered city after the valued dog. From Ovid we have the names of Actaeon's dogs (who, the myth goes, tore him to pieces), including Aello (Whirlwind), Arcas (Bear), and Laelaps (Storm). The collars of dogs in medieval funeral effigies held names like Jakke, Bo, Parceval, and Dyamant. Chaucer gave us Colle, Talbot, and Gerland in the "Nun's Priest's Tale." Recommended names for hunting dogs of the Middle Ages included Nosewise, Smylfeste, and, ironically, Nameles.

By the 1870s the question of the naming of dogs was of sufficient moment that an opinion piece could be quasi satirical on the topic, declaiming that a dog's name "should hold, as it were, implicitly in itself all the elements for a conversation

---

* In Greek, *Styrax*, *Bryas*, and *Hybris*—which have also been translated as Spike, Lively, and Riot.

with (the dog) on its character." So a poodly mutt called "Frantic Scrabbler" could be either "Frantic," "Scrabbler," or "F. Scrabbler," enabling different sorts of conversations. Sporting newspapers ran a "Names claimed" section: lists of dog names and provenance for the record. On August 19, 1876, a man named Carl claimed "the name of Rock, for my field trial setter out of J. W. Knox's Dimple, by his Belton." Dudley, Rattler, and Beauty were also claimed that day. In 1888, one foxhound fancier detailed instructions for naming: names should always be two- or three-syllable names, "accentuated on the first syllable."* Moreover, they need be "euphonious and well-sounding words, which come freely from the tongue when uttered in the loudest voice."

Today, only the American Kennel Club, the organizing body for registered pedigreed dogs, proposes—and enforces—serious rules of naming. Should you want to register your purebred dog, the AKC has some news for you. You can't name the dog Champion, Champ, Dam, or Sire; nor Mr. Dachshund, Mme Whippet, or any breed name. Your name must top out at thirty-six characters, spaces included: exactly the length of *Frantic Scrabbler o' American Kennel*, except that apostrophes and kennel names are verboten. (You can pay ten dollars more and write out "of the.") No Roman numerals, no obscenities, no umlauts. And if thirty-seven other dogs have, in the history of naming, been named your dog's prospective name, you are out of luck.

Still, a goodly number of unusual names have been given to dogs over the years. Browsing an AKC stud book—the

---

* In American English, as your ear probably knows intuitively, most di- and trisyllabic names have an emphasis on the first syllable, so this is not much of a requirement. Longer names, by contrast, rarely emphasize the first syllable, as phonological rules prohibit a word ending with three unstressed syllables in a row.

complete listing of registered dogs—from 1922, I came across
the Pekingese section. At the time, naming your dog Chee
Kee, Chinky of Foo, Chumy chum, Clang clang, Lao tze, or
Yum-yum of wee kee was apparently considered perfectly
okay. This moment of oblivious offensiveness marks something of an odd spot in naming history, though. Names have
changed character, but most are functional, descriptive, and
good-hearted. A 1706 book on hunting hounds includes those
named Bonny, Caesar, Darling, Fuddle, and Gallant. George
Washington had a Dalmatian named Madame Moose, a New-
foundland named Gunner, and spaniels Pilot, Tipsy, and Old
Harry for hunting; the house dogs were Chole, Pompey, and
Frish. Nineteenth-century foxhounds named Captain, Tick-
ler, Knowledge, and Light are recorded; there was a Chase,
various Rifles, and even a Fox. At about the same time, Mark
Twain kept dogs named I Know, You Know, and Don't
Know. The favorite dogs of Sir Walter Scott and Lord Byron
were Maida and Boatswain, respectively. Nineteenth-century
children's magazines give a glimpse of the naming of the time,
with letters and stories about dogs named Bess and Blinky;
Jack, Jumbo, and Joe; Towser, Spry, and Sport. The *Louis-
ville Courier-Journal* of 1875 lists Jack, Jip, Carlo, Fido, Major,
and Rover as some of the most popular names among locally
licensed dogs (with at least one Bunkum, Squiz, and Duke of
Kent represented); the *Chicago Times-Herald* in 1896 found
a Peter Kelley, Rum Punch, and Billy Sykes living on the
South Side. Among the pedigree English setters listed at the
time of the first dog show in Chicago in 1874 were an Adonis,
Afton, Arron, two Bangs, a Baron Peg, and a Gooenough [sic].
Human nicknames were used for pets, and once in a while
dogs were even given the surnames of their owners.

While these sources are glimpses into dog names, Hartsdale Pet Cemetery, a thirty-five-minute drive from New York City, functions as a five-acre monument to them. It began as a dog cemetery in 1896, when a friend of the owner of the land was looking for a place to bury her beloved and expired dog.* It now houses all manner of pets, including chickens, monkeys, and one pet lion—as well as several hundred pet owners who asked to be cremated and buried by their pet's plot. The cemetery resembles a human cemetery scaled down: ornate iron gates opening to fields of tombstones of all sizes and varying levels of extravagance, some topped with a pebble or decorated with clutches of flowers; only the plots are smaller. And the tens of thousands of stones are engraved: amazing evidence, to anthropologists like UC Berkeley's Stanley Brandes, who has studied the cemetery, of the changing place of pets in the home. As he reports, over time, more and more inscriptions allude to the place of the deceased animal in the family, including giving the pet the owner's surname, and referring to the surviving owners as the pet's *mom* or *dad*. Even religious identity is extended to pets, who have "Gone to Eternal Rest," are "In God's Care," or have Stars of David decorating their stones.

The earliest gravestones sometimes have no name at all, or mention "my pet." But before long there are dogs named Brownie and Bunty and Boogles, Rags and Rex, Punch and Pippy commemorated. Short of one pet (species unknown) named "Robert Burns," the majority of the names until the 1930s were not human names. Nor are they gendered names: Teko and Snap may be male or female; perhaps it didn't matter much to their owners. But after World War II, many more

* Though her request inspired the land owner to create the cemetery for similar bereaved owners and their deceased pets, the woman's name, the dog's name, and the dog's tombstone are all lost.

human names come into the mix. Sure, there is Champ, Clover, Freckles, Happy, and Spaghetti. But there also are Daniels, Samanthas, Rebeccas, Olivers, and Jacobs: peoples' names, and also clearly distinguished by sex.

Forty years on, in 1985, *New York Times* columnist William Safire posted a call for dog names and their naming stories from the readers of his "On Language" column. Over several months, Safire received 410 letters, some with just one name, others with several dozen, the letter writers having done neighborhood sub-surveys of their own. The result was a snapshot of mid-eighties American dog-owning philosophy. In that year, Max and Belle topped it (Bella came later, apparently), with Ginger, Walter, and Sam nipping at their heels. Apart from peoples' names, Safire lists cartoon characters as common, plenty of food and coat-color names, names ending in diminutives (like a large dog named Binky), and dogs named obliquely after their owners' profession (tennisball-retrieving Topspin, long-suffering lawyer's dog Shyster, and a sound engineer's dog Woofer).

Now, three decades later, had dog naming changed? I was curious to find out. While I do like a handwritten epistle, I suspected there were easier ways of getting the information.

I began asking dogs. Or, rather, people with dogs. All I needed to do was leave my apartment in New York City to encounter the full range of domestic quadrupeds and their people. By virtue of the convention that walking with a dog gives others license to open a conversation with you—about the dog—I began an informal survey.

Soon I ranged farther afield. One summer evening, at an exhibition of art made for dogs in New York—to which dogs were invited—I sent my son out with pen and paper to gather names from the dogs' owners. The sampling of names with which he returned, including Nashville and Tosh, was perhaps a bit overrepresentative of dogs who go to art exhibit openings, but our list was growing. Back at the office, I emailed the owners who have volunteered their dogs to participate in studies at my Dog Cognition Lab and asked for stories of How Their Dogs Got Their Names. Hundreds of names streamed in.

And then I hit the survey jackpot: Twitter. Rather, dog Twitter. I tweeted out a call for the what and why of people's dogs' names and, as the little twittering bird does, it caught the breeze. A political commentator with a million followers who also is an ardent dog devotee, Keith Olbermann, re-tweeted my call. Twelve hours later, I had two *thousand* responses. A few days on, I stopped updating the spreadsheet after passing eight thousand entries.

Should you ever feel downhearted or despairing, the resulting listing of names and origin stories that I gathered should be at the top of your reading list. The alacrity with which people responded to my request was the first indication of what I might find: of the pure, openhearted goodwill of people keen to share something about their dogs. *Let me tell you about my dog.* And rare is the story that is not funny, sweet, silly, or poignant. The collection of all of them mirrors just the fine qualities we admire in our dogs: devotion, cheer, unwavering affection. From the very moments we bring a dog into our homes, it seems, we begin pouring at them just what they are pouring at us; we begin treating them like kin from the get-go. They wag and lick and wiggle and gaze at us; we gaze admiringly back, minus the wag and wiggle. But in these names are sometimes that wag—that cheeriness, that care. You don't come up with "Stella Poopers" without a good dose of affection joined with mirth.

That many of the dog names are cheerful does not under-mine the overall emotional heft of reading this list: many sto-ries of how people named their dog are, frankly, moving. The moment of the stories comes out of their personalness.

So it is that I came to see an astonishing truth: in the US, naming a dog is done with as much, if not more, care as nam-ing a human child. Sure, I have a story of my son's naming. Pregnancy is nine months, I have to assume, in order to pro-vide the time for the expectant parents to read every baby-name book, heatedly argue about the unacceptable name that one's partner has suggested, and try out and move on from a dozen names. In the end, the name matches the person who emerges. There is a story, but it is not a silly one. It is given the gravity accorded to the appearance of a whole human being from between a woman's legs.

With dogs, on the other hand, there may be arguments, and there may be (I learned) baby-name books read, but the end result may be "Mr. Pickles"—and everyone is just pleased as punch about it. Your dog's name reflects, more often than not, something about you and your family—something you share, find endearing. The process of naming is itself part of the history of the dog that you are creating with them. Many of the stories are dense with emotional highlights; the resul-tant names meaningful twelve ways to Tuesday. A not-atypical story goes like this, of a dog named Rufus Marvel:

> *Rufus because we found him on Rufus Thomas' birthday. Rufus Thomas wrote and sang FUNKY CHICKEN. My last dog before Rufus was named Chicken. Marvel because Rufus Thomas named his son Marvel.*

And of a pup named Cash (one of four "Cash"s in the list):

*He's almost all black . . . and not fond of 99% of people, so
I went with "Cash" after Johnny Cash (and his black ward-
robe)! It seemed fitting because of his color as well as the fact
that my first dog was named "Rose," after the (Johnny Cash)
song "Give My Love to Rose."*

Rufus Marvel and Cash's origin stories hit on some of the
recurring kinds of explanations for how people came to their
dog's name. Many, many dogs are named for famous people
(Jimmy Carter, Harper Lee, Mark Rothko, and Tina Fey, consider yourself duly honored). Those people's sports successes
("Trick" for a hockey player's hat trick), song lyrics (the Kinks'
"Lola"), and book characters ("Paddington"; both "Watson" and
"Sherlock") also wend their way into dog names. Personality—
Sassy, Moxie, Hammy ("he was a big ham"), Pepper ("she's a
spicy girl")—accounts for some names; and coat color, responsible for untold numbers of "Blackie"s through the ages,
accounts for a goodly handful of namings still. The attempt to
connect a past dog and the current dog also represents a clus-
ter of namings. It is not uncommon to find, as explanation for
one name—such as Franklin—an attempt to coordinate with
past or present dogs' names—Faraday and Edison. Some dogs
are in fact given the name of a past dog outright—usually a
beloved, or first, or beloved first dog. This honoring doesn't
stop at the canid, though. And in this way there is a distinct shift
from the Safire sample of 1985. Many dogs are named for—and
expressly to honor—a person: a friend or, often, a deceased relative.* Grandmothers are well represented.

To coordinate the names of one's dogs, and especially to

---

* The Tlingit people in Alaska preceded us in this form of honoring: as Bob
Fagen described to me, "If someone doesn't have a child on whom to bestow a valued
personal name, it is permitted and not infrequent to bestow the name on a dog."

name a dog for a relative, is to treat the dog plainly as family. Consider the literature PhD married to a man whose surname is Hyde: she named her dog Jekyll, and their *family* becomes Doctor, Jekyll, and Mr. Hyde. Or the mother of Julian and Juan whose dog is named Jupiter, to match. Many dogs "take"—or are *given*—their person's surname, and their naming follows some of the same codes for honoring others who are close to us as baby-naming does.

The trend of giving human names to dogs is no longer a trend: it is the *way*.* In the listing of nearly eight thousand names, there are in fact many non-human names—Addendum, Fizzing Whizbee, Honey Bee, Oreo, Razzmatazz, Sprocket, Toblerone. (I should say *non-human-for-now*: one never knows.) But only one person offered an objection to giving a person's name to her dog (although in fact the name, Daisy, is a person's name). More common was the sentiment of "Donald"'s owner: "I love human names for dogs . . . HE IS NOT NAMED FOR TRUMP." "I always wanted a Lucy, whether child or dog," says Lucy's owner. Many future-daughter's names were apparently planned, and now, for reason of only-sons or never-had-children, there are dogs with the intended names: Zoey, Gracie, Greta, Chloe, Sylvia.† "I wouldn't call my kid Bowser, so why would I name my dog the same," says Silas' person. (The one dog named Bowser on the list is in honor of a video game character.)

---

* . . . in the US. But not all cultures follow suit. In Taiwan, for instance, few dogs have a Chinese given name. In one survey, the most common type of name was a reduplication, such as *mao mao* (furry), *pao pao* (bubble), and *qian qian* (money). What is shared is the affectionate nature of the names given.

† In forums on baby names, it is not unusual to hear that a name came about as an alternate, after a friend or family member preemptively gave the name to their dog. Few are happy about this. While the practice of naming dogs after people has proliferated, naming a person after a dog would still be aberrant.

All but one of the twenty most popular dog names in my sample are plainly human names: Lucy, Bella, Charlie, Daisy, Penny, Buddy, Max, Molly, Lola, Sophie, Bailey, Luna, Maggie, Jack, Toby, Sadie, Lily, Ginger, and Jake. You have to go down by leaps before you get to all the Peppers, Bears, Luckys, Peanuts, and Busters that are more (if not exclusively) *Canis* than *Homo*. Notably, many of these top names have spiked in popularity among baby names recently, too, and were not as popular when the owners were named by *their* parents. Thus there is no owner named Bella and but one person named Lucy among thousands of submitters—though both have made the Social Security office's top one hundred baby names every year for the last decade.

While there are clearly trends in naming, the singularity of the names bespeaks their idiosyncratic origins. Nearly three-quarters of the names in the list are the *only* example of the name. There is *one* Schultz, *one* Sonja, *one* Studmuffin (the world likely could not handle more than one Studmuffin). Given how charmingly convoluted the explanations can be for a dog's name, this singularity makes sense: a dog's mother's name (Callie) leads to thinking of California; add to that the dog's gray coat, leading to thinking of the California band Grateful Dead and their song "Touch of Grey"; whose lyrics include the line "I will survive," which when translated into Italian is "Sopravvivrò," which, simplified for pronunciation's sake, becomes the dog's name: Soapy.

What I find most becoming in these stories is the meaning poured into them. It is as if, when a dog first enters our lives, we begin the relationship by handing to the dog well-plucked bits of ourselves: the books we've read, the people we've known, the feelings we have about different chocolate bars and Harry Potter characters. If we have a partner or children, maybe each member will contribute a part of the whole.

He likes Zelda the video game character; she likes Zelda Fitzgerald: ta-da, Zelda dog. She is a devotee of the philosopher Stanley Cavell and the poet Stanley Kunitz + he loves (Stan) Laurel and Hardy = a dog named Stanley. Even if the meaning is sometimes opaque: "I wanted Marvin, my wife liked Oliver. We met halfway with Sherman," one person wrote.

Various other categories of names emerge after I've pored over the list for hours, my vision blurring and my own dog, Finnegan, looking at me with bemusement. Dogs in a family of neuropsychologists might find themselves named after neurotransmitters; a science teacher's dog is naturally a Nimbus Cloud; dogs whose environments are filled with the strains of music are themselves Timbre or Coda; be a dog of a chef, and you may be named Mignon. Let your children name the dog and you have just increased the odds that you are living with a Sparkles, Shaggy, Sprinkles, or Doodle Butt for the next fifteen years.

The dogs themselves are often part of the naming process. "She told us her name," some people replied; others called out names and waited for a response of any sort from the dog. A large chunk of naming happened because the name "just suited him," a category that includes my own bemused Finnegan. What I find most pleasing about this kind of name is that it implies that dogs already have personalities, prior to their lives with us, and we are starting out on the road to discovering who they are, name first.

Many declare that their dog "looked like" a Charlie, Monty, or Missy, or like another animal—bear, bunny, koala, fox, teddy bear (okay, animalish). A bouncy dog may be named after a grasshopper; a stout dog, Tank. A dog's toothless, peaceful, lame, or simply female character leads to names matching those attributes. A German breed may be named

Fritz; an Irish breed, Murphy. Through this list I learned that Krekel is Dutch for cricket, Tasca is Italian for pocket, and Saburo is "third son" in Japanese.

There is plenty of silliness in naming, too. I'm reminded of one of our research projects at the Dog Cognition Lab, in which we asked people to send in videos of their play bouts with their dogs. We reviewed them all and transcribed what dog and person did into long lists of behaviors, to gain more understanding about how dog-human play works. Though I was in the solemn business of looking at the videos scientifically, there were many lovely all-out, rough-and-tumble, giggly play bouts that made the whole experience gleeful. People succumbed to face-licking, howled like wolves, crept up sneakily behind their dogs, and generally behaved wonderfully half their age. Dogs inspire silliness. William Safire wrote in his *New York Times* column about the German shepherd he had named after Henry A. Kissinger (who made Safire particularly irate). "I wanted to be able to say 'Down, Henry!' with impunity"—and he no doubt got many an opportunity. There are dogs named *Stellllaaaaa!*; dogs named Irene (enabling "Goodnight, Irene"); dogs named *Luuucy!* (said with Desi Arnaz's mock outrage). Along the Henry lines, there is even a Damnit. Exclamation point implied.

That said, even with the frivolity, it is clear that most namers took the business seriously. Indeed, many respondents alluded to the importance of a name with "dignity"; others focused on a name according the dog the "respect" deserved. A few dogs pre-named by a previous home or shelter had their names changed, under these terms:

> *Biffy's shelter name was "Beefaroni", which we thought was cruel and unusual . . . (but) it looked like he was responding*

to "Beef." So we changed it to the more fashionable "Biftek" (steak in Turkish/French), which quickly became Biffy.

And others had their former names maintained, in order to not cause any more distress or anxiety in a pup whose life had already had her fill. Of Gordon:

It was the name they had given him at the shelter where we adopted him. We didn't want to change it and cause him confusion.

But the ultimate convergence of respect and levity might come from the final category of names: the full names with titles, slobbery tongue in jowly cheek. Misters Biscuit, Tibbs, Barns, Dog, T Bree, Big, Wilson, and Waddles are joined by Mss. Moneypenny, Mini Cooper, and Kitty. I so look forward to the day when I get to announce the canid arrivals at the ball.

I hereby present:

Macaroni Noodle the Famous Goldendoodle
Abigail Heidi Gretchen Von Droolen-Slobben (AKA "Abby")
Mr. Tobercles, the Magnificent Muttness (AKA "Toby")
Cobber Corgwyn's Gwilym the Red Rapscallion
Grover Nipper Leaky Puccini Fuzzy Muzzle Mucho Poo-
    cho Miller Shanner
Tchoupitoulas Napoleon
Sir Pugsley
Sir Franklin Humphrey
Sir Charles von Barkington
Baron von Doofus
Bubby von Forza

Doctor Frederick von Doom
Maximillian Von Salsburg
Otto von Bisbark
Theodore von Kíçrmíçn
Baron von Schnappsie
and
Dr. Pickles

• • •

Before Finnegan was "Finnegan" he was "Upton." We'd liked
the name, and relished giving it to him, but we didn't know
much about our dog yet. So we tried it out for a week—calling
after this small new slippery form racing through piles of
fallen leaves; cooing it at him while bending down for an ears-
back face-licking greeting. It just . . . wasn't him. This dog was
a *Finnegan*, and once we changed the name, it was clear how
well it suited him.

Five years later, though, we met our Upton. Well, he was
"Nicholas" at the shelter, and another name before that. A
grown dog with a goofy smile, no experience with leashes, and
an urgent need of ACL surgery, he had been returned to the
shelter from which he'd been adopted years before. We have
the photo from his first adoption, showing a sweet-faced long
puppy who we only would come to know as a sweet-faced tall
adult. This time the name took and we had our Upton.

Today, a dog's name, like the dog behind it, is no longer an
afterthought. The very particularness of *your pup* is matched
by the particularness of their name. In some cases the name fits
the dog, and in others, perhaps, the dog comes to fit the name.
In both cases, the name is a set of spectacles that zooms you in
to the fact of the animal's singularity. You begin to see what
it is that is specifically "Xantippe"- or "Teddybear"-like about

the dog, to notice their fears and pleasures, to see their habits and quirks. Some suggest that a name predestines a person to a certain life; the same may be true of dogs as well. For a dog is that paradoxical creature who is at once created in interaction with their person, and is also their own dog. When I imagine future dogs I hope to know in my life (and I do), I imagine their names. A dog gets her name, and she becomes one of us.

Owning Dogs

You own your dog. They are one of quite an array of items that you own, including perhaps: the chair you sit on; the car you drive; the clothes, watch, or glasses you wear; and this book in your hands (library books excepted: owned by libraries). To say that you own your chair is to say that you have absolute rights to do with your chair what you'd like. You have rights to sit on it, turn it upside down; re-upholster it in orange velvet; keep it un-sat-upon in the basement for twenty years; or toss it out. Your chair has no say in it. It cannot complain, sue you, or, for that matter, make any decision at all. Should you cut off its legs, or cover its seat in a plaid kaftan, it must simply suffer through it.

Weirdly, while we consider dogs to be family, not furniture,* the same is more or less true of your dog as your chair. Though dogs, unlike chairs, make decisions, feel pain, suffer when abandoned, enjoy rolling around in fallen leaves and snow, and presumably want to not be sat on or donned in kaftan, they also have precisely no rights in the matter. There are *some* constraints on our behavior with our pups: animal-cruelty laws forbid injuring animals and forbid throwing them away. The asterisk on both of these admonishments, though, is astronomical: harming a dog is allowed, if it is "justified"; so is throwing the dog away, as long as it's in the direction of another set of arms (such as relinquishment to a shelter). Even when cruel behavior veers into the criminal, penalties are remarkably minor. In the eyes of the law, a dog is a chair is a dog. And a fairly low-end chair, at that.

And the law does gaze at dogs. As chair-equivalents, dogs are treated more or less nonseriously when they come up in legal settings. In adjudicating divorce cases in which a dog or dogs are at issue between the unhappy couple, judges typically dismiss the case, and are fond of writing things like "After all is said and done, a dog is a dog." "[D]on't ever bring a stupid issue like that before me," one judge responded to the possibility of a pet custody case. "Go out and buy another dog."

In such disputes, dogs are "assignable property," and may be granted to one or the other spouse, along with all the other domestic possessions, under the "equitable distribution" laws of whichever state the dog (and the couple) resides. A five-year-old chocolate Lab is "marital property," the judge in one case says: "chattel." Seeking custody or visitation rights of Barney, a rescue dog, is equivalent, another judge writes, to "a

* Though dogs have their own kind of furniture: a genetic variation in some breeds leads to extra hair, especially forming a mustache, beard, or bushy eyebrows, which is called "furnishings."

34

visitation schedule for a table or a lamp." Dogs Gracie, who had a shoulder injury and cataracts and was eleven, and Roxy, both suffering through the split of their parents, were ruled the property of one parent only, based exclusively on the detail that she was the one who "harbor[ed]" the dogs most recently. Gracie's age, medical condition, or preference did not matter in the case, for which she was simply the property of a person.

In response to an application asking for "exclusive interim possession" of Kenya and Willow, nine and two years old, respectively, the judge assigned to this divorce proceeding observed that the dogs were essentially equivalent to silverware—and the application was just as absurd as asking for exclusive ownership of cutlery. Should a judge grant one party ownership of "the family butter knives," he asked, dripping sarcasm, "but, due to a deep attachment to both butter and those knives, order that the other party have limited access to those knives for 1.5 hours per week to butter his or her toast?"

One hopes that the butter-knife judge did not live with dogs himself. In fact, the effect of dog ownership on the judiciary is not insignificant. In the case of a young miniature dachshund named Joey, living in New York with his divorcing parents, the judge ruled that, "wonderful" though dogs are, his fate did not "rise to the same level of importance" as a child custody case. (The judge mentioned his own pit-bull mix Peaches as representatively wonderful.) Custody cases of dogs would be "a drain of judicial resources," he claimed. But he did concede that a brief hearing, not to exceed one day, should be undertaken to determine what would be best "for all concerned"—including but not limited to Joey—regarding Joey's fate.

Cases that meaningfully consider the dog's perspective are virtually absent. And when considered as more than butter knives, it is such contingent factors as the recent possession of the dog (who took the dog after the split), the original owner-ship of the dog (who impulsively went to the shelter or breeder that day and walked out wide-eyed with a new animal on a leash), or even who had taken the dog to training classes (where what counts as a "class" is undefined, and its usefulness is uncon-sidered) that determines the rightful "disposition" of the warm-blooded, slobbery, gentle, loving property. In the thirteenth century, one tale goes, disputes between two people as to right-ful ownership of a dog was determined by which one could get the dog to come when called. Even that would be a step up from our twenty-first-century legal approach.

Even before tens of millions of American households had a dog, the clash of ownership and family membership popped up in the courts. In 1944, a judge heard a case about the proper disposition of an unnamed Boston bull terrier, whose value was placed at twenty-five dollars, after his owners' split. In ascer-taining the dog's age, the judge waxed anthropomorphic: "it is apparent that he is now about to enter the mellow years when those qualities most to be desired in a dog are at their peak, and the natural springtime inclination to roam, common to all males of whatever specie, is on the wane." Despite this, the judgment found the dog's age and all other particulars of the dog to be irrelevant, since he was simply among the (ageless) property to be distributed from the previous couple's estate.

Admittedly, when the attempt to decree who should take possession of the dog is left to the owners, their testimony is sometimes no less incongruous than the law's treatment. One member of a divorcing couple in Tennessee claimed she should have custody of their Dobie-retriever mix, since she had, in her account, kept him away from "ill-bred bitches." The moral upstandingness of her dog was further exhibited by his attendance at his owner's in-home Bible study class and the owner's vigilance that no one drink alcohol in his presence. The husband, for his part, argued for custody on the basis of the fact that he had taught the dog a lot of tricks, including riding on his motorcycle—and that, for good measure, he had abstained from beer in his dog's presence. (The judge awarded joint ownership, only to have the woman abscond with the dog: she was found with the dog out of state—in a beer hall.)

Casually inserted in all of these considerations is the language of *ownership*. We own chairs, cars, butter knives, dogs. But is it accurate any longer to speak of us as dogs' owners, in the same way that we own chairs, cars, and butter knives? Or are we their parents—or, are they our sisters, brothers, uncles, second-cousins-once-removed? Are we their boss, or their friend or buddy? Are they our companions? Or are they only our *things*?

The law says "things"; my heart says no. And I am disposed to listen to my cardiac organ over the organ of government. If I consider the dogs in the room with me—really gaze at their forms, curled up on pillows on the rug, sharing the space with my son—they are clearly more akin to my son than to the pillows. Like children, dogs have interests, have feelings, and have experiences. Even if a child cannot articulate what she wants, we nonetheless think it is important to imagine and satisfy her wants; though she cannot be, clearly, responsible even for herself, we have responsibilities to her. So, too, with dogs. Dogs are unequivocally family—even if there is not a simple familial term to capture their relational role.

The inaptness of the twenty-first-century American dog's legal status as property is plain. Dogs are family not just to me but to the 95 percent of people polled in the US—to the millions of people who share holidays, vacations, beds, birthdays, and play with dogs—just as we *don't* do with our chairs,* however lovely a tone of green and how envelopingly cushioned they are (though thank you, my stout green armchair, for all you do).

Our laws, reflecting and reflected by our culture, don't express this sense. And thus dogs' treatment in the hands of the law is dissonant. Our society abandons, legally, millions of dogs to shelters each year. In fact it's not illegal to abandon your dog in the *street* in some states (though it is illegal to so abandon your old car). The bioethicist Bernard Rollin wrote that at the beginning of his career, in the sixties, it was not unprecedented for people to take their dogs to be euthanized before they went on vacation—as it was cheaper than paying for boarding.† Nothing about this act was illegal. Even in the nineties, living in a rural area, a veterinarian observed that one solution to the separation anxiety I was worried my young dog Pumpernickel was experiencing was to "put her down." This veterinarian remained my veterinarian until the conclusion of that sentence. Today the idea of ending a dog's life when it is expedient to the owner may be abhorrent—but it is not criminal.

The legal status of dogs actually enables behavior ranging from neglectful to inhumane. Though we claim to consider dogs to be members of the family, we are allowed to treat them otherwise. Certainly there is much less "vacation euthanization." But from their infancy we commonly leave them alone (a daily occurrence for most dogs); we fail to give them sufficient stimulation (leading them to find other of their owners' possessions to chew in their absence); and, in grievous but not

---

* If you bring your chair on your vacation or to your bed, that's on you.

† And there remains a phenomenon called "convenience euthanasia," as when a dog gets old and too much trouble or expense to care for.

rare cases, we abuse them, abandon them, or kill them.* Dogs' child-like status makes this treatment especially pointed. Not only do many owners see dogs as their children, dogs' ability to take care of themselves is child-like, at best: they are entirely dependent on us and must simply accept the life we give them. We take advantage of their cooperativeness to, in large part, ignore what we see as their non-urgent needs—or to dispose of them when they are inconvenient.

• • •

In my mind, the next order of business is plain: figuring out how we got to this paradoxical state, and how we can align the way our culture, with its laws and habits, treats dogs, with how we think of dogs.† Why is our family considered property, and how can we resolve this two-headed hydra into one with a single, suitable, head?

To do this, we go back in time. Our habits today spring from our habits yesterday and every day-before-yesterday. The incongruity of the dog's current legal status in a country where they are also dressed in hand-knit sweaters—and the sweater is more valuable than the dog—is directly traceable to the beginning of thinking about animals, and to the beginnings of our legal system. Our legal system evolved from English common law, which dates

---

* While illegal, dog fighting—starving, prodding, and torturing dogs until they will fight another dog to the death—is still widespread today, over a decade after NFL quarterback Michael Vick was jailed for his involvement in a dog-fighting ring.

† The paradox I'm highlighting is one visible in Western culture—in particular, contemporary American culture. In the Americas, there have been dogs living with and among humans for thousands of years—but the attitude toward dogs which has shaped our current culture came with the European arrival on the continent. I'll note, too, that the majority of dogs alive at this moment are not American; for the moment I will leave the puzzles of their existences in their respective cultures to people native to those countries.

to the Middle Ages, and civil law, which shows the influence of Roman law. Our use of animals is not re-thought every month, but plainly rises from how we formerly used them—as workers or recreational show dogs—with the pressures of our work and idleness in mind. Their ability to be "used" at all is traceable to early ideas about man's place among animals and the natural history of what animals are.

> *"Be fruitful, and multiply, and replenish the earth, and subdue it: and have dominion over the fish of the sea, and over the fowl of the air, and over every living thing that moveth upon the earth."**

Much of the Western attitude toward animals, legal and more broadly cultural, comes from the idea of dominion. The notion of animals being at the service of humans—existing for our use—still resonates clearly in today's laws. Curiously, as the author Matthew Scully points out, the next line of Genesis, after the famous "dominion" line, instructs humans to see the fruits and seeds of plants as "meat"—not those living, moving animals. It is assiduously ignored. Other sections of the Old Testament describe humans' duty to act responsibly toward animals: that "a righteous man regardeth the life of his beast"; even describing mankind's "covenant" with animals—"the beasts of the field, and with the fowls of heaven, and with the creeping things of the ground." These notions of duty, attention, and inclusion have not had the same resonance historically as the idea of dominion. We adhere to the word in one place and dismiss the calls for a broader reading.

As historian Keith Thomas has written about modern

---

* Genesis 1:28, King James Version.

England, even the tractability—the ease of dealing with and the amenability—of domestic animals was seen as evidence of human dominion: we can tame them, so we must be their superiors. In the eighteenth century, domestication was seen as good for animals: it "civilized them" and allowed their populations to grow. The language of the human master's "dominance" over dogs, as is often stated, evokes dominion again—and both come from the same Latin root.* The *Catholic Encyclopedia*'s entry on "animal cruelty" specifies that humans "may lawfully use [animals] for our reasonable wants and welfare, even though such employment of them necessarily inflicts pain upon them."

While the use of animals was given to us by the Old Testament, our way of thinking about natural objects, legally, comes from Roman law. To ancient Greeks and Romans, the world was designed for humans, and all law, writes legal scholar and attorney Steven Wise, "was established for men's sake." And by "men," they meant *men*—specifically, *white men*: women, as well as children, slaves, nonhumans, and the insane, were property that could be owned by men. Men had rights, and could be owners. Property did not and could not. Notably, Wise comments, the place of animals in current US law is precisely the same as it was over two thousand years ago in Rome.

Within this framework, philosophers (first) and then scientists (eventually) have considered whether those early distinctions between humans and non-humans hold water. Descartes thought so: animals are like "automata or moving machines," he held; they are not sentient. The dog writhing and howling in pain as Descartes and other like-minded folks vivisected them was a squeaky wheel, a broken horn, a watch whose spring had

---

* Per the Oxford American Dictionary, "Latin *dominium*, from *dominus* 'lord, master.'"

sprung. Kant, more than a century later, acknowledged animal sentience, but claimed animals were not due consideration, given their perceived irrationality and lack of self-awareness.

In the twentieth century, such blanket statements about animals began to be questioned by scientists. After Darwin proposed the now-accepted notion of continuity between species—"the difference in mind between man and the higher animals, great as it is, certainly is one of degree and not of kind," he wrote—the door was cracked open to imagine that human animals were just versions of animals, and one could expect to see our abilities reflected in them to some degree. In the last fifty years the question of animal pain (they feel it), rationality, and self-awareness (some show it) has been posed and answered scientifically. Alas, the law does not reflect most of what we now know.

Anglo-American law and Western culture before the nineteenth century have no consideration of animals in and of themselves: only as "things," as "man's instruments." The question of whether there was a better or worse way to treat a dog was not in the air. Dogs were not moral agents; they had a moral status "no different from that of inanimate objects," as philosopher Gary Francione writes.

Paradoxically, dogs were granted more agency than an object has in one case: when they behaved badly, killing or maiming another animal or a person. Such a dog was deemed dangerous, guilty of a crime, and was summarily executed. Per their status, though, the dog was not really thought to be the morally responsible party; the owner was, and was fined.* Owners of the accused breeds were made out to be "social

---

* Much the same still happens, in the case of a biting dog: a dog's act leads to their execution, and the owner is fined. In medieval times, a dog might be hung in public for their transgressions, after a public trial. Now we don't give them the trial.

deviants" sharing the "violent tendencies" claimed of ostensibly violent dogs. Likewise in nineteenth-century Britain, at the time of a rabies crisis, when any suspicious-looking dog was rounded up and killed, in case they carried the disease. Owning such a dog identified one as suspicious or suspect oneself, since people were considered responsible for forming their dogs' nature, especially when it was ferocious or dangerous.

• • •

As these notions of animals' place, use, and nature simmered, Western society went ahead and made a mess of animals. Cruelty was widespread. Dogs were not singled out for harassment, injury, or killing; all animals were cruelty's object. Dogs were pets, dogs were guards, but mostly dogs were just *around*—not yet specially *among*.* In American legal history, dogs made their first significant appearance in animal-cruelty statutes—but not before other animals had. Animal-welfare laws date to the nineteenth century, with early statutes protecting horse, cattle, sheep, and pigs from willful mistreatment. These took up from English philosopher Jeremy Bentham's conviction that animals' ability to suffer requires that they be treated humanely. He lamented that "on account of their interests having been neglected by the insensibility of the ancient jurists, [they] stand degraded into the class of *things*," instead of on equal footing with humans. He imagined that "The day may come, when the rest of the animal creation may acquire those rights which never could have been withholden from them but by the hand of tyranny."

---

* This may be said of many animals—rats, raccoons, pigeons, squirrels—considered pest animals today.

That day did not come in the next century. While at first pass it seems apt to talk of the rise of "animal welfare" in the nineteenth century, this descriptor disintegrates under scrutiny. Notably, the select animals were protected from being intentionally mistreated; but they were not protected from mistreatment at all. The first statute in the country, in Maine in 1821, made it a crime to "cruelly beat" cattle or horses. By implication, the legislature acknowledged that it was still perfectly okay to harm the animals otherwise: by laming them, say, or killing them. And so they were: lamed, and killed.

In 1829, New York passed a slightly expanded law, forbidding anyone to "maliciously kill, maim or wound any horse, ox or other cattle, or any sheep, belonging to another," or "maliciously and cruelly beat or torture any such animals, whether belonging to himself or another." That is to say, the law expressly allowed a person to maliciously kill, maim, or wound their *own* horse or ox—just as long as it wasn't by beating them.

In both laws, it is an adverb that does the thrust of the work. It is the adverb that defines and circumscribes the limits on cruelty: "cruel" or "malicious" beating is unallowed—but not beating per se. Similarly, only the "wanton infliction" of pain, "with no reasonable purpose" is unlawful—but not the infliction of pain at all. This mandate is nearly synonymous with the language of the animal-cruelty laws of today. The human-centeredness in the law is flagrant: perhaps it was assumed that the human financial interest in the animal would restrict the owner's behavior to the non-malicious.

This was a time in New York when dogs would be found wandering every city street, ducking under wagons, stealing food, and darting from human grasp; when horses moved people and commerce; when chamber pots were evacuated out the window and pigs roamed the streets subsisting off household garbage; when the city could be smelled from an arriving ship before being seen. Zoos held elephants in cages only slightly bigger than the elephants; horses who fell lame were often left on the street to die. Dogs, other pets, and wild animals were not protected at all. The protected animals were ones with commercial value to humans: farm and work animals. That said, the legal language was intended less to actually protect the animals than to protect the animals' owners from loss of their material possession (thus exempting the ownerless wild animals). At the time, dogs had no "socially recognized value." Dogs were dispensable, and could be discarded, stolen, neglected, or beaten.

Still, having a law protecting animals at all was a sea change. The advancements here were to begin to use the words "cruel" with animals, and to consider, legally, that some human behavior should be curbed. Eventually, due to the guidance and enthusiasms of diplomat and philanthropist Henry Bergh, who would go on to found the ASPCA, the law was changed and expanded; by 1867, it included all animals, not just those who were commercially valuable. The kinds of cruelty made illegal stretched to "overdriving" or "overloading," tormenting, and needless mutilation. Still, plenty of adverbial hedging about what counted as cruel remained: while causing injury "unnecessarily" or "needlessly" was outlawed, the ostensible "necessity" or "need" was dictated by the human actor, not the animal. So if an animal "had" to be whipped to make it move, so be it; if an animal were too sick to be useful, it could be killed. But the spirit of the law, which spread outside New York with time, made advances: the law included sections prohibiting the use of animals in fighting or baiting sport;* criminalized the abandonment of disabled, old, or infirm animals; and introduced requirements to not just avoid cruelty but to affirmatively care for one's animal by providing sustenance and water. At last, the animals were becoming the concern. The law mandated that dogs (and other animals) had the right to a life free of unnecessary pain and suffering.[†]

Oddly, it was only after these laws, in the early twentieth century, that dogs gained a legal status: the status of property. Before that time, only farm animals, or animals that were "useful," could be property, and so needed protection. In some states, the designation was long in coming: Virginia only began calling dogs (and cats) personal property in 1984. As with farm animals before them, the dog's legal status was intended to protect against *loss* of property: thievery of a dog was considered a real crime against the owner of that dog.

But as far as the dog is concerned, becoming legal property is not necessarily an improvement in stature. With their new designation, dogs became legally equivalent to furniture. Furniture that you cannot beat to death, but still furniture.

So current law does not represent a categorical improvement for dogs' welfare. Today's New York State laws—fairly representative of most states' laws—expand upon the early statutes in ways that testify to the bizarreness of human

---

* Fighting was still common after the law, and even reported on in the newspapers: "If there were any member of the fancy in the three cities who didn't know that there was to be a dog-fight early yesterday morning, it was because he was either broke or blind or deaf and dumb," the *Cincinnati Enquirer* said of the meeting between the dogs known familiarly as Thursday and Dan. (As usual, it was a fight to the death [Thursday's].)

† An understanding of what dog "suffering" might include has advanced considerably in the last century. An 1890 *Baltimore Sun* article noted that "The indiscriminate poisoning of dogs is not permitted in Baltimore. The humane way of getting rid of worthless curs is by drowning." Drowning was the method of choice for dog catchers in New York City and elsewhere for many decades.

behavior: there are now restrictions on tattooing and piercing your dog, prohibitions against keeping dogs outdoors in inclement conditions, and proscriptions against surgically cutting dog ears without using an anesthetic.* The primary sections detailing forbidden behavior toward dogs (and some other animals), though, remain nearly identical to the statutes seventeen decades ago. Any person who "overdrives, overloads, tortures or cruelly beats or unjustifiably injures, maims, mutilates or kills" a dog, or deprives them of "necessary sustenance, food or drink" is guilty of a petty misdemeanor. Punishment is a fine, of similar criminal gravity as swiping a bag of marshmallows from a grocery store: "the bare threshold of criminality," as legal scholars David Favre and Vivien Tsang have written. In that time, the cultural attitude about where dogs should rest at night has changed from thinking they belong on the street or chained outside to welcoming them under the four-hundred-thread-count sheets of the owner's own bed (or, minimally, on a monogrammed plush dog bed).

A newer category of "aggravated cruelty"—wherein someone, "with no justifiable purpose," "intentionally kills or intentionally causes serious physical injury" to a dog—that is, with intention to cause extreme pain or done "in an especially depraved and sadistic manner"—is now a felony. I cannot even allow myself to imagine the kind of behavior that counts as aggravated cruelty being delivered to any dog I've ever met. In New York State, a sentence for a felony conviction is just

---

* Looking at the anti-cruelty statutes is demoralizing through and through. For while they forbid people from keeping dogs in dangerously hot or cold conditions; killing animals sadistically; dyeing chicks to be sold as babies; electrocuting animals for their fur; selling disabled horses; throwing glass or nails with intent to harm animals; clipping dog ears without anesthetic; selling dog flesh or fur; and so forth, this is to say that each of these acts has been done frequently enough to warrant a law prohibiting it.

two years' imprisonment on the outside. Most convictions will result in much less jail time.

Notably, the language of the statutes—especially the modifiers ("unjustifiably") and specifiers ("with no justifiable purpose")—still allows for the cruelty, if humans think that cruelty can be explained away. Hitting and corporal punishment of a dog not cooperating with your request to "sit," couched as necessary, justifiable discipline, are completely accepted by the state. "How hard do you hit the dog?" the Monks of New Skete, authors of many books on dog training, ask in advising you to give an "unruly" dog punishment. "A good general rule is that if you did not get a response, a yelp or other sign, after the first hit, it wasn't hard enough." Courts have found that "willful" mistreatment means "something worse than good intentions coupled with bad judgment." "Statutes enacted for the protection of animals from cruelty were not intended to place unreasonable restrictions on the infliction of such pain as may be necessary for the training or discipline of an animal," one wrote. Only "an evil state of mind" shows malice, in this interpretation. Thoughtlessness, ignorance, neglect: all can be used to justify cruelty.

Moreover, the statutes spend as much time laying out the numerous exclusions as they do detailing forbidden behavior. Exempt from even aggravated cruelty charges is anyone with a weapon who comes upon a dog perceived to be sick or a threat: the dog can be shot (by the weapon-carrying non-expert). Researchers are exempt from charges in the context of scientific experimentation using dogs: one can conduct research with live dogs, which is, by all criteria, preposterously cruel. As long as the study is conducted "properly," it is justifiable, says the state.

Just as in the 1800s, animal-cruelty concerns in these laws

are about human use, not the health and happiness of animals. There is no federal animal-cruelty law.* Recently, the FBI did begin collecting information about animal-cruelty cases. But they are concerned not with the animal, but with the person who is cruel. For it is often the case that an animal abuser will go on to commit murder or sadistic crimes against people.

These statutes exist in the context of the overarching legal view of dogs: as property. Those who study the law, like David Favre, describe property law as fundamental to the legal system, because of humans' abiding interest in being able to "control, direct, or consume things." That urge leads to a simple conceptual division: to the law, things can be property or they can be persons.

Well, dogs aren't persons.

Yet.

• • •

The oddness of thinking of dogs as ownable objects pops up whenever there is policy and prose about what you can do with your owned objects. "Add a Bike, Pet or Golf Clubs to Your Trip," Amtrak, the train company, cheerfully suggests when you book a ticket. And by the way, your dog must be "odorless, harmless, not disruptive and require no attention during

---

* There is a federal Animal Welfare Act, intended to regulate animals used for research; and where interstate commerce comes into play, as with animals transported as part of a fighting ring, Congress has enacted laws. These do not amount to true federal cruelty protection for animals, however—and in recent years enforcement has dropped precipitously. As I write this, the House of Representatives is *considering* a bill, called the "Preventing Animal Cruelty and Torture Act," which would make it a federal crime—a felony—to participate in conduct in which an animal is "purposely crushed, burned, drowned, suffocated, impaled, or otherwise subjected to serious bodily injury" (with the exception of activities which inflict "customary" injuries, such as hunting, medical research, slaughtering animals for food, defending oneself, and so on).

travel"; and travel in a pet carrier on the floor or *under* your seat. This is a perfect description for how to convey luggage—I try to carry odorless luggage at all times*—but comically inapt for a living creature. "Winterize your dog," the *New York Times* writes, helpfully adding dogs to the list of objects, like boots or cars, that must be prepared for winter. The home-furnishings concern Ikea opened a dog parking area outside their stores in Germany (made less galling by their opening of Manland in Australian stores, a lounge area for non-shopping male members of a couple). The equivalence of the warm bodies and individual personalities that we know with golf clubs or vehicles is inapposite in the extreme. My bike hangs upside down, tires flattening, in a locked basement storage unit, covered in a layer of dust. My dog has just polished off a snack of scrambled eggs in our heated apartment.

Some of the consequences of dogs' status as property are surprising. Dogs can be currency. You can use your high-priced Labradoodle as collateral for a loan, because she is property.† There is not yet a futures market in designer breeds, but there could be.

Indeed, the dog's value as commodity—their breeding value—is high. The extent of the dog sale market is, as biologist Patrick Bateson observes in a 2010 Inquiry into dog breeding in the UK, "astonishing." Breeding farms can produce thousands of dogs in a year. In tiny Wales, a country of three million, nearly one thousand dog breeders are known: that's potentially a million new Welsh dogs right there. This density

---

* Except for my husband's cheese when returning from France. Sorry about that.

† This is not exclusively Western, nor recent. For instance, animals were a prominent source of capital in rural Egypt of the early nineteenth century, according to historian Alan Mikhail. People bought futures in animals, shares of animals, time-shares of animal labor, and sold and separated the rights of owners of parent and offspring.

would be roughly like having three thousand dog farms in New York City alone: thirteen hundred more breeders than there are public schools. The vast majority of dog breeders in the UK (and the US) are exempt from fulfilling *any* designated standard of welfare for animal businesses, including standards of veterinary care. Even those subject to regulation simply require licensing, veterinary care and disclosures, and a "lemon law" guarantee to take back a "defective" puppy. The sale of dogs is an essentially unsupervised business. As with all owned dogs, cruelties unseen by others' eyes go unpunished.

The government's assessment of the dog's value, once they come into your home, is that it is virtually nil (don't expect much collateral). The "fair market value" of a dog is a kind of replacement cost: what you paid for them. If you bought your dog from a breeder who overcharges for ostensibly designer pups, that might be a few thousand dollars. If you rescued your dog, it's the cost of adoption—probably less than one hundred dollars. On top of that you might receive back the cost of de-sexing, vaccinating, or training classes. In other words, the official "value" of the dog includes all the non-dog things about the dog. Against all intuition, "replacement" value does not take into account replacement of the *actual individual animal*: the Finnegan who looks at me balefully until I let him in under the covers at night, or who breaks into a spastic dance when he realizes we're going for a run. He is invaluable, which is not to say without value. I could not fathom a "replacement cost," but it would be decidedly non-zero.

Another consequence of being property is suggested by the fate of the chairs: they can be *used*. Millions of animals are used each year in the US for basic research, product testing, medical experimentation, and in classrooms. These animals are mostly rats, mice, and birds (which are not even considered "animals" for purposes of determining they have good welfare), but a nontrivial number are dogs. It's long been so. Although Ivan Pavlov is not known for performing humane experiments on dogs—after all, he operated on them without anesthetic—relative to the physiologists of the time, he was downright gentle. Claude Bernard, a near-contemporary, was a vivisectionist extraordinaire, of the kind who believed that experimentation on live animals as *spectacle* was appropriate. His university lectures on animal physiology often included a demonstration on a live dog, whose vocal cords would first be severed, after which Bernard would remove the animal's internal organs, observing the results, until the animal (inevitably) died. Bernard and his colleagues dispatched of countless dogs in this way.

How many dogs? Does it matter? Isn't one dog—a sweet-faced small dog with floppy ears and a tail that wags at the sight of a friendly hand reaching through the cage—too many?

There is one dog, known as "brown dog," vivisected on multiple times over more than two months before finally dying, who is memorialized by a statue in Battersea Park, London. The dog of the statue* is familiar: eyes alert and inquiring, floppy ears each flopping distinctively. Her fur, though rendered in stone, is scruffy. She sits awkwardly. She is someone's pet. "Men and women of England, how long shall these things be?" the plaque originally read.

How long, indeed. While the plight of research dogs may be well known, as researchers try to wrangle with their moral responsibility, other people have come up with a new and different way to use dogs. They've created an industry of farmed

---

* The second: the first was intentionally destroyed after protests about the statue and vandalism, including by outraged medical students who wanted to do their dissections.

dogs. Not for meat, or for animal products. But for their eggs, or their uterus: as players in the new business model of cloning dogs. When Barbra Streisand misses her deceased dog, Samantha, a dog of the Coton de Tulear breed, she can now do a business transaction—to the tune of fifty thousand dollars—to try to get a simulacrum of Sammie back. Ownership of the first dog translates not only into ownership of a second (quite unlike the first), but also into the keeping of numerous dogs. Dogs are used as egg donors and dogs are used as surrogate mothers in which to implant the denuded eggs filled with cellular material from the beloved dog. These dogs are behind the scenes, in the lab: no one's pet. They do not go home with Barbra. Countless other dogs are produced in the cloning process who are not viable, and die after a short or long time, or who are simply not identical enough looking to the original to be used. They are otherwise disposed of.

Or: maybe we could try not using dogs that way.

•   •   •

Round about April every year there is a convergence of weather and mind in the northeastern US. As the cold loosens its grip, jackets are left unzipped, legs are occasionally bared, hair is freed from its woolen-cap bindings. There is a lightness of step. Bright young green shoots, having plotted for weeks, begin their plucky journey through matted leaves, sprinkled with the detritus of winter. Children may skip; passersby smile.

And something happens in the space between the ears, too. As warm breezes catch that loosened hair and skirt hem, one feels a lightness of thought. There are *prospects*—one could finish that book, begin that yoga practice, free the closets and the basements of the burdens of physical objects no longer coveted. There are chances for *change*.

At the college at which I teach, the semester is ending, and I hold the last few classes of my seminar in Canine Cognition in an increasingly stifling room in a building made to contain heat, not to allow for free flow of thoughts. My students are wrapping up fourteen weeks of learning about the history, genetics, physiology, and behavior and mind of the dog, and I ask them to reflect on one thing more: the future of the species. What should we do for the dog? I ask. This creature, who observes our comings, goings, and in-betweens with reverence and attention; who we count on for emotional support, companionship, and even for our health—what ought we do for this species in return?

The room is silent. Maybe, a voice offers, we shouldn't have pets. Everyone groans. Eyes dart around, catching other gazes, confirming it must be a joke. We've all read about inherited disorders, the social and emotional abilities of the dog, their cooperativeness, our misreading of them: the dog as subject. We've studied the dog under the assumption that we will always be able to live with dogs.

Someone else pipes up: surely there are inadequacies in our way of dealing with even this favored animal that we can fix right now, today. Stop dangerous inbreeding. Don't leave your dog isolated and alone for most of her life. Learn to read the dog's behavior to find out when he's asking for something, scared, in pain, or confused. Everyone relaxes a touch. That's what we should do.

But what about that suggestion, made by a brave student and some others. What if dogs shouldn't be our property? What if we shouldn't own dogs? *Shouldn't own* because it does not befit humans to be leaving others vulnerable to suffering. But also *shouldn't own* because . . . dogs perhaps shouldn't be property, *ownable*.

Philosopher Gary Francione wants us to stop living with dogs—or, more to the point, to stop *having* to live with dogs, because we have stopped making new dogs. In his view, the abolition of animal use, including their use as pets, is the only justifiable action society can take, once we acknowledge the moral status of animals: that they deserve moral consideration. They become moral agents—animals for whom things matter—because we know they are sentient, able to experience pain and suffering. Francione believes their legal status not only ignores this fact, but contributes to its dismissal out of hand.

We have a "moral schizophrenia" in dealing with animals, Francione thinks, which is due to their status as property. Because animals are chattel property, the standard of animal welfare will always be very low. "It costs money to protect animal interests," he writes, "which means that those interests will, for the most part, be protected only in those situations in which there is an economic benefit in doing so." His way of thinking is that regulatory laws, like animal-cruelty laws, serve to solidify their status as property, as subject to our ("justifiable") use, telling us not to treat the dog with respect and without cruelty for its own sake, but for the sake of avoiding punishment. So, he thinks, we should no longer use them at all.

Under this view, we should not release our current dogs into the night, but must continue to live with them and treat them with dignity. Given that we humans brokered their place at the table, we have to allow them at our table. But to Francione, "nearly all of our animal use can be justified *only* by habit, convention, amusement, convenience, or pleasure."

While Francione's logic is sound, the result is grim. I feel a visceral rejection of any scheme that blanketly prohibits living with dogs. And I also worry about the kind of "un"domesticating that Francione proposes. If we erred in domesticating dogs and other animals, as he seems to suggest, should we feel so confident in saying what is best for dogs next? Not only are we not good at planning species' futures, we are not even that good at determining what dogs and other animals want now, when they are right in front of us.

Moreover, the abolition route would lead to, eventually, the extinction of dogs as we know them. I don't want to live in any world that has no dogs in it.

One might sympathize with Francione's outrage at the treatment of animals that being "property" enables, but see a different remedy. If there is a dissonance between family and property, why, simply change the property status. It is antiquated and no longer reflects the prevailing culture or science of dogs.

Proposals exist, and come in two flavors: within the present system or extending it. Attorney Steven Wise takes the former view, though he works the system by challenging what is meant by the terms. Wise is perhaps best known for arguing that chimpanzees should be considered legal persons. With his organization, Nonhuman Rights Project, he asked the state of New York for a writ of habeas corpus—usually used on behalf of the imprisoned, granting relief from unfair captivity—on behalf of a chimpanzee named Tommy, who is owned by a person who keeps him in a cement and steel cage outside a trailer in upstate New York.*

Personhood for chimpanzees—or dolphins or elephants or dogs—is not as peculiar as it sounds. To the law, being a member of *Homo sapiens* is not what makes you a legal person. Corporations can be persons. Limited liability companies, trusts,

---

* Three other chimpanzees, called Kiko, Hercules, and Leo, are the subjects of concurrent suits using habeas corpus.

consortiums, partnerships, unincorporated entities, associations, joint stock companies, or, in legal terms, entities "of any nature whatsoever" can be persons. Being a person means you have certain interests that are significant. It does not mean you are a person.

Starting with Roman law, "persons" had rights and interests; "things" were the property of "persons," and lacking any rights. At no time have only humans been persons (and, for too long a time, many humans were not considered persons). Even from Roman times, though, there has been confusion about the human/person distinction. "No rights exist as between man and beast," Cicero wrote, quoting another Stoic philosopher that "men can make use of beasts for their own purposes without injustice." Vagueness was seeded from the get-go about who or what was really meant to be the vessel of the rights. Wise sees an opening there. His approach first cites the demonstrated social cognitive complexity—and similarity to human persons—of chimpanzees. Chimps are, after all, nearly human genetically. And he takes advantage of the historical application of habeas corpus in disparate ways having nothing to do with its primary legal use. Its flexibility allows Wise to challenge chimpanzees' status as legal "things" that can be kept.

The courts have denied the writ.* Tommy remains captive. But in 2016, a chimp named Cecilia in an Argentinian

---

* In May 2018, the State of New York Court of Appeals denied the leave to appeal of the lower court. But in a concurring written opinion, Judge Fahey expressed concerns about "[t]he inadequacy of the law as a vehicle to address some of our most difficult ethical dilemmas is on display in this matter." Of the question of treatment of animals, he wrote that "[u]ltimately, we will not be able to ignore it. While it may be arguable that a chimpanzee is not a 'person,' there is no doubt that it [sic] is not merely a thing."

zoo was declared a non-human legal person and ordered released to a sanctuary.

Might personhood allow dogs to escape their thingness? "Throughout legal history," Christopher Stone writes, asking *Should trees have standing?*, "each successive extension of rights to some new entity has been, theretofore, a bit unthinkable. We are inclined to suppose the rightlessness of rightless 'things' to be a decree of Nature, not a legal convention acting in support of some status quo." In 2017, the Whanganui River in New Zealand was granted personhood. Shortly after that, the Ganges and a tributary, the Yamuna, in India, became legal persons.

•   •   •

Or, extend and revise the terms. David Favre has introduced the idea of "living property," which would be a subtler but profound revision. The idea of personhood for animals, he told me, "is trying to break down the wall," whereas the notion of living property simply removes "a few bricks" from the wall. It harks back to the conceptual division of objects as property or legal persons and suggests that to imagine all objects, animate or not, as fitting in one of two categories is limiting. While human beings fit nicely in the category "persons," it is unsurprising that fitting nearly everything else in the category "property" makes less sense. For instance, not all things are clearly the property of something else—for being property is a relationship between objects and persons. The sun, the moon, and the giant sequoia are not property of a person. Ah, but the sequoia might be in a national park, in which case, despite its having lived from hundreds of years before our government was formed, we have slipped the colossal tree into the property tent: property of our government.* Favre is interested in the fact that these divisions are human constructs, not features of the sun or sequoia in and of themselves. Given that, the assignment to one category or another can be adjusted—as, for that matter, can the categories themselves.

For instance, on that grand tree one might find perched a white-headed woodpecker (*Picoides albolarvatus*), which makes its habitat there. Is the woodpecker the sequoia's property? Plainly not, because property is owned by persons, and the sequoia is not a person. Is the woodpecker the property of the park? Potentially. But Favre makes the case that as long as it stays in the park, the woodpecker, who is in the control of no one, is more aptly described as "self-owned." The park's administrators may have responsibilities to attend to the general well-being of the woodpecker: protecting him from hunting, or attempting to maintain his environment. Similarly, a newborn baby, who is the full responsibility of her parents, is not *owned* by them, but neither is she quite a legal person, in that she barely has control of her own body. She may, too, be "self-owned." Parents will set limits, manage her behavior, and make many choices for her. She doesn't have total freedom, nor should she.

Here's where we come to dogs. Favre suggests that dogs might best be considered more like wild woodpeckers and newborns than like sequoias: as owners of themselves, even if they are still, in the law's binary view, property of another. Right now they are more sequoia than child. As magnificent as the conifer is, we think of it differently than the warm, furry magnificence nosing me right now. Our current "ownership"

---

* Too, there is a way in which saying that we "own" a tree that so precedes us is like saying the sun is "our property" based on our having set our eyes skyward.

would become more like "guardianship." The term "guardian" is already used in some cities—including Boulder, San Francisco, and Amherst—to better describe the relationship between human and dog.* The legal status only needs catching up with the name.

•   •   •

The first living creature I see this morning, before my husband or my son, is my dog Upton. Noticing me stirring, he paws me once for a belly rub. Across the bed, Finnegan responds to my sleepy gaze by rising, shaking down to his tail tip, and approaching to greet me. Both dogs linger on the bed until I am ready to get up; they follow me down the hall, offer me toys, communicate with the cat, check in on my son and his breakfast, and pursue their morning stretches. They will be part of our family's day. I spend the afternoon meeting new dogs—as subjects voluntarily participating in a study at my lab, brought in to this new place under the careful watch of their persons. Each dog arrives with trepidation, delight, or curiosity; cooperatively sits with their person; sniffs and examines what I show them, acting out their individual personalities; and, finally, looks to their person when they finish. I will end the day sharing a meal with my family—the dogs eat when we eat—and we will retire on the rug or sofa to read, play (Finnegan likes one particular small squeaky ball; Upton is currently partial to a stuffed pig), watch a movie, wrestle (Upton will joust and rumble with anyone as long as we stay

---

*I find this title imperfect, but more suitable than "pet" or the now-popular "companion," as widely used in the phrase "companion animal." (Yes, they keep our company—but they are companions who eat separately, are completely on our schedule, and must wait in suspended animation for us when we are away. Some company we are.) Some, like philosophers Sue Donaldson and Will Kymlicka, argue that domestic animals might, alternately, be extended *citizenship*, with its accompanying rights.

on the red rug; Finnegan is more of a bench player, coming in only when the activity is heated), or just sit, in contact with each other (Finnegan will want to be closest).

With this scene in mind, the current status of dogs as property—as chattel—is unbefitting. My dogs are perfectly person-like: they are individuals.* We differ by species only: I am their person and they are my dogs. If there is possession, it is two-way: us of them and them of us.

Laws change to reflect the thinking of our time. Two states—Alaska and Illinois—recently changed their statutes to include considering the "well-being" of a dog as relevant in determining where the animal should live after their persons' divorce. Those considerations could include noting with which person the dog is more bonded; any stress for a dog in changing homes or losing dog friends; a dog's age and health; or the relative responsibilities taken by each dog parent. The changing laws are a subtle nod to what is not at all subtle about dogs: that they are living; that they live; that they have lives.

What would it mean to thus assign dogs the status of "living property," as Favre has suggested? It would oblige an improvement in dogs' lives; it would represent, he thinks, a forthright acknowledgment of the real concern for their well-being. We would actually have to keep the dog's interests foremost in mind. This is not just reasonable; it highlights how peculiar it is that we haven't had to keep them in mind up until now.

We already acknowledge that we have *some* obligation to dogs—to not be cruel, at minimum (as laws also dictate), but

---

* As, certainly, are other animals, although those who do not live around farm animals are slow to extend individuality to farm animals, and those who have not observed or interacted with wild animals are slow to extend individuality to wild animals.

also to behave responsibly toward the dog. Living-property status would reflect the commonsense understanding of what "responsibly" means, when it comes to something that has a life with its corollary, experience—and whose very existence massively improves humans' lives. We have no duty to inanimate property: as nice as a chair may be for sitting in, we have no duty to it. We do have a duty to dogs. Moreover, the duty is owed to individual dogs, not to the state—as is the case with cruelty laws. Each dog is due her right to be a dog. "At this point in history," Favre has written, "the non-human animals of our Earth are not our brothers, nor our equals, but like our children."

We'd have to pay attention to what matters to dogs: it would then matter to us. Anti-cruelty laws gesture at the concern to avoid dogs experiencing some kinds of suffering (or, more likely, lightly punishing those who inflicted it); some states have provisions for "sanitary conditions," periodic exercise, and veterinary care when needed. But to stop here is to equate *living* to the absence of neglect. Living, for humans and non-humans, is not about avoiding suffering. It is about pursuing meaning, happiness, engagements.

Dogs should be allowed—enabled—to experience the potential of the species: full dogness. A bird should be flying, a pig should be snuffling in the mud; a dog should be

playing
pursuing
finding
running
resting
chasing
chewing

rolling

tumbling

mounting

nosing

touching

digging

smelling the world ad lib

They should be with and among dogs; with and among people. They should see new places, meet new dogs, engage in new activities. They should be allowed to make choices; to decline to participate in some enforced activity: to be participatory in conducting their own lives.

Admittedly, some of the natural behaviors dogs often express may cause owners to blanch: James Serpell, at University of Pennsylvania's Veterinary School, highlights their "appetite for garbage, sexual promiscuity, olfactory preoccupations, toilet habits, and occasional naked hostility towards strangers and visitors." Our willingness to indulge dogs their behavior is usually limited to those behaviors that don't disgust and discomfit us. While I will stop short of endorsing that we all let our dogs hump each houseguest to their heart's content, I wonder what kind of *animal* we think we've got with dogs. While we profess to love the animal, we seem to despair at their animalness.

What a dog needs to be a dog—the essential elements of life—should be attended to. Despite decades of being told by the pet industry that the elements were, roughly, to train them, to feed them, and to walk them, these requirements are perfunctory and wholly inadequate. Furthermore, the relative ease with which those guideposts can be met (take a few classes, put down some kibble, strap them to a leash for a walk around the block), dangerously misrepresents the inadequacy of that life experience for a sentient creature. It doesn't bother to imagine, let alone to meet, what the dog wants, needs to, or even *can* do.

The last two decades have seen a trickle of research into dog cognition become a river, and the results of that work can be used to inform what the dog can do and should be allowed to do. That certain breeds are predisposed to pursue, round up, and usher along other animals (sheep or, lacking sheep, children); that some breeds are triggered by the sight of a fleeing object to sprint in pursuit; while others are restricted in breathing and do better at moderate paces, with ample rest; that long-nosedness comes with keener vision across the horizon (equipping them to follow that bouncing ball) while short-nosedness comes with keener vision in the center of the eye (focusing them on any human face that may be nearby)—all of these should be accounted for in the dog's world. We now know that dogs are highly skilled at, and enjoy, unpacking smells, that they identify people and other dogs by odor, and may in fact become less good at sniffing if we pull them away from smells. How can we but let them sniff, then? We understand the importance of social companionship— whether person or canid. How can we but give them company, then? We should appreciate that dogs are right-pawed or left-pawed (and thus biased in ways that we might have neglected), that they don't like being pet equally over their body (and thus simply endure with good humor the head-pats and aggressive rubbing . . . until they don't)—in short, that they are individuals, who indeed have *ways that they feel*.

It would mean changes in ownership of dogs, to be a right (or a privilege) we can lose. We *get* to own dogs. But not if we treat them any old way. Individually, should a person demonstrate that they can't provide a suitable life for the dog, the dog could be transferred to others' care and ownership. We do this now, with animal hoarders—but they are only the most egregious cases of inability to suitably keep animals.

Moreover, not all legal persons may be "appropriate owners," as Favre puts it. Some (such as corporations) "do not have the interest or ability to take care of their property." Puppy farms fall squarely within this frame. The particulars of the lives of the pups or parents at a large-scale dog breeder matter to that breeder only insofar as they continue to make money for them. The dog "matters"—but only as a product, commercially; not as a dog, per se. If it's easier to keep many dogs in a small cage, remove pups too early from their mothers, or to isolate dogs for convenience, they will. Any ostensive welfare is only in service to their business.

What if, as living property, it was no longer acceptable to see dogs as currency? It would be no blow to the economy to prohibit the selling of dogs. The pet overpopulation that is in some good part due to large commercial dog breeders would be eliminated. Breeding would be done by people who have no commercial interest in the dogs—giving the hands-on and time-consumptive nature of breeding right. This could discourage all but those who already concern themselves with the well-being of dogs for the dogs' sake. There should be no profit to be made in breeding, and distributing, sentient creatures whose population exceeds our society's ability to care for them.

If money *is* involved, a different distribution may be due. Should dogs be used in a productive way—be "employed"— they would be owed a share of any monetary value of their labors. As a tool to find an undesired pest for clients, for instance, a percentage of any profit could be put aside for costs related to their welfare and well-being.

As we face the need to revise antiquated legal notions of animals, we are walking with dogs into a changed but improved world for them. The very "use" of dogs—one of the legal terms that walked us into our current paradoxical relationship with dogs—might be restricted. While we could own dogs, we could not vivisect them. We could keep them, but not if we just keep them alive. Should they be put to a use for which they are not suited, the owner would be relieved of the dog. This would not give dogs free rein; it would rein in our freedom to treat dogs any way we like. Though a gain for dogs, this would not be a real loss for us—not for those who do not benefit from or willfully flaunt the mistreatment of dogs. It is not a zero-sum game.

My sweet, earnest dog sits on my soft, comfy chair, and I see the two of them as completely different. Our dogs look at us; we are seen by them. I want my actions—our culture's actions—to be worthy of that gaze.

Things People Say
to Their Dogs

"What is it about dogs that makes intelligent men, gifted women—great minds—look at them and say [in baby-talk voice], Who's a good boy? ... Wooj a whajeejeeb?"

(Stephen Colbert)

Although they are stoically silent in response, we talk to dogs. Happily so, for there is little bleaker than seeing a person reading notifications on his phone while dragging a dog at the end of a leash out on "her walk." It's so natural to talk to dogs that for a long time I wasn't even aware when I did it. But just as surely as I put on both shoes this morning, buttoned my coat, and checked the door after I locked it, I surely talked to my dogs. I have no memory of doing any of these; only evidence that my shoes are on, the coat is buttoned, the door is locked. And now? Now I have evidence that I talk to my dogs.

For now I'm listening.

For several years I've been listening—to what I and the rest of my family say to our dogs, first, but also to what *you* say. Everywhere I go I encounter dogs: on the sidewalks, in the parks, in stores and airports, at readings, at my lab. And most of the dogs are with people. It is, thus, not long before I hear people talking to their dogs.

> *You're so cute and so smart.*
> *And worth money! I could marry you.*
> (Woman to her goldendoodle, September 13)

As wildly anthropomorphic as talking to dogs might seem at first pass, we've talked to dogs long before we began dress-ing them in hand-knit sweaters (cable-knit, alpaca for softness) and celebrating their birthdays (custom peanut-butter-and-liver cake, decorated). Dogs were but one animal we spoke to. Hundreds of years ago in the early modern period, what we now consider farm animals were ubiquitous in towns, living around and among city-dwellers. Pigs walked alongside pedestrians (occasionally knocking over and injuring children), chickens were welcome in the house, and it was not unusual to see cows milked in the streets. Unburdened by concerns about keeping our distance from animals, the animals were often spoken to—for why should they not understand? The conversations were decidedly one-sided, and more often commands than conversation starters: one might say "Coom biddy," "Yuly, yuly," or "Bawk up," to the cow being parked in her place. In some sense, animals shared a common language with their owners, as working horses *understood* "Gee" to mean giddyup; "Heit" to mean turn to the left; "So boy, there boy," as a statement of praise. Or so they seemed to understand: a good horse was one whose behavior was in line with the request (and one whose behavior wasn't would not last long).

Historically, the language spoken to animals reflects the biblical notion of dominion, of man's place above animals. Talk is telling or commanding, not asking or wondering. In a post-Darwinian world, though, the idea of dominion is not only scientifically bankrupt, it is simply inapplicable to the relationship we have with animals, especially pets. While we might command a dog to *sit* or *come* (whether the dog does sit or come is another question), commands do not a conversation make—and when we speak to dogs now we *are* in a sort of conversation with them. As one of us, your dog is in on the dialogue: spoken with, not just ordered-to.

That conversation has never been, though, the kind of talking to animals practiced, famously if fictitiously, by Hugh Lofting's Doctor Dolittle, who forsakes a human medical practice when he realizes that he has a communicative in with the animals. (Plus, they're nicer.) Dolittle's exchanges with animals inspired me, as a child, to imagine the possibility of talking to animals—and having them talk back. For in his world, animals talk, well, exactly like humans, and Dolittle speaks to them as if they were friends or colleagues. "Well, well!" he says to the dog, Jip, who is busy smelling out where a missing person might have gotten to, "You know that's really quite remarkable—quite . . . I wonder if you could train me to smell as well as that . . ." Dolittle's "well, well!" is just the kind of marker one might use in, say, an early twentieth-century British adventure story. It turns out to be exactly *not* what we say to our dogs, however—even when we are being formal. Formality calls for "Mr. Jip, of the Jip Jipsons," or, in our house, Upton's full name: "Upton Horowitz Shea . . . ," not "Tell me, my good dog, might it be time for a walk?" Nor do we carry on, ruminating or commenting with dogs the way we might with a partner or friend: notable, since the dog, at least, is a captive audience.

Thanks so much. Thanks, dude.
(Man to Finnegan, who's sniffing him, December 5)

On the other hand, this doesn't mean that the conversation we're having with our dogs is just simplified speech. It's not precisely that of parent and pre-verbal child, for instance. Thinking of dogs as owners' children is deep-seated. It's in our language: dog owners are spoken of as the dog's "mommy" or "daddy" (common parlance at the veterinarian's office), and people refer to their fur "babies." And it's in our brains: one fMRI study found that mothers had the same patterns of brain activity when looking at photos of their dogs and of their children. It's even in our cultural stereotypes: popular (but incorrect) opinion is that dogs have roughly the intelligence of two-year-old children; young couples may consider getting a dog as a trial run for having children.*

But we don't speak to dogs exactly like we do to babies. There are certainly overlaps. In both cases, we use baby talk—

---

* An impulsive search of academic journal papers finds dozens of appearances of the particular construction "like children, dogs" (". . . did not always abide," ". . . exhibit behavioral traits," ". . . use their caregivers," ". . . explore the environment," ". . . are notoriously unreliable").

or what researchers thereof call "infant-directed speech" (which sounds way more academic than studying *baby talk*). When we baby-talk to babies, the pitch of our voices is higher—*Hi, baby!* is first soprano—and singsongy, with lots of variation. Our voices are all harmonics, more like a child's voice than that of an elderly person. So, too, to dogs.* Imagine rendering *Hi, puppy!* as James Earl Jones: preposterous. Even Jones would be forced into a falsetto. We use a fairly limited vocabulary with infants, and with dogs, too. Rarely have I discussed forgoing any perambulations due to precipitation (as tongue-lollingly-satisfying as those words may be) with my infant son or my pups. Instead, we tend to repeat words, slow our speech, shorten phrases, and outright drop some categories of words, such as articles. Speech is telegraphed: while I now say *Will you go find the ball so we can play catch?* with my eight-year-old, we *Go get bally!* with nearby babies—and with our ten-year-old dogs.

Talk to puppies (or grown puppies) differs in other ways: when speaking to infants, we hyperarticulate our vowels: exaggeratedly saying *Look at the doggeeeeee!* to babies—but not nearly as much to dogs. It's a subtle but key difference that marks a rift in our ways of thinking about kids and pups. Hyperarticulation seems to be didactic: a way of teaching a growing human our language. By contrast, when we are talking to dogs, we are under no illusion that they will grow up to use the language themselves.† So we do the attention-getting, positive-affect parts of baby talk, but drop the schooling.

---

* And even more to baby-dogs: "puppy-directed speech" exaggerates this effect. Puppies respond with alacrity to these speech sounds—much more so than to the rest of the stream of language above their heads.

† True to form, we use hyperarticulation in speech directed at foreigners learning English as a second language: one part condescending, another part (intended as) instructive.

On the flip side, ever since living with three males age ten and younger—only one of them human—I realized that though I treasure my dogs and have the utmost respect for their dogness, there are things I will say to my dogs and not to my son. I probably utter *C'mon!* daily to Finnegan and (especially) Upton, but if I'm going to ask my son to get a move on, I couch it in something more grandiose: *Come on, sir slowpoke; Will you come with me, kiddo?; Let's get going, please.* In the same way, my eyebrow-raised, high-pitched *What's this?* is exclusively doggo; same with the *Go to your bed!* request that precedes their getting a treat. Were I ever to bark *Sit!*, it'd be to dog, not boy (I tend not to ask: who am I to insist on a particular spot for their rumps?). I caught myself saying *Good boy!* once to my son when he was still an infant—and have never done so since.

What are you even doing? I don't understand you.
(Woman to her very sniffy black-and-white dog, October 22)

I do talk to my dogs, though, quite a bit. On awakening, the two dogs warming either leg may be the first creatures I speak to in the day: *Hi fellas, how're you doing this morning?* I wonder after their dreams, but don't ask after them. Instead, I might request that Finn creep closer for a scratch in the body-stretching way he does—front claws gripping the bedsheets to pull him forward, back legs extended as though in pure flight. I'll ask Upton if a walk or breakfast is in order. Thus begins a day of talking to the dogs.

Of course I do not expect that they will respond. Nor do I worry that they will. If I thought they might, it would change what I'd say. At least one culture that is not filled with dog-talk *does* so worry, and that's why their members remain quiet. James Serpell reports that the Yurok Indians of California, despite highly valuing their hunting dogs and granting them a ceremonial burial at their deaths, did not talk to or name their dogs, "in the belief that they might answer back, thus upsetting the natural order and provoking general catastrophe." As though if they did respond, the important distance between dogs and people would be broached.

Or perhaps the dogs would simply have horribly nasal voices and say radically smart (or stupid) things, and we'd rather not have to face the consequences of this. But pure quietness in the presence of dogs unnerves me. Not everyone talks to their dogs, but if they don't, I will. Though I'm happy simply coexisting in a room or on a forest path with a dog, I consider the dog an agent, worth addressing.

I don't know, you'll have to ask him. They're his.
(Nonchalant dog's owner to another dog sniffing
at his pocket, June 7)

When I began listening for other owners' dog-directed soliloquies, I found they were ubiquitous. Heading down a city sidewalk in the morning, when sleepy dogs and people stumble out for the dog's morning micturition, I might catch two or three conversational snippets on a long block. Indeed, it began to seem as though the act of a person walking by sometimes *prompted* an owner's conversational opening to her dog— as though to emphasize how not-walking-slowly-alone-down-the-sidewalk she was. Not at all alone: she was *with* someone.

I began writing down each overheard snippet.* Five steps after passing a woman leading two small dogs, both in sweat-

* You can find some of these on Twitter: #ThingsPplSayToTheirDogs.

ers, one of whom has lifted a rear leg to aim directly on a construction scaffolding post, I stop, pull an unopened envelope out of the top of my bag, and scribble down her words: *You're going first: excellente! Awesome job!*

Not only could I not make her lines up, I probably could not recall them a minute later. Without memorializing her bilingual and unusual enthusiasms at once, they would be lost. Neither the dog nor, likely, the woman herself was listening. No one else seemed to pay them the slightest mind as they headed deeper into their walk. After a tepid reverberation on the underside of the scaffolding, her words disappeared into the morning din. I stuffed the envelope back into my bag and glanced back at her. She and her little dogs turned the corner and were gone.

Several hundred scribbled overhearings later, I began to notice a pattern. Most of the dog-speech I heard fits into one of a few categories. Not grammatical categories or even useful conceptual categories; rather, they are a breed of distinctly dog-directed categories. The woman praising her peeing, sweatered dog is a member of the first: the Mom Commentary on behavior. Eyes fixed on the dog, she sees *everything*. And she's gotta talk about it.

> *You've got a lot to learn! A lot to learn!* (Woman to her dachshund puppy on the sidewalk)
> *What's with all the grass this morning, dog?* (Woman to dew-licking long-haired mutt)
> *Did you make a friend?* (Woman to her approaching, wagging dog)
> *I know you got excited when you saw another puppy . . . but I need my arm to remain in the socket.* (Woman to leash-tugging retriever)

74

Oh! You're a humper! (Woman to humping dog)

You sure love *testosterone, doncha girl!* (Woman to her dog eyeing male dog on the other side of the fence)

You can sit all you want when we're home. (Woman to dog not going anywhere)

You are B-A-D. (Woman to possibly keen-spelling dog)

You really don't like pigeons, do you? (Woman to indifferent beagle)

Appropriate to the category, most of these speakers are women. In fact, among my notebook scribblings, the speakers were women about six times as often as they were men. Women speak more often, speak more quickly, and speak longer than men—on the sidewalk and in scientific studies of dog-talkers. They repeat words more and are not shy about dropping in a term of endearment. This is not to say that men are immune from the Mom Commentary:

Be nice! When you get tired, you get nasty. (Man to rambunctiously playing dog)

Oh come on, now, give me a break. It's just me. (Man to barking dog)

Buddy, you can't stop in the middle of the street. (Man to loitering dog)

Okay, I got it kiddo. I can definitely hear that. It's coming any minute now. Almost there. It's very exciting. (Man to dog howling for a treat)

Common to both genders—common to humans—is commentary reflecting the profound difficulties that the vision-centered biped at one end of the leash has in understanding the olfaction-centered quadruped at the other:

Come on! It's a lamppost. (Man to dog enjoying the finer
   olfactory pleasures of a rainy evening)
Two-dog butt-sniff! Wow! (Woman to yellow Lab being
   well investigated)
I just don't see what's so interesting. (Woman to nose-on-
   the-ground Pekingese)

Madam *Excellente* actually bridges categories: she's also a
member of the Cheering Squad gang of dog-talkers, encour-
aging and pulling for their team:

Good stop. I really liked that halt, guys. (Dog walker to her
   five charges, upon navigating a street corner)
At least down the block, baby. (Woman to her large,
   unmoving bulldog)
C'mon, you made it the whole way. One more step! (Man
   on top step to puppy sprawled on second-to-last
   step)
Let's lead! Leader! YAY! (Woman leaving house with tiny
   dog)
Go on, get a good sniff of his wisdom. (Woman to dog nosing another dog's graying muzzle)

Given that new dog owners are instructed early on to teach
their charges commands—to *sit*, *stay*, *come*, even, for reasons
beyond me, to *roll over*—it's not surprising that another category is Instructions. I heard many a *Sit! Stay!*, but what struck
me was how perfectly implausible most instruction is. It is
quite outside of the usual roster of commands:

Okay you guys: share. (Man to two dogs being given a
   plate to lick clean)

No pizza! No! (Woman and Yorkshire terrier ogling fallen slice on the sidewalk)

You're not going to go? Okay, let's go. (Woman to dog who apparently understands polysemy)

Stop! Those dogs are bigger than you. Tut, tut. (Woman to two barking dachshunds)

No coyote scat before breakfast, dogs. (Woman to inadvertent scat-detection dogs)

Listen up, we're just having a pee. No dogs, no nothing. (Woman explaining)

If you make it to the end of the fence, you get a biscuit. If you lie down, no biscuit. (Woman to corgi who's probably not going to make it to the end of the fence)

Not now. We'll smell that on the way back. (Woman to dog intent on particular patch of sidewalk)

Go run! Go play! Wait, not in the mud! (Woman—futilely—to Labrador)

Stop! Go play with the other dogs. Go on! (Woman to poodle trying to play with her)

Come now, do what you have to do. (Woman to little dog at curb)

You guys are going to have to get coordinated. (Woman to two dogs pulling in different directions)

Hurry up! We're late! (Woman to not-particularly-feeling-it dog)

Heads-up! Heads-up! Keep your eyes on the road! (Woman to chocolate Lab running sideways toward me)

Let's go this way. I know there's no vegetation or garbage but guess what? There may be a doggie! (Woman to wiggly puppy)

Go get the ball! Get the ball! Get the . . . Okay. I'll get it. (Woman to non-retrieving retriever)

Let's get organized, ladies. (Woman to bevy of terriers)

A little privacy, man. (Woman to dog ardently sniffing pooing dog)

Allez! Clarence is going the other way. Allez vous. (Woman to Shiba Inu)

Be part of the solution, buddy. (Woman to misbehaving dog)

I see you doing weird stuff. Cut it out. (Woman to one of her four small dogs)

You just have to tell me how you're feeling! Are you constipated? (Woman to dolorous dog)

Leave it. We have better ones at home. (Man to dog desperately searching for lost tennis ball)

Mind your manners. (Man to seemingly polite dog)

And, mixing instructions with not just the implausible but the impossible:

Come on. Be a man. (Man with baseball hat and bulldog being sniffed)

Often those instructions are repeated to a degree that would be extraordinary in any other conversation:

Go go go go go, let's go, let's go. (Woman to dog nosing curb)

STOP. STOP IT. STOP. STOP. STOP! (Woman with ball to Labrador barking for ball)

Kill it! Kill it! Kill it! Kill it. Kill it, yay! (Woman, dog, and soft toy)

Gimme paw! Gimme paw! (Elderly man on the street to three-legged dog)

In the spirit of conversation that requires only one voice, we turn question marks toward our pups, engaging them *as if* they might respond—and then waiting a beat to give them due time to so reply. They don't, though, and we are rarely sad or blue when they don't. This is the realm of Forever Unanswered Questions:

Am I still interesting? (Woman to puppy, interested in something else)

What, are you reinventing the poo? (Woman to long-pooing dog)

Did you get a new toy? Did you get a new toy? DID YOU GET A NEW TOY? (Woman to dog waiting with toy in his mouth)

What's your name, baby? (Woman to "Spike")

Is it over here? How about over here? Are you sure it's that one? Are you sure? (Handler to dog, near beehives)

Are you coming to the park? Or am I going alone? (Man to long-eared, sad-eyed dog)

Would you guys like to be in a book group? (Woman to dogs in dog park)

Why do you always do that when she's sniffing? (Man with two dogs, one pulling eastward, one nose downward)

Hi, honey. Did you vote? (Woman to pleased-looking dog outside voting center)

Behind every unanswered question is the feeling that we might already know the answer, given that we and our dogs live together, see each other naked, and obviously *know everything about each other*. Hence the reliable appearance of the "we've discussed this"s: implicitly using the dog's full family name, we roll our eyes at their pretense of not understanding exactly what they're supposed to do:

> *We both know we have to go now.* (Woman to dog gamboling in snow)
> *Seriously?* (Woman to long-peeing dog)
> *We've talked about this: no eating stuff you find on the street.* (Man to foraging dog)
> *You remember how we were going to cooperate? Good girl.* (Woman to unresponsive dog)
> *Hey! Stop it! [whispered] We talked about this yesterday.* (Woman to lunging dog)

● ● ●

Even as I had become preternaturally attuned to the moment an owner began speaking to her dog a half a block away, for many months I did not bring that attention to myself. One day, I heard myself talking to the dogs, happily unselfconsciously. Soon enough, I realized that I was talking to them not just every day, but many times a day. I turn out to be a classic dog-talking owner—and the things that come out of my mouth, well, they are often cross-category utterances, to be sure:

> *Maybe he lives here all the time, that's strange, huh?* (Me, as we enter an already-occupied elevator and my dogs address the occupant nose-first) . . . *I mean, they might be thinking* . . . (I add, for the man's sake)

We talk to dogs differently when others are around. Most of the talk I hear is *over*heard—not intended for my ears. But when we talk to dogs around others, it serves as a social lubricant, a way to open up the possibility of talking to each other. *What's your name?* said dog-ward is never, never answered—except, obligingly, by a dog's owner.* Dogs are not only reflections of us, they are social intermediaries for us. Any hesitation I may have about a person approaching me on the street is deflected by Finnegan's smiling, wag-filled greeting of nearly every kind and manner of human being. And both the approaching person and I can continue to deflect any discomfort or awkwardness we feel by talking not to each other, but to the dog. *Hi, you! What a great day for a walk!* Many greetings involve exclamation points, the kind of stranger's greeting likely to get a devout New Yorker's hackles up: living in such close proximity to millions of other people works partly by not having to admit we actually see each other. But brandished toward the dog, the exclamation point pierces the conceit of our mutual invisibility. We each acknowledge the other through our shared admiration for the dog. *You're so shiny!*, he (I?) often gets. To which I respond, *Thank you; I polish you nearly every day, don't I, Finn?*

At a dog park, the "new dog" is greeted by the noses of the old-hand dogs—and by the attentions of the old-hand dog owners. *Who are you? What a sweetie you are. Oh, you're a jumper!* After talking to the dog—while looking at the dog—the "regulars" can raise their heads up to the owner. Even after

---

* Often, owners' relationships, which were initiated by their talking to each other's dogs, develop without the people ever introducing *themselves*. Years have passed before I've learned the names of the familiar human faces accompanying dogs I've known, tickled the ears of, and seen grown up. (Then, promptly and inevitably, I forget the persons' names.)

the humans are in conversation, the episode will be ended via the dog: *Bye-bye Max; See you tomorrow, little guy.* As a bridging device bringing humans into contact, dogs and their habits and foibles are far preferable to the weather. More slobbery, though.

You, you, you, you, you.
(Woman to well-mottled dog, November 11)

It's not only strangers who can be looped in by dog-talk. We talk to our relatives—our human relatives—via our dogs as well. Remember the dogs in Baatombu communities, in western Africa, named and spoken to as a reply to another person's behavior? US linguists have seen something similar in talk directed to the dog in lieu of, say, one's partner. Linguist Deborah Tannen observed a couple arguing, and then: "The man suddenly turns to their pet dog and says in a high-pitched baby-talk register, 'Mommy's so mean tonight. You better sit over here and protect me.'" The dogs enable the speaking; they are not really the spoken-to.

I think you're being a little bit too pushy.
(Woman to her great bearded dog, August 5)

Through all our talking, dogs are silent. Some scholars think this represents a "human fantasy" of how communication might go: all listening, no talking back. More charitably, it is simply a relief from the nonstop verbal world we live in among people. But soon enough, we fill in their side of the script. "We like our pets' silence," Erica Fudge suggests, "because it allows us to write their words for them." By Victorian England, owners were taking this idea seriously, and writing dog autobiographies—for show dogs, lost dogs, old dogs, escaped dogs. The trajectory that these autobiographies follow is strikingly similar to human autobiographies: detailing the pup's youth, upbringing, adventures, misadventures, and the advent of wisdom in old age. One collie, Luath, telling his tale, notes, "'What can dogs know about death?' some humans ask. A deal more than such humans imagine." Nineteenth-century dogs apparently wrote to their doctors—"I feel 'real sick' this morning . . . you must promise not to tell mother, but she gave a dinner last evening, and I *did* enjoy myself . . . Do you think it is possible for [that] to have made me feel as I do? . . . Your grateful patient, . . ." They wrote poems: "I hate to walk alone—/my eyes grow very dim; / I'm hard of hearing, too—a fly/Might knock me down, so weak am I/In ev'ry trembling limb." And they were whistleblowers, calling out the "evils" and "abuse of animals" at the newly formed dog shows.

Instagram dogs are today's autobiographers, their humans expressing their thoughts as much in image as word. A French bulldog, dressed in striped pajamas, sits up in bed with plumped pillows, a fresh newspaper, and a plate of croissants; the caption "best slumber party ever" is meant to represent her thoughts at this scenario. Her person's thoroughgoing lack of interest in anything like the dog's actual thoughts is highlighted by her purported recommendation of a bottled water drink (price, eight dollars for sixteen ounces; link to manufacturer supplied) placed between her front paws. Instagram dogs model clothes, sponsor everything from cleaning products to collars, and, no surprise for a dog with hundreds of thousands of followers, often have an agent. All this dog-talking is less *to* the dog than *for* the dog—a whole nother, spurious outgrowth of talk around dogs. Humans voice the dogs' supposed thoughts, and are themselves silent. While not engaging in a dialogue, this kind of ventriloquism expresses the same urge to include the dog in the conversation.

We do something similar with each other, at times. Most interpersonal interactions involve conversation of one sort or another—largely verbal.* Sometimes the other person isn't in a position to speak: she is a four-month-old baby, for instance, or caught in the grip of Alzheimer's, or simply preoccupied with something else. In those cases, we speak for our interlocutor. Sociologists suggest that, further, people with power or authority tend to translate their charges' speech into the "true" meaning: a parent for a child (*He is wondering if you'll share your toy*, a mother explains of her toddler grabbing at another child's treasure); an employer for employee (*What you seem to be saying . . .*). Dogs fit perfectly in both slots: we talk for them, translating their feelings and experience, or filling in the space after a question. Lying down at the vet's: *"Oh, I'm so tired, I just have to lie down here"*; anticipating the vet's exam: *"We aren't going to like this at all"*; noticing their surroundings: *"Hmm, I am sensing a smell that's not mine."* We comment for them, make requests, report their moods and hopes and fears. In all of it, the dog is the center, the principal: it's their point of view we're after. When we speak for dogs, we at least make an attempt to imagine their perspective—which is to grant them a perspective worth imagining.

Don't even think about it.

(Woman to thoughtful dog, August 10)

---

* . . . but also nonverbal: a nod of greeting; a smile of appreciation for a door held open; a mutual eyebrow-raise marking two strangers' shared proximity to an amorous couple on the subway.

If our speech to dogs isn't typical adult dialogue, nor quite the same as our speech to children, and if we don't expect a response, who are we talking to, then? I think the answer is: ourselves. The language-speaking child in ourselves. It's as if our private speech, the conversation we're having in our heads, has slipped out. This talking-to-ourselves is far from trivial: it's been connected to problem-solving (muttering your process aloud can speed it along) and as an integral step in language-learning. The psychologist Lev Vygotsky, formulating his theories of child development, described a stage when children internalize conversations with those around them—social speech—into a conversation in their own heads. He called it "inner speech" and thought it enabled children to use language to reflect on and consider their own behavior. We keep on that monologue with ourselves as we age into adults. It's not quite the way we'd talk to those around us, though, with its cropped syntax and a "note-form" shorthand that represents your familiarity with your own thoughts. But it's just like what we're saying to our dogs—as if they were *in our heads*.

They are, of course, the preoccupation of our minds: we hope for them, are concerned for them, and care for them. We narrate our thoughts while we watch them, and their thoughts while they accompany us. Of course, it's in all our heads—only, some of us let the words escape through our mouths.

You had better stay your bottom right here, sunshine.
(Woman to sunshine pug, October 7)

I've walked around for years listening to people talk to their dogs, and hearing myself talk to our own. Between me and the two dogs, sometimes I don't shut up. Much of what we say to dogs is nonsense, presuming much more comprehension than we have any right to expect of a dog. But the more I listen, the more charitably I hear. The novelist Donald McCaig writes about a famous Scottish sheepdog trainer, who, asked if one should talk to dogs, replied: "Of course you should talk to your dogs madam . . . But you must talk sense." On the contrary, I think the pleasure of the best talking is that it can be *non*sense—but we feel that our dogs are in on the joke with us. We know they will not respond, but we include them in the conversation nonetheless.

One of the things we say to our dogs daily—two-thirds of us, according to one survey of North American pet owners— is *I love you.* Even the simple sound of our voice is an expression of that love, regardless of the content of the words we say. Through talking to them, we let them into an intimacy with us. They hear our secrets, our private thoughts.

Now you know: pass me on the sidewalk, and I may be listening. You have become aware that there might be eavesdroppers on your conversations with your dogs on your nightly walk, or as you wait at the veterinarian's office. Please: don't let it stop you from talking.

It's the moment when you are at your most human,
and you wear it well.

(Dog to you)

The Trouble with Breeds

*"His stature is dignified, his expression pensive . . . (He is)
rectangular in shape . . . a gentle, loyal and affectionate
dog . . . An intelligent and independent thinker, he displays
determination and a strong sense of purpose while at work.
A dog of dignity . . ."*
(Clumber spaniel breed standard)

Picture a dog. It's likely a breed, or recognizably breed-like.
People identify with certain breeds; love the breed they grew
up with; are drawn to the expressions, impishness, regalness,
humanness, or simple improbability of a type of dog. Dogs
as we know them—the idealized portrayals of Dog—are the
result of selective breeding. The astounding range of sizes,
skills, and personalities of this single species is due to our

distant ancestors' eye for diversifying dogs into functions, and, more recently, breeders' eyes to diversifying dogs by form.

Encountering a dog on the sidewalk, we become amateur genealogists. *What breed is your dog?* is such a common query that owners have long established go-to responses. If your dog is purebred, or what is called a "designer" dog (two purebreds mixed), you have the breed name at hand—and maybe some history and endorsement of the breed or breeder. If your dog is a mutt, there's the chance for some creative license. Guessing the combination of breeds that explains that charismatic tail, the short legs–big head combo, the winsome smile, is an art form practiced by all experienced dog people. Or a breed name is invented: my husband used to call his pit bull–type dog Zoe a "Brooklyn shorthair," given the ubiquity of dogs of her ilk where he lived (and the desperate need for the dogs' reputation to get a boost). A shelter in Costa Rica, hoping to increase adoption rates, piggybacked on both the cachet of a breed name and our sense of the intrinsic individuality of each dog, and began giving each mongrel pup a singular breed name: "Bunny-tailed Scottish Shepterrier"; "Freckled Terrierhuahua"; "Fire-Tailed Border Cocker."

For years, shelters and re-homing centers have been in the dubious business of breed-eyeballing. Our last three dogs have been so eyeballed: Finnegan and Pumpernickel were billed as of the ubiquitous "Lab mix"es; Upton, as a Plott hound and Great Dane. No doubt none of these is accurate; instead, they were simply a means by which we could begin to give our dogs a history, a past.

Our keenness to know our dog's breed has introduced a new, widespread owner behavior. Among the unpredictable changes to one's life upon welcoming a dog into your home (rising in the depths of night to take your dog to pee; willingness to search in the bushes for a beloved slobbery tennis ball; surprising expertise about the ideal substrate for pooping) is finding yourself taking a cotton swab and massaging it between your pup's gums and cheek to gather enough saliva to saturate the thing. But you may. And you likely will, because of one of the features of dogs that got us to this waggy, urinous, saliva-filled place to begin with: our fixation on the story of who our dogs are, via their breed.

Big business, aided by a burgeoning field of genetic testing, is ready to scratch your itch to know. For the skeptical purebred dog owners and the mixed-breed owners alike, you can now mail that cheek swab away, and, in the dog-genealogy companies' words, prepare to "understand and care for your dog like never before." "Knowing your dog's ancestry," another claims, "can help you create a tailored wellness program to fit their one-of-a-kind needs."

And so we may do it. The question raised by this kind of exploration into the "ancestry" of your dog, though, is rarely posed. And that is this: what would the answer actually tell us?

Thinking of dogs in terms of breed is limited, limiting, and sometimes dangerous. Our typological thinking prefigures a serious trouble with dog breeds today. Now, no member of a breed is themselves liable for this trouble. It has happened *to* dogs, and, to some extent, it has even happened to breeders.

What has happened is the celebration of improbable and unsustainable variations on the theme of Dog. By breeding to limited standards, we have created extraordinary specimens, with many alarming medical problems. Natural selection was displaced by artificial selection—domestication—and, currently, by a woefully misguided selection: our choosing which dogs to breed from within a closed genetic pool. What's driving that selection in the breed world? It's driven by a judge at a dog show handing out a Best in Show trophy. That's what's driving selection.

•   •   •

"It is a robust, but elegant and racy, pursuit dog with
no exaggeration of length of body or limbs, muscle
development, angulation, nor curve of loin . . .
not a fragile dog, but is also a dog with class and grace.
The attitude is noble and somewhat aloof, and the
expression of the dark eyes is gentle and melancholy."
(Sloughi breed standard)

On a warm September day, I enter the bedlam of midtown New York City at lunchtime. Office workers mid–phone conversation project onto sidewalks from revolving doors; bankers in matching suits trot in lockstep in front of me; walkers juggle cell phones and sandwiches. I slip into an unprepossessing office building on Madison Avenue and step onto the elevator. On the fourth floor, the doors open to a marbled and carpeted lobby lined with short pillars. Atop each pillar is a small statue under glass: each of a different breed of dog. In the corner is a life-size statue of a German shepherd dog painted as the American flag. Turning down a hallway, nearly a hundred small dog heads peer out at me from atop nearly a hundred walking sticks, jostling for a treat or pat from a passerby.

A room opens in front of me. There are dogs everywhere, but the only noises are the hum of air-conditioning, the measured sliding of bookshelves on tracks, and muffled honking from four stories down. I pet a small statue of a snuffling basset hound, share a gaze with doleful setters and alert fox terriers rendered in oils, and meet Belgrave Joe, the "Abraham" of fox terriers, who died in 1888. His full mounted skeleton, tail curved into a hook, rests under glass. I have arrived at the American Kennel Club library.

For a person interested in dogs, the library provides the excellent continual surprise of finding yet another book or magazine about dogs at every turn. There is *Dog World*, *Dog Fancy*, *The Dog Fancier*, and *Dogdom*; *Kennel World*, *Kennel Review*, *Western Kennel World*; *Dog Craft*, *Popular Dogs*, *The Dog News*. Bound volumes of *Schnauzer Shorts* and *Springer Bark* sit peacefully alongside the *Doberman Quarterly*, *The Bulldogger*, *Dane World*, *Puli News*, *Boston Barks* (featuring the Boston terrier), and *The Barker* (featuring the Shar-Pei), regardless of how their respective real-world exemplars would behave. I also sit. In front of me are thirty years of American Kennel Club stud books.

With the founding of the kennel clubs, stud books became the key literature securing the superiority of kennel-club dogs. For the books list all the registered members of the pedigreed class: the genealogy, via an exponentially expanding tree, of each breed. (Well over fifty million dogs in the US, as of the turn of the twenty-first century.) Their distinction was that the books were, soon, "closed"—that is, only accepting breed membership from dogs born of other purebreds. In this way, each breed is itself literally a club whose membership is limited: granting no new members except for progeny of current and past members. Initially, some out-breeding was allowed: to soften a bulldog, say, one might pair her with a terrier. Early American dog shows even listed "Cross bred" setters as an official category of entrant. But eventually, to be registered with a club, the requirement for a dog was that they be a traceable descendant of the foundation animals. In other words, a dog's parents, grandparents, and up through the various great-grandparents need to have been from the founding dogs. This is attainable by one means: inbreeding, or mating within a closed gene pool.

Just as had been intended with bred horses, poultry, and cattle, purebred dogs were meant to have fixed characteristics. Before this point, breeding was not entirely willy-nilly: at least for people with working dogs, they aimed to breed their dogs with other good-behaving specimens they might come across, just as cattle breeders wanted animals generating more and better meat. "The country gentleman, he'd have a pack of fox hounds. If he saw a guy with a great dog at another hunt, he'd say, 'I've got a bitch coming into heat, how about getting her together with Prince here?'" Stephen Zawistowski tells me. Zawistowski is an applied animal behaviorist, was Science Advisor to the ASPCA for many years, and has written extensively on the history of dog behavior and ownership. A foxhound with a keen nose, focus, endurance (the dogs needed to run one hundred miles a week) and a fine baying call would be prized, and found a mate to continue the line. People kept some records of the pairings of highly valued animals. Still, this kind of breeding was haphazard: it was neither completely controlled—most puppies were the result of dogs being dogs—nor concerned with aught but the best-behaving specimen for the breeder's particular need. The mate needn't always be aristocratic, or even another foxhound. Pairing a dog with another "breed"—a dog being put to a different purpose— might lead to a new feature in their pup, Zawistowski says. "Some guy breeding coonhounds or beagles in Kentucky who wants to put a little more foot in his dog"—making them speedier on the trail of rabbits, say—"would potentially breed into the coonhound, then you would continue to backbreed into your beagles." As author Bronwen Dickey reports in her book *Pit Bull: The Battle over an American Icon*, bulldogs, used for dog fighting or hunting vermin in the 1800s, were sometimes crossed with terriers to make a more "agile" dog for the functions to which they were being put.

Purebred breeding changed this somewhat casual approach, and added a different emphasis: dogs were bred not for best function, but for best form—more refined, most superior, most pure. What counted as the "best form" was sometimes sensible, but often capricious. What good is a breed designed for form over function? "It is a stupid question," wrote Clara L. Dobbs, a Chihuahua fancier, in the 1927 *AKC Gazette*. "What is beauty good for?"

·   ·   ·

"He is an attractive dog of handy size, exhibiting substance without coarseness."
(Welsh springer spaniel breed standard)

Purebreeding began in the late nineteenth century in Victorian England, and took off like gangbusters. Your purebred German shepherd, if registered with the American Kennel Club, can trace her parentage back to the spark in one Max von Stephanitz's eye in 1889: a dog nobly named Horand von Grafrath (née Hektór Linksrhein) who he chose to begin breeding to create a more perfect version of what was then simply a shepherd's or shepherd dog. Horand is the first named German shepherd. Von Stephanitz's description of the dog reveals something of his aspirations in breeding him: Horand had "beautiful lines," he wrote; was "clean and sinewy in build" and was "one live wire." Moreover, he possessed "the straightforward nature of a gentleman with a boundless zest for living." A photograph of Horand in the midday sun shows an alert and athletic dog, proportioned healthily, with a bushy tail draping casually behind him. While a bit scruffy, he is not overly long and his back does not slope, and while recognizable as a German shepherd, he would never win Best in Breed today.

The rise in the popularity of purebred dog breeding can be traced to the appearance of the first dog shows: one, an exhibition, in the Zoological Gardens in London, featuring only spaniels; the second, a proper dog show in Newcastle upon Tyne in 1859, including only pointers and setters. The Newcastle show piggybacked on an ongoing poultry show; indeed, dog shows were modeled on long-standing shows of other domestic animals. Among the aristocracy, breeding of farm animals was a way of establishing a pedigree for the finest specimens; breeding horses with attention to ancestry began a century before.

The winner at Newcastle among the pointers was "by Lord Derby's Bang out of his Dora"; the winning setter was a Gordon setter named Dandy. Perhaps not coincidentally, the setter winner was owned by one of the pointer judges, and the pointer winner was owned by one of the setter judges. Each was awarded a "celebrated double-barrelled gun" made by the sponsor W. R. Pape.

Though early breeders might have felt sure they knew beauty when they saw it, confusion reigned, at first, as to who the "best" dog might be in the shows. "In many cases," one sports journalist wrote, "the choice of points is wholly arbitrary." What might be a plus in one breed was considered a fault in another. Not only to determine who should win at the shows, but also to distinguish the best show dogs from the execrable common dogs, breed clubs developed breed standards. "Where there was a name, there was a breed, and where there was a breed, there had to be a standard," historian Harriet Ritvo writes. So the bulldog, once used for bull baiting (the "sport" of a dog worrying a bull through chasing and biting, in order to soften up the meat that would be produced therefrom), had its reputation rehabilitated by a standard that changed its shape. "The dog conveys an impression of determination, strength and activity," reads the standard of 1892: with a massive protruding lower jaw, a "strikingly massive" head, a face "as short as possible," and skin "deeply and closely wrinkled"—to the point of favoring what a breed enthusiast called a "good broken up face"; as for the skull, "the larger the better." The "broad, slanting and deep" shoulders were to bear the weight of a very wide chest and "capacious" breast or "brisket"—sufficiently wide as to be crippling. Arguments were had, not over whether these deformities were useful or kind, but over whether features like the light-colored "Dudley nose" should be permitted. (It was not.) Collies transformed from shaggy sheepdogs into moviestar beauties with long, glossy coats and excessively pointy noses, whose distended faces, dog-show reviewers commented, left little room for brains.

In breed standards, a dog's size is often specified: both the ideal weight of the dog, but also the length of the dog's particulars. The Sussex spaniel's nose is to be three to three and one-half inches; the Gordon setter, four to four and one-half inches "from corner of eye to end of nose." An early publication of dog-show results includes a photograph of one of the champion Gordon setters, called Belmont. In the same book is a profile of Harry Malcolm, who formed the Gordon Setter Club and bred Belmont. He wrote the first standard for the breed, specifying that the eyes, "full of animation," should be colored "like the ovary of the Italian bee." Belmont's photo, black-and-white, fails to reveal his bee-ovarium eyes, but he is a beauty: lean and confident in pose, his eyebrows raised expectantly. The text accompanying Mr. Malcolm's photo describes him as "wiry in physique . . . active . . . of great endurance." Both man and dog have bristly hair around the muzzle.

Many standards allude to the greatly desirable trait of bodily "symmetry"* and some to the very proportions to be desired: the Clumber spaniel should be two and one-half times as long as high; the cocker spaniel, twice as long "from nip of nose to root of tail" as they are high at the shoulder; the mastiff, one-third wider in girth than shoulder height, its head exactly two-thirds as wide as long. Of the English pug, the standard insists, "The pug should be *multum in parvo*"—literally "much in little"—with a short, square muzzle, round head, strong, straight legs, and cobby body. Their coats should be glossy; wrinkles, "large and deep"; as for the tail, "the double curl is perfection." A satirical cartoon of the time, titled "Dog fashions for 1889," shows a woman dressed in the muffler and skirted costume of Victorian England and accompanied by a reptilian dachshund dog, a floor-sweeping terrier-type, a bulldog with an outsized head and underbite, a pug with a tightly spiraled tail, and a giant, leonine wolfhound. Satire aside, some of the dogs are not unlike what pass for fine members of their respective breeds today.

Dog shows were an instant hit, and within a few years there were international shows and shows with more than a thousand dog entrants. Breeding and showing dogs became the "dog fancy"; the owners, "fanciers." Competitiveness and the advent of monetary prizes led to owners cheating by doctoring their dogs—dyeing the dogs' coats, fashioning "correctly" shaped

---

* With the exception of the humble Irish water spaniel: "the symmetry of this dog is not very great."

ears or tails with scissors—or tampering with competitors' pups. To combat this nefariousness, a formal Kennel Club was formed in London in 1873 to, as quoted by Ritvo, separate those "who breed to win and to whom pecuniary questions are no moment" from the hoi polloi by instituting a method of tracking pedigreed dogs and their owners. An American Kennel Club soon followed in Philadelphia in 1884.* The club's constitution, bylaws, and rules and regulations allude to the requirements for dog membership (a registered name and established heritage), set terms for participation in certain classes of competition, and note absolute exclusion of dogs "with mange" from the proceedings.

The original fanciers began with only a handful of breeds, all considered "sporting" (alluding to their former field work running down or retrieving game), given the honorific pedigrees: a handful of setters, spaniels, pointers, and a retriever. Hounds of the basset, blood, deer, dachs, fox, and grey varietals soon joined them; within a decade, so did the unlikely club of bulldogs, pugs, Great Danes, mastiffs, and terriers Bedlington, Irish, Skye, and Yorkshire. By the nineteen-aughts there were nearly three dozen more breeds—terriers in particular sprouted new and fanciful varieties—as well as such now familiar breeds as Chihuahuas, Dalmatians, Chow Chows, and poodles.

From a pedigreed dog population of zero in the mid-nineteenth century, nearly 200 AKC-recognized breeds—nearly 350 worldwide—have sprouted today. More are added

---

* Though the US dog shows began much later than in the UK, I found evidence of an early dog show in our country, in May 1862, run by Phineas Taylor Barnum, the great showman: "a competition among the EDUCATED PERFORMING DOGS!" featuring "FOUR THOUSAND CHOICE DOGS, including OVER FORTY DISTINCT BREEDS." Crufts, the UK Kennel Club's dog show begun in the late nineteenth century, modeled their shows after Barnum's.

regularly by the AKC; numerous other new breeds, not yet registered nor pedigreed, pop up with the seasons: various poodle-spinoff -oodles, including one Golden-mountainberdoodle; XXL pit bulls; cavachon and cavapoos—Cavalier King Charles spaniels bred with bichons or poodles.* Cavapoos can be purchased on spec online in a shipping bundle that includes an "apothecary" health kit, designer collar, and "special puppy pacifier."

In this way, the dog, already plucked from the kingdom of wild animals and domesticated, changed irrevocably by their tolerance of and cooperativeness with us, underwent a second ice age. The last century and a half marks the dog's development from an animal to a showpiece. The question of *whether* someone should get a dog slipped into not whether, but *what kind*. A dog's breed becomes a status indicator, identifying the dog's person as sensitive or as dignified. Lists of most popular breeds in the city of New York trace how people in various parts of the city want to be seen. Guess where pit bulls are popular? Not on the Upper East Side, home to the storied Metropolitan Museum, impossibly clean sidewalks, and highly competitive, $32,000-a-year preschools. Bedford-Stuyvesant, Brooklyn, home of one of that borough's most recent gentrification-induced socioeconomic mixtures, prefers the pits. The Upper East Side has the Shih Tzu, whose breed club describes the dog as "[b]efitting his noble Chinese ancestry as a highly valued, prized companion and palace pet . . . proud of bearing [with] a distinctively arrogant carriage." The

---

* From the pedigree perspective, any dog that is crossbred (a mix of two purebred dogs) is not actually a pure breed. Perhaps to the chagrin of some goldendoodle (et al.) owners, this dog would thereby best be described as a "crossbreed" or a "mixed breed," if the crossing has happened more than once, not a new breed. Our society's esteem for breeds is thus shown to be undercooked: we barely know what is meant by "breed," and instead let others define it for us.

more liberal Upper West Side features the slobbery, loveable Labrador ("style and quality without over-refinement, and substance without lumber or cloddiness").*

That century and a half is further notable not only for hurrying dogs into the revered position they occupy in our homes, but also for normalizing deformities as cute and even desirable. Breeding is responsible for the latter, and at least witnessed the former: could we imagine there being a Rin Tin Tin without the noble, magnificent, German shepherd stars? Or imagine 101 average-looking dogs; Dorothy and her little cur, too; the Little Rascals and an undistinctive-looking Petey. It is perhaps not coincidental that so many dog stars—themselves responsible for up to decade-long upticks in each breed's popularity post-movie (of Old English sheepdogs after *The Shaggy Dog*, Labrador retrievers after *The Incredible Journey*, and, of course, the inevitable result of *101 Dalmatians*)—have been purebreds. Identifiable, charismatic, with distinctive humanlike personalities, dog movie stars have helped to create dogs as persons. Only: persons who you could get a copy of on Saturday afternoon by following the ad in the paper for *Collie puppies, finest breeding*, or *Toy French Poodle puppies: snow-white, long silky coats, long ears, and jet black eyes*, and driving to the Cute-Name Kennel in Bucolic Smalltown, Big State that gives you one, with the ears and the eyes and the coat.

There's the trouble.

• • •

"Faults: Too heavy head . . . / Too narrow or small skull / Foxy appearance / Presence of an apparent stop [area where

---

* Today, just as there is an elitism in choosing to buy a member of a storied breed, there is also a hint of self-importance in having a "rescue" dog. (For the record, I am a member of the class of rescue-dog people.)

the muzzle meets the skull] / Missing pigmentation on nose,
eye rims, or lips / Eyelids round, triangular, loose or small /
Overshot, undershot, wry mouth."
(Great Pyrenees breed standard)

A breed is less a scientific designation than it is a way of looking. Two dogs who look sufficiently distinctive from each other—the towering Great Dane, long of snout and tall of shoulder, and the Chihuahua, decidedly petite, on delicate legs—are still both the same species, but they are said to be of different breeds. While they are genetically distinguishable in important ways, their commonalities overwhelm their differences. Currently, what we usually mean when we say "breed" is "purebred"—especially those with a continuous ancestral history back to the moment when one person, usually a man, decided to mate two good-looking dogs together and name them "Beagle" or "Bloodhound."

What we called "breeds" hasn't always been purebreds. This isn't to say there weren't distinctive-looking dogs, or dogs called by names now appropriated by purebreds, like *greyhound*, *mastiff*, or *spaniel*. Before the nineteenth century, there was plenty of talk of breeds: there was a beagle-*looking* dog breed, and no one confused them with bloodhoundy types. "Mastiff, greyhound, mongrel grim, Hound or spaniel, brach* or lym"† Shakespeare rhymed in *King Lear*, giving us evidence of a couple of recognizable breed types in the late sixteenth and early seventeenth centuries. Even "mongrel" was a breed (a status that might make a modern show dog blanch). An eighteenth-century history of dogs adds dogs of

* a female scent hound.
† *Lym* is short for *lyam*, leash, and the dog at the end of that leash was something like a bloodhound.

various locales—Siberia, Lapland, Ireland—and even divides up breeds of mongrels, including the "Turk mongrel-dog," the "greyhound with wolf's hair," the "blubber-chops dog," "the pug-dog," "the small shagged dog," and "the dog [who] got between the bull-dog and mastiff."

What breed is the oldest? No pedigreed dog can honestly defend that storied claim. The assertions by some purebred dog breeders that their breed is the "most ancient" breed rely on slipping from one meaning of breed (distinctive-looking types) to the other (purebred and pedigreed). Various types of dogs, distinct in form or function from one another, existed for thousands of years before purebreds. These "landraces" arose as a combination of geographic isolation of different groups of dogs—leading to dogs adapted to their own climates—and genetic drift. Ancient humans preferred dogs who chased the deer they wanted to catch, found the pheasant they'd felled, or barked ferociously when a stranger approached the hut. This preference is, inadvertently, a selection for certain physical types: those of the gait, size, coat, and keenness of sight or smelling to out-hunt or -guard the other dogs.

By contrast, most of the breeds we see today were "created out of whole cloth, or something very close, in the not-too-distant past"—less than two hundred years ago, Ritvo writes. These purebred dogs are, as old breeds were, identifiable and distinctive physical types; the difference now is that they result from specific selection by means of inbreeding.

Still, purebred enthusiasts try to parlay the similarity in appearance of recent purebreds and ancient dogs to lend credence to their feelings of the superiority of their preferred breed. Some of the histories cooked up for purebreds are on their face ridiculous, as the claim that the Afghan hound—then the Barukhzy hound—was one of the dogs on Noah's Ark. (The regal Afghan's breed standard still toys with this assignment, calling them the "king of dogs," with "eyes gazing into the distance as if in memory of ages past.") The AKC and breed-club websites for the Xoloitzcuintli, a small, nearly hairless dog with oversized erect ears, claim that the dog "accompanied man on his first migrations across the Bering Straits," even while acknowledging that the breed was recognized by the AKC in 2011. Kennel-club membership isn't a prerequisite of breed membership, but deliberate selection of the dog is—and that simply didn't happen until the nineteenth century. Even putting stories of the Ark aside, the archaeological record of ancient breeds and the genome of current breeds don't align: the oldest dogs genetically aren't the ones at the oldest archaeological sites.

We have an inkling of what the early, loosely defined breeds looked like, via ancient relics. Walking down the long entrance hallway at the Met, in New York City, I always visit a small bone dish from ancient Egypt meant to hold cosmetics. The dish is carved as if to be the belly of a solemn resting dog. The pup's ears flop and forelegs cross like the hands of a prim lady. This face is no doubt the image of a dog who walked the land some 3,500 years ago—to my eye, something on the order of a well-fed Labrador. Elsewhere, an ash-preserved figure of Pompeii, one of the tempestuous Mt. Vesuvius' many victims nearly 2,000 years ago, was probably a guard dog, despite his small frame, as he was found chained to a house. Mosaics captioned "Cave Canem,"* of muscular but underfed long-nosed dogs with erect ears and snarling lips, might have been his cousins.

The history of art gives us a record of the dogs hanging around the studios of the historical artist. Medieval tapestries and paintings show panther-like, lean dogs accompanying

---

* Latin, literally "Beware the dog."

horses on a hunt or voyage. A small dog with the head of a Pomeranian and the body of a terrier stands in the shadows at the feet of Jan Van Eyck's matrimonial scene from 1434: likely a lap dog, not a hunter. Jan Fyt's hunting scenes include various dead ringers for setters, spaniels, greyhound types, beagles, and even a Dalmatian among the many extravagantly displayed dead hares and peacocks. A hungry wirehaired pointer–type caught in a defecatory crouch steals the scene in the seventeenth-century Rembrandt etching *The Good Samaritan*. Medieval and Renaissance dogs were not usually honored with a portrait, to be sure, or even a place in the frame. Dogs were intended to be at the behest of humans, for one or another work task, or were nuisances.

The first known list of types of dogs, published in 1486, lists a handful of "houndes," including the recognizable Grehoun, Mastiff, and Spanyel, as well as types that have disappeared or changed names, like Mengrell, Myddyng dogges, Tryndel-taylles, Prikherid currys, and "small ladyes' poppees." These would have been breeds that formed more or less naturally, with humans merely keeping around and feeding the ones they liked and culling or casting off the ones they did not. The first complete listing of "Englishe dogges," nearly a hundred years on, specifies seventeen types of dogs according to what they do. So there are Terrars, terriers who pursue fox and badger on the ground; various hounds like Bloudhoundes, known for scenting the blood of injured prey; and the Spaniel-gentle or Comforter dog, "to satisfie the delicatenesse of daintie dames . . . instrumentes of folly for them to play and dally withall, to tryfle away the treasure of time." Dogs with various non-hunting jobs: the Tynckers Curre, who carries a tinker's mending supplies; Turnespete dogs, responsible for keeping the meat rotating on the spit by running in an attached hamster-wheel; and Daunsers, "taught and exercised to daunce in measure at the musicall sounde of an instrument . . . showing many pretty trickes by the gesture of their bodies." There were Mooners, known for "bawing and wawing"* at the moon; Tumblers, who "turne and tumble, winding their bodyes about in circle wise"; and Stealers. The fifteenth-century Book of Saint Albans included small dogs that "bear away the fleas" as a category. Linnaeus listed thirty-five breeds—in addition to naming them all *Canis familiaris*, thus indicating that the listed types could and did interbreed, and were not of different species.

In all events, dogs were to have purposes for humans. And nothing about that changed in the nineteenth century, with the arrival of kennel clubs and the sport of breeding dogs for show. What changed was that the purpose was more to reflect the human and his place in society via his perfect dog, rather than solely to engage in a job like hunting, herding, or guarding. Such was the development of a society with just a hint of idle time and extra money.

• • •

*"Neither a Roman nose nor a dish-face is desirable . . .
A black nose is a disqualification . . . A two-tone
or butterfly nose should be penalized . . . Drooling
to be heavily penalized."*
(Brittany breed standard)

Behind the designing of dogs is a rumble of something more distasteful. The breeders' ambition was, as befits the name of the product, purity. "They didn't want polluted ani-

---

* I assume this is more or less what howling sounded like in the Renaissance.

mals. They didn't want proletarian animals. They wanted purebreds," Peter Sandøe, a professor of Bioethics at the University of Copenhagen, put it in an interview. As the move to restrict membership in a breed indicates, by formalizing breeding, fanciers were separating the respectable dog wheat from the unholy, scurvy dog chaff. "No dog can win" in a class, one nineteenth-century breeder's guide cautions, "unless pedigree of sire and dam be of undoubted purity."* The assigning of "papers" to purebred dogs echoes the question of the standing of immigrants to the country. And the language of purebred advocacy sometimes veered into the language of eugenics. In her comprehensive book *Pets in America*, Katherine Grier quotes an early twentieth-century veterinarian: "Many ill-bred 'mutts,' like so many human waifs, actually develop by their own natural abilities into remarkably bright, attractive, and worthy beings. But . . . it is the well-bred dog which is commonly looked to for natural development along reliable lines—the ones from which something can be expected . . . as a class [mixed breeds] can never hope to equal the true, pure-blooded animals with their generations of unmixed blood." Perhaps not by coincidence, you can find a 1905 advert for the American Institute of Phrenology's† next meeting among the listings of dogs for sale and for stud in the popular turn-of-the-century breeders' magazine *Dog Fancier*.

The means chosen to achieve "purity" were simple: inbreeding dogs very, very similar genetically—matings between siblings,

---

* The late nineteenth century also saw the rise of the idea of "purity" in other respects, such as in milk production and handling: the so-called hygienists aimed to purify milk through heating, to address the bacterial contamination likely with raw milk.

† Phrenology, by which one ostensibly could determine a person's character by examining the topography of their skulls, has often been linked with eugenics, given the connection drawn between morphology and merit.

or parent to pup. As anyone with at least a distant memory of biology class remembers, reproduction between close relatives can cause a recessive gene to be matched with another recessive gene, thus allowing latent genetic problems to suddenly pop up in an individual, and in their young, too. Charles Darwin demonstrated that outbreeding or crossbreeding—pairing a member of a species with one whose genes are dissimilar—leads to healthier offspring. He called this "hybrid vigor." But once a trophy is handed out, once a standard is penned, the aim of dog breeding is to ignore the genetics lesson and to produce more dogs *just like* that—via inbreeding.

The founder of the German shepherd dog, von Stephanitz, exalted in the results: "creatures of pure blood, where by proper breeding all unevennesses have been eliminated, far surpass all mongrels," he wrote, then went on to say, falsely, "Darwin shows in an abundance of conclusive examples, that crossbreeding leads to deterioration—and that a connection by breeding between unrelated races, or between races whose qualities have been developed in opposite directions, leads to ineradicable degeneration. On this subject he remarks; 'Crossing eliminates the virtues of both parent races, the only result is the true mongrel, whose chief characteristic is lack of character.'" Notably, von Stephanitz got the laws of inheritance, the views of Darwin, and the quote from Darwin wrong: the quote appears to have come from Alfred P. Schultz, an advocate of racial purity, in his book *Race or Mongrel*.* (Darwin's *On the Ori-*

---

*. . . whose subtitle is generous in educating the bookstore peruser what she is in for: "A brief history of the rise and fall of the ancient races of earth: a theory that the fall of nations is due to intermarriage with alien stocks: a demonstration that a nation's strength is due to racial purity: a prophecy that America will sink to early decay unless immigration is rigorously restricted."

gin of Species was published in the same year as the first dog show, but mentions nothing about mongrel dogs' character, or lack thereof.) Moreover, von Stephanitz added, "We can compare our shepherd breed dog without exaggeration with the Human Race . . . Thus the dog is a reflection of his master."

That about makes the point. Surely a desire for a beautiful specimen of dog need not be a mark of racial intolerance. What early fanciers did have in common, perhaps, was a longing for an ideal dog: the consummate collie, the supreme spaniel. The unreality of a quintessence of Dog; the utter lack of tidy connection of extant dogs to ancestral types; nothing deterred these breeders. They were joined, as well, in their distaste for the mixed breed,* the mutt, the mongrel, the cur.

On the matter of mixed breeds, an early article in the AKC club magazine, the *Gazette*, is entitled "Dogs That No One Should Own." Another, "What's All This Talk About Mutts?" quoted the writer and breeder Albert Payson Terhune as saying that a registered dog "guarantees its quality"; moreover, if pedigreed, "puppies are much more valuable." As to the "heroism, war-work, better temper, greater health, cleverness, and faithfulness" that were often attributed to the mutt, the author dismissed them out of hand. Such virtues are *expected* of purebreds. If a "circus trainer" who performs amazing stunts is said to prefer mutts, why, the writer suggested, it's just that he didn't have the money for a purebred.

To the fanciers, mongrels were responsible for "ninety per cent of all the mischief" done by dogs; they were dirty, useless, "rubbish," "degenerate," and thought to "contaminate" pure stock. The word "mongrel," initially applied to animals of

---

* "Mixed breed" is really a misnomer, as before there were purebred dogs, no dog was the result of the "mixing" of two purebreds. The phrase is widely used to describe, simply, dogs of no clear heritage—before and after the rise of pedigreed dogs.

mixed heritage, quickly came to mean a person of mixed racial or social background—and never with kind intent (the word *mutt*, too, is short for *muttonhead*, which was not intended as a compliment to sheep or human intelligence). The word then bounced back to impugn mixed-breed dogs as well: "Like a true mongrell, he neither bites nor barks, but when your back is towards him."

Putting aside the fact that every dog in the mid-nineteenth century was a literal mixed breed, it is acknowledged that to begin a breed line one has to start with mixed breeds. A mongrel dog was identified with the street, and thus with people of the street: the infirm, the downcast, the impoverished. "Nobody now who is anybody," the *Dog Owners' Annual* declared in 1890, "can afford to be followed about by a mongrel dog." "The value of a mongrel," a nineteenth-century dog fancier wrote, "[is] just a trifle less than the price of the rope you would purchase to hang him."

Something of this attitude continues today. The website of the UK Kennel Club has a link to click if you want to find a "rescue" dog, the current euphemism for "mutt waiting in a shelter to be adopted." Click it, though, and you are directed to input "the breed you would like to search for." What follows is a list of Kennel Club breeds—not breed-rescue organizations, but the breed clubs. There is no linking for breed-rescue sites, or to the thousands of shelters for dogs who are not purebreds: the majority of dogs who need homes.

The Kennel Club presumably knows that even if the dog is a purebred, re-homing a dog will not lead to further registration fees for the club. The "information guide" to getting a rescue dog that I found when visiting their website in 2018 does a preposterously passive-aggressive job of discouraging this option. "Do not consider adopting a rehomed dog if you have a busy life, or very young children," the guide opens, "as it may need special care unless you know it is 'bomb proof' and the people rehoming it can give you a full history." It goes on to list the various behavioral and temperamental and physical problems that the dog "may" have, the rigorous application process you "may" face, and the difficulties you will face when the dog, having survived an (assumed) "trauma"—("Some will have been found wandering the streets cold and hungry")—will need to "learn to trust again." "Separation anxiety, fear of noises, and attempts to run away are common."

And oh, the responsibilities: are you up to the task of having such a damaged dog? "Be prepared to walk the dog at least twice a day and to clean up his/her waste," they admonish. "Can you really afford the time and expense of dog ownership?" Presumably this marks these dogs as distinct from the purebred dogs they advocate for, who miraculously walk themselves and are self-cleaning. Their attitude is based, one can assume, in an interest in self-perpetuation: if people did not buy breeds and register them, kennel clubs would no longer exist.*

•   •   •

"His courage is proverbial."
(American Staffordshire terrier breed standard)

Living with dogs sometimes feels like an exercise in collecting and characterizing *Who They Are* and *What They Do*. I have memorized the particular way Finnegan's ears fold on

---

* Ten months after I publicized this fact in January 2018, the Kennel Club changed their site somewhat to include mention of "crossbreeds"—still directing the rescue-dog-interested to breed-rescue sites, not shelters. Their information guide has been replaced with a perfunctory web page describing the "behavioral 'baggage'" you might get with dogs "who have been rejected at least once, and, in some cases, a number of times."

themselves, the left-handed curlicue in Upton's tail, the gentle curls in the feathering on Pump's legs. When I try to enumerate the distinctively-Upton behaviors that have happened *today*, I am overwhelmed: his placement on the bed overnight so geometrically ideal so as to force me into a fetal position in one corner; the thump of his tail when he sees me rising to greet him; his lopsided trot down the hall; the combination openmouthed-smile and circular-tail-spin that projects him to find me in the kitchen; the half-leaps of his eighty-five-pound frame as I put down breakfast; the galumphy way he greets the cat, curled in a box; the attention he pays to any noise out the window; the way his lip snags on a left tooth when he is pensive; . . . and that's only by 8 a.m.

There is pleasure in the predictable behaviors of our pups. In fact, many of the "tricks" we ask dogs to do are exercises in predictability: we say *sit*, the dog sits. We say *shake*, the dog shakes. Our discontent at a dog's willful uncooperativeness is really discontent at the undermining of predictability. It gives the lie to the feeling of control we have when we know what they are going to do; when we cannot pull that magic out of the hat, we balk.

Advertisements and descriptions of breeds intentionally appeal to this desire for predictability. As a result of their ubiquity, we've been left with flawed typological thinking: as though one retriever can be said to be, on some level, like every other retriever. To be sure, looking at weeks-old puppies, bodies splayed on each other and exploring outward in ever-expanding circles, at first they do all look alike. They are squeaking, snuffling, tumbling fur puddles. But then one pup breaks away and aims for your outstretched finger. Another notices a shoelace dangling off a shoe and fumbles after it. A third burrows into their mother's belly; a fourth climbs on the third. You notice the pink nose of one, the seeming furrowed brow of another. Already, they are distinct, and every moment they will grow more into themselves.

In our perseverance in talking about breed, in our fore-grounding of typology, we're missing each dog for who they are. Yes, each dog is as a member of a species, a breed (or a mix)—but an individual most of all. A focus on the important unit of variance being the breed, not the dog, is where the danger lies. Having a dog of a particular breed seems to assure predictability, but it does not. On many tests of a dog's behavioral tendencies, in ways that matter to living with them, there turns out to be as much variation between dogs of the same breed as between dogs of different breeds. Dogs differ widely in trainability and in their responsiveness to people—again, not by breed; by the dog.

Along one dimension breeds *do* seem to be distinct—and, alas, it is one that many people overlook. On measures of "reactivity," or general excitement to stimuli, breeds matter. While all dogs have the olfactory and visual equipment to see a rat, only some—we call them ratters, or terriers—find themselves compelled to ferret out the rat from whatever rat hole he's hidden in. My own dogs see sheep, surely, and approach them, wonder at them, and sniff enthusiastically. They do not, however, "show eye" (locking their gaze on the sheep), stalk closer, and move to corral the sheep to move back toward their pen as any Border collies meeting sheep are inclined to. And there are some behaviors that are more reliably seen in some breeds than in others: hounds bay, pointers point, retrievers retrieve—whether a felled feathered bird or a tossed fuzzy ball.

Genetics matters in setting predispositions, in changing susceptibilities. Somehow, though, the common understanding of breed distinctions is applied selectively: a pit's a pit, anti–pit bull people will say, and can't be changed. But that same person may bring a Border collie into a small apartment and assume that they will be quiescent. Weirdly, many people ignore just those genetic tendencies that had a place in the working history of the breed type, but that do not have a place in their new role as companion dogs. Every trainer knows a family who brought a Border collie into a small space, and are chagrined that she's herding the children of the house, or harassing passing skateboarders. What was once the desired behavior in the dog we now call "misbehavior."

Whichever way we cut it, our thinking about who a dog will be is deeply imperfect. By imagining that a dog's description in a breed standard will serve as a guarantee of behavior, we set the dog up to disappoint us. Most breed standards include commentary on the breed's temperament and character: it is *loyal* or *aloof* or *independent*. These traits are not built in, though: at best, they are generalizations; at worst, they are wildly idealized. A goodly number of standards claim *intelligence* as a feature of their breed—though many couch it as an "intelligent expression"; if not claimed to be quick-witted, the breed is doubtless "bold," "noble," the epitome of "dignity" or "grace," "devoted," or "affectionate." All lovely features, but none reliably distinguishing one breed from another.

The standard for the golden retriever declares that the breed is "friendly, reliable and trustworthy. Quarrelsomeness or hostility towards other dogs or people in normal situations, or an unwarranted show of timidity or nervousness, is not in keeping with Golden Retriever character"; the AKC website declares them "good with children." Indeed, I've known many exceptionally friendly golden retrievers, as exhibited by their fulsome greetings and enthusiastic weaving around and through my legs. They very nearly smile. And yet watch a toddler toddle over to the dog's favorite stuffed toy, or try to ride the pony-sized dog, and you may well see a dog who is good with children bite a child in the face, as happens with some regularity. One research study comparing golden retrievers with breeds thought to be dangerous (Doberman, Rottweiler, pit bull–type dogs) found no difference at all in the amount of aggressive behavior of the breeds.

•   •   •

"[A]n aristocrat, his whole appearance one of dignity and
aloofness with no trace of plainness or coarseness."
(Afghan hound breed standard)

Legislation has followed from our ways of characterizing members of the species. For instance, dogs have always had restricted access to some places and been outright banned from others. They still are. Typically, the ban involves prohibition on the species level: it is *dogs* we don't want in our restaurants (New York City, twenty-first century) or in our city (Reykjavík, Iceland, twentieth century). The specific prohibition of particular breeds runs parallel to this. Over time, hugely different breeds have become the bête noire of the moment. In 1876, a dog called the Spitz—a small, pointy-nose Pomeranian-type, of the sort one could easily stash in one's purse—was disparaged. "So far as morality is concerned, the Spitz is thoroughly and irredeemably corrupt," wrote the *New York Times*. "He is a tireless and shameless thief, and exhibits a perverted skill in obtaining access to forbidden cellars, and in stealing the reserved bones of honest and frugal dogs, which is truly vulpine"—which fox the dog is accused of resembling in his "treacherous face." This calumny was due to the breed's being a new immigrant to the US, and coincident with the spread of hydrophobia—now known as rabies—in New York City.

The now well-loved Saint Bernard also had a stint as the canine bugaboo in the nineteenth century, as did the dastardly dachshund and the bone-chilling Cuban bloodhound—the latter not a bloodhound at all, but a "short-haired, black, red, yellow, brindled, or spotted dog, or any colour . . . with a head, breast, fore-legs, and shoulders like a light-made mastiff, and snout somewhat elongated, ears erect, like a greyhound." The breed was imported by the state of Florida "for the purpose of hunting the wretched Indians whom they wish to expel from the country," according to a newspaper of the time.

The singling out of breeds took a new turn in 1991. Two years prior, an eleven-year-old girl was killed by a pair of Rottweilers in the UK, igniting "a wave of hysteria," as noted animal researcher James Serpell writes. Owners of Rottweilers were, suddenly, harassed in public when walking their charges; the dogs themselves did poorly in the nation's press: "Terrorists on four legs," a headline shouted about these "devil dogs." In response, the UK created breed-specific legislation—now sufficiently ubiquitous to earn its own acronym, BSL—under their Dangerous Dogs Act. The Act expressly forbade ownership of four breeds of dogs: three of which (Japanese Tosa, Fila Brasiliero, and Dogo Argentino) were virtually nonexistent in the UK,* the fourth being pit bulls. Oddly, Rottweilers were off the hook.

BSL has been catchy. Australia, China, and various European countries have caught it. Doberman pinschers, German shepherds, Chow Chows, and myriad other breeds have been banned. Banned dogs are either confiscated and killed,

---

* Except one Japanese Tosa.

or allowed to live out their life if tattooed, registered, spayed, and leashed and muzzled at all times, regardless of the dog's history. The US is, as usual, a mélange of different attitudes toward dogs, but various forms of legislation have been enacted spottily throughout, ranging from bans on pit bull–type dogs in Miami-Dade County and in Denver in the 1980s, even before the Dangerous Dogs Act, to current regulations in public housing in New York City that forbid any dog over twenty-five pounds.*

Today, one breed, more than others, bears the brunt of the characterization of certain breeds as irredeemably evil: the so-called pit bull. It was not always so for pits. Pit bulls were cover dogs three times over in *Life* magazine—featured because they were winsome, not because they were wicked. Teddy Roosevelt had a bull terrier named Pete in the White House—albeit one who treed the French ambassador and bit a Navy Department clerk before being killed by another dog, as the newspapers sympathetically reported. But, as Bronwen Dickey describes, the dog tumbled from its position as a well-loved dog to being cast as a menace, hardwired to kill. Dickey reveals that a few pit bull attacks, including a child's death— tragic and also statistically not unusual—generated a flurry of hyperbolic press reports that demonized the dog while ignoring various other relevant factors in each situation (cases included such details as a toddler left unsupervised, an abused and starved dog, and a negligent owner).

Breed-specific legislation relies squarely on the spurious idea that behavior is determined by breed—that genetics determines behavior—exactly in the way breed standards

---

* A side effect of which has been communities dealing with the peculiarities of living with small dogs, who can be harder to manage in non-obvious ways: they can be more vocal, and some owners do not walk or socialize their toy dogs, for instance.

imply. A pit bull—any pit bull—will act "like pit bulls do"; which is allegedly different than how a dachshund—and all dachshunds—will act. Pits are a telling example of the emptiness of the claim, for with pits, there is no there there: it is not a pedigreed breed. They could be an American pit bull terrier, American Staffordshire terrier, Staffordshire bull terrier, American bully—or, for purposes of the legislation, any dog with "one drop" of any of these breeds' blood in him (which proportion is determined by our gaze, not by drawing blood).* "Pit bull" is used more as a "social caste" of dogs than it is a description of a specific breed or breeds, Dickey tells me: "It's a short-coated nondescript dog not otherwise specified"—with either a blocky head, stocky body, brindle coat, or a "splash of white on the chest"—a mongrel of any heritage. "It becomes like Prince: the artist formerly known as . . . ," she says: they are the dog formerly known as the pit bull terrier, but now are any dog you want to malign. In 2016, Montreal moved to ban various pit-like breeds, as well as dogs with "characteristics" of the breeds, after a woman, sadly, was killed by a dog. A boxer.

Most dogs identified as pit bulls are *not* actually pit bull in any way: half of the dogs so labeled by dog professionals do not have any genetic relationship to any of the breeds considered pit bull–like. Shown a photo of one square-headed, black dog, her erect ears folded over themselves, shelter staff and veterinarians in one influential study unanimously identified "pit-bull type." Her genome identified "Irish water spaniel" and "Siberian Husky." Conversely, some dogs identified as *not* being pit bulls actually have some of these bully breeds in their ancestry. Dog experts in the US, where rhetoric about pit bulls

---

* Taken from, or evocative of, the Racial Integrity Act of 1924, in which Virginia, determined to keep people of different races from marrying, defined "white people" as those who have not even one drop of non-white blood in them.

has reached a fever pitch, are much more likely to label a dog as "pit bull" than UK experts.

Another problem with breed-specific legislation is that we are notoriously poor at determining what breeds a mixed-breed dog has in them simply by looking. Even experienced professionals cannot reliably identify the breed of a dog by sight when parentage is uncertain (as with the ubiquitous shelter mutt); nearly 90 percent of breed identifications at shelters have been found to be incorrect. One study found dog experts—including shelter staff, vets, and behaviorists—not only didn't agree with each other about various mixed dogs' ancestry; they also rarely identified *any* of the breeds that appeared in analysis of the pups' DNA.

These inexactitudes represent a lack of understanding of genetics more than a lack of understanding of dogs. Against our assumptions, the first generation of pups from two different purebreds often look nothing like each other, and nothing like either of their parents. In John Scott and John Fuller's famous study of the influence of genetics on behavior, they mated breeds with different appearance and characteristics and then examined the result in their offspring (called the F1 generation) and their offspring's offspring (F2 generation). The F1 pups of a basenji and cocker spaniel pairing have a floppy-eared, hound-Lab look; none of the F2 pups with these genes look remotely like cockers or basenji. A photo lineup of the F2s show black pups, tan pups, pups with dark tails dipped in white paint; black with white spots, and white with dark spots; some with broad heads, some with small heads. None is her parents or grandparents; each is her own dog.

Nor do breed bans work to reduce dog attacks. An exhaustive Danish study looking at the number of dog bites from before and three years after a "dangerous dog" act prohibited ownership of any member of thirteen breeds,* found that the number of bites slightly *rose* after the breed ban. Recent research from the UK, Ireland, and Spain has found the same: breeds are being targeted indiscriminately by the bans. Any dog with teeth can bite. And as James Serpell and his colleagues have shown, dogs responsible for the most reported aggressive acts are . . . *dachshunds*. I tell the dachshund I meet in the elevator of my apartment building this, as he barks and tries futilely to jump higher than his own knee. His owner hushes him and drags him, his legs locked and unyielding, skating on his toenails out the door.

•　　•　　•

". . . well developed hips and thighs . . . with the whole rear assembly showing strength and drive . . ."
(Boykin spaniel breed standard)

The strangeness of our thinking about the reducibility of dog to type finds its most ludicrous result in the appearance of businesses that will, for a large fee, clone your beloved pup. On its surface, the motivation for pet cloning is deeply understandable: anyone who has lost a pet can summon that grief. And we commiserate: what one wouldn't give to have the dog "back"! Ah, says the business model, what if you *can*?

Genetic clones can in fact be developed. A hair clipping, some petri dishes, a surrogate mother dog, and fifty thousand dollars, and you're on your way. But clones do not look identical to the original: genes express at different rates in different environments. And they do not act the same as the original:

* (and requiring muzzling of the dogs already owned)

behavior emerges from that precious set of genes waltzing out the door and into the world. What one puppy has experienced of life—the dogs, people, squirrels, and butterflies; the smells, sounds, sights, and tastes; the comforts, dangers, alarms, attractions, confusions and pleasures—is impossible to replicate. The clone will turn out to be her own (doubtless quickly irreplaceable) pup. She will be a good dog. What she won't be is a reincarnation of the last one.

The premise of cloning is flawed in the same way as the premise of a breed's predictability is flawed. A dog is treated, unintentionally, as an object, not an individual. An object can be bought, replicated, thrown out. And, sadly, so can dogs. Are we far from the day when a particular genetic type—the perfect breed—will be trademarked and mass-produced, available online with next-day shipping? Cloning is but one step from this dystopian dog future.

The urge to clone a dog winds up being, on examination, more incongruous than reasonable: the whole point of having a relationship with a dog is that it is a relationship *that you grew with the dog*—not that the dog came a certain way and you are just visiting their personality. You make each other; the bond between you is forged together. And so the business of cloning—which raises expectations that no dog can fill; which treats the dog as a commodity rather than a living being; which takes advantage of our grief at losing our dogs—is indefensible.

• • •

"Closely set eyes are to be faulted. China or wall eyes are to be disqualified . . . A pointed muzzle is not desirable . . . A dish-shaped muzzle is a fault . . . Too many wrinkles in

the forehead is a fault . . . A spotted nose is not desirable.
A flesh colored nose disqualifies."
(*German shorthaired pointer breed standard*)

When I ask Amy Attas, a veterinarian with a wide-ranging practice, which breed suffers the most for having been selected for form, she does not hesitate. "Bulldogs," she says. This breed is definitely one of the most stricken by the effects of selective breeding. Seeing the English bulldog in 1866 and today, the breed looks to have been in a significant traumatic accident. "If you look at photos of old Westminster or Crufts [the big UK dog show]," Stephen Zawistowski says, "the bulldog had a *face*"—a clear, noticeable muzzle. No longer. Today, the muzzle on this wonderful dog appears to have been run at high speeds into something unmoving: it is dramatically smashed upon itself, the nose jammed backward, the jaw thrust forward as though on the receiving end of an uppercut. Pendulous skin, pushed into the face, drapes and folds upon itself, curtaining the eyes and extending into long jowls.

The phenomenon facing the bulldogs, and all purebred dogs, is the rise of inherited disorders—and the high number of inherited disorders is due to inbreeding. Moreover, the breed standards have encouraged an exhaustive refining of the shape of the animals, with deleterious effects. For many dogs, the result has been profound. For instance, the standard for the bulldog in 1892 insisted that the dog's skull should be "very large—the larger the better." Now, because of their disproportionately large heads, bulldogs cannot fit out of their mother's birth canal, and must typically be birthed by Cesarean section. The breed has other genetic medical problems, many visible. Because of their skin rolls, they tend to have chronic skin infections and soreness. Because of their bulging eyes, their eyelids either roll in or out, damaging the cornea and causing insistent irritation. Their stocky body and short legs lead to painful and sometimes debilitating movement issues.

The long word for the short-nosed dog, like bulldogs, is brachycephalic. Breeding for a shorter nose* has changed the shape of their entire skull and all the soft bits the skull protects. Wolves are the opposite: dolichocephalic—classically canine in profile. Humans are brachycephalic, too, in a manner of speaking. And that may be why dogs with flatter faces have been bred: as a species perhaps uniquely narcissistic, we humans like animals that resemble us. Selection for shorter noses, alas, raced way ahead of evolution's ability to redesign the sinuses, hard palate, and other tissues to fit in the cramped space. As a result, bulldogs, and all brachycephalic breeds, often have severe problems breathing in the heat, or with the least amount of exercise—which includes "walking." "French bulldogs have a ton [of problems] too," Attas continues. "Brachycephalic problems." Attas, who confesses she was imprinted on pugs—another brachycephalic breed with a squashed nose—when she met her first dog as a three-year-old, tells me about another rescued pug she recently adopted: herself a three-year-old from Chicago. "It wasn't a hot day when I came to get her, but she just could not breathe: she was panting, making noises indicating that she was really have trouble getting air in. I flew her home with a fan in my hand, blowing cold air on her, because she couldn't maintain her body temperature." Attas soon did surgery on her dog to open her pug's nasal passages, including cutting the alar fold (the tissue ringing the nostrils) to make enough space for air to simply get into the nostrils, a soft palate resection (removal of

* 1892 standard: "The Muzzle should be short, broad, [and] turned upwards."

the soft tissues jammed tightly together in the throat, in order to make a space to breathe through), and removing the dog's saccules—tonsil-like sacs in the larynx. "If you breathe with effort, like pugs do, the saccules evert from their crypt"—a surprisingly apt term for where the saccules, turned inside out, sit—and obstruct the airway even more. "It's like breathing through a straw," Attas says. Soft-palate resection surgery is now commonplace for the brachycephalic breeds.

And yet bulldogs are the fifth most popular breed registered with the AKC; three other brachycephalic dogs (boxers, French bulldogs, and Yorkshire terriers) have for several years joined them in the top ten. "People don't think, 'I want to get a dog with eye problems who can hardly breathe.' They probably think, 'This type of dog is cute!,'" says Zazie Todd, who writes about pet-human relationships. In point of fact, the most popular breeds today are not the ones that exhibit the best behavior, have the easiest personalities, are the longest lived, or are the healthiest. Puzzlingly, the most popular breeds have more inherited disorders than less popular breeds. What is more puzzling is not that they are diseased, per se; it's that it is *we* who made them sick, and we are either oblivious or frankly cruel.

I'm going to choose "oblivious," because the effect of our growing awareness is visible. The problems with brachycephaly have gotten sufficient attention that national airlines ban nearly two dozen identified brachy breeds—or any "snub-nosed dogs of any 'mix,'" as American Airlines' website puts it, with odd snideness—on the plane as checked luggage, as dogs usually travel. Putting aside the question of whether it makes sense to treat dogs with any sort of nose more like checked luggage than like the family members we consider them to be (which family presumably rides in the cabin),* the policy reflects the realization that in hot or stressful conditions where airflow may be restricted, these dogs are more likely to suffocate.†

Inherited physical disorders afflict the majority of pedigree dogs, though, even those whose looks do not reveal them. The same genes that create the "ridgeback" in Rhodesian ridgebacks can also lead to dermoid sinus, a neural tube disorder that leads to crippling neurological problems. The preposterous swayback and splayed and short "frog feet" of the German shepherd dog lead to musculoskeletal disorders and debilitating hip dysplasia. The Cavalier King Charles spaniel's skull is so small that its brain, which grows too large for the allotted space, can swell in an extremely painful way, a condition called syringomyelia. Simply being gigantic—consider the massive Great Dane— or diminutive—widespread in a recent trend of saucer-sized "teacup" dogs—causes orthopedic problems from hip dysplasia to kneecap dislocation. Pugs' bulging eyes can lead to ulceration; basset hounds are prone to disc disease; Dalmatians to deafness.

The source of these genetic disasters is inbreeding—which means the responsible parties are inbreeders. AKA breeders. This is not about good or bad breeders. It is about an adherence to the idea that pedigree dogs must be inbred, as well as breed standards that glorify disease and deformity. Some stan-

---

* I do not believe that it does make sense (and I do not truly put this aside: see *Owning Dogs*, ch. 3).

† The policies followed the discovery that most of the dogs who died on airline flights were short-nosed, and reflect either good welfare or good business sense (or both).

dards have also changed over time for the worse. A male Dane of 1889 was meant to be around 120 pounds; today, the AKC lists the weight of the dog as "140–175 pounds": extra weight that taxes their bones. Change the standard—let, say, Ridge-backs without the ridge on their backs into the breed; or allow outbreeding, mixing in a separate breed occasionally—and rates of the negative effects of inbreeding will tumble. But the pedigree dog world is built on that standard, that closed line. (And what is called "line breeding," wherein breeders ostensi-bly choose mates more carefully from among the pedigree, is no better: "a distinction without a difference," as biologist Pat-rick Bateson writes.) It wasn't always so, remember: before the closed stud books, good breeding involved lots of outbreeding. There is resistance to that now, Stephen Zawistowski tells me, citing a well-known case with Dalmatians. This breed has an inherited urinary tract disorder—which co-occurs with the perfectly black spots of the canonical Dalmatian. One fancier wanted, naturally, to breed it out of the dog. So he brought in a fresh blood line, selecting against the disorder: "he bred a pointer into his Dalmatian line, then backbred repeatedly," breeding the crossbred dog with purebred Dalmatians, Zaw-istowski relates. Though the crossbred's pups, which lacked the disorder, were initially approved for registration with the AKC, "there was a point where they said, You can't register them." The dogs couldn't have papers if they came from a crossbreed outside the pedigree line, even if it reduced the chance of the disorder.* "It wasn't like he was breeding with a skank dog on the street," Zawistowski adds, with some rue.

Even a conscientious breeder who nonetheless simply fol-

---

* In 2011, the descendants of the crossbred Dalmatian were finally allowed into the AKC, some thirty years after the breeder's first request. In the meantime, none of his defect-free Dalmatians were allowed to sully the pool.

lows the standard is unwittingly exposing their dogs to disorders. In his inquiry into dog breeding practices, Bateson writes plainly of what we can expect when we inbreed: "reduced fertility both in litter size and sperm viability, developmental disruption, lower birth rate, higher infant mortality, shorter life span, increased expression of inherited disorders and reduction of immune system function." Impotence, abnormalities, ill health, and death. Nothing to crow about.

The inquiry was funded by the UK charity Dogs Trust and the UK Kennel Club after the airing on BBC One of a documentary called *Pedigree Dogs Exposed* that shone a light on the perils of inbreeding. Its reception was dramatic: BBC canceled its longtime contract to air the Crufts dog show, and others withdrew their sponsorship. The power of the documentary was its exposure of the consequence of inbreeding for individual dogs. Former RSPCA veterinarian Mark Evans minces no words: we celebrate, he spits out in the film, "mutants, deformed, disabled, diseased animals." Damnable video, hard to watch, shows a Cavalier in spasms of pain from its swollen brain; an epileptic boxer in seizure; and numerous breeders and judges who casually disavow any harm to the dogs. I instinctively avert my eyes at the footage of a Pekingese named Danny, his face nearly hidden behind his blow-dried fur, running around the show ring at Crufts in 2003 for the umpteenth time. His tongue curls up in his mouth, his eyes, large and bugging, dart frantically. Even while still in the ring he is placed atop an ice pack: due to his brachycephalic airway obstruction, he had become critically overheated. That year, he was awarded best in show. (In 2016, his grandson—whose continually flopping, panting tongue confirms his lineage—was crowned the winner of the Toy group.) By 2008 Danny had had some eighteen litters; each of his offspring has a high chance of suffering the same respiratory difficulties that kept him on ice.

• • •

"Set almost flush, the eyes are comparatively small and almond shaped with tight eyelids. The color is a warm tone of medium to dark brown, dark amber but never yellow. The expression is keenly alert, intelligent, direct and quizzical."
(Irish water spaniel breed standard)

When an anatomical travesty is our "best" dog, I fear we have entirely lost our way. We can't stay in this place—not while knowing how troubled breeds are. Given the prized place dogs have in our culture, our complacency about their welfare is deeply disquieting. Miraculously, simply by cross-breeding dogs—something that the phenomenon of designer dogs has, ironically and unintentionally, flirted with—we could make them healthier.* Period. After *Pedigree Dogs Exposed* was aired in the UK, the Kennel Club made some changes—for instance, eliminating father-daughter matings. Not enough. Kennel clubs and breed clubs have had health on their radar for years. As long as fifty-five years ago the British Veterinary Association specified ten genetic disorders due to conformation to standards. Still, until health—and not appearance, nor purity, nor best in show—is the priority, there will be inbred disasters. Why not put health first? Every dog

* This is not to suggest that designer dogs are necessarily healthier: if bred improperly, or if the first generation is extended through inbreeding, they are just as bad. But if one continuously mixed breeds each generation, then that's a good start. If a cockapoo is amorous with a goldendoodle, and their offspring extend the circle, why, then we'll have some swell pups.

owner wants their dog to live longer; no owner wants their dog to suffer, as they now are. If big agriculture were developing plainly diseased animals—a genetically engineered headless chicken or a massive super pig, researchers have observed, "society would shut them down. Is doing it to our companion animals"—for that is what we are doing to dogs—"any more justifiable morally?"

Don't worry, everyone: crossbred dogs will still be fantastic. Look at mutts, simply crossbred many times over: adorable, individual—plus just those traits we want in our bred dogs: "intelligent," "loyal," "affectionate," and, in the case of my dogs, terrifically "noble" (if with a touch of goofiness) in their own way.

We can begin by de-commodifying breeds. As much as dogs are loved, they are also a business proposition: people make money from selling inbred dogs, from selling unhealthy dogs, from selling a false promise about what a dog will be like to people who are entirely unprepared for the reality. Most everyone knows to rail against "puppy mills," or large commercial breeders, where pups and parents are often kept in unsanitary conditions; the mother bred until she can breed no more and then is killed; the pups isolated and unable to have the critical socialization needed for successful life with humans and other dogs; everyone underfed and deprived of reliable water or medical care. "All large puppy-breeding operations," Grier writes, "whether a run-down rural puppy mill or a scientifically managed puppy farm, treat dogs as livestock." But some ten *thousand* puppy mills, by the ASPCA's estimate, continue to exist because . . . people buy puppies from them. Not directly, or even intentionally, at times, but often: it is widely recognized that virtually *all* pet stores—yes, all; yes, including that nice store near you; yes—get their dogs from puppy mills.* As with agriculture, dog breeding has gotten too big: it doesn't scale, and corners are cut, usually into the well-being of the products—the dogs themselves. To that point, the AKC, reemphasizing its mission to take "whatever actions necessary to protect and assure the continuation of the sport of purebred dogs," weighed in on puppy mills, or what they call "high volume breeders." None of the final recommendations made by a committee investigating the problem was "getting rid of puppy mills." Instead, though, the committee unanimously recommended that the AKC explore the possibility of providing registered breeders with the incentive of "an attractive registration certificate suitable for framing." Well, that ought to do it.

Humane societies and shelter workers speak plainly to the point: *Adopt, don't shop*. To simply walk into any shelter, where one or many dogs' barks ring through the hallways, is to appreciate the poignancy behind the slogan. Each face peering out, meeting your gaze, pleads with you. Dogs lying curled upon themselves, or a litter curled around each other's bodies, seize my heart and melt it. Imagine a restriction on breeding until every one of those faces was placed in a new home. Eventually, though, "you can't help breeding," Peter Sandøe has suggested. "The future of domesticated animals is in our hands—whether we like it or not." As long as we want to live with dogs, we can't avoid it, because it is only where they are free-ranging that they get to choose the terms of their romantic life: owned dogs' pairings are at the behest of the human holding the leash. Stephen Zawistowski agrees: "I estimate that on an annual basis we need eight to ten million dogs,

---

* Unless you've seen the parents yourself, assume that puppy with "papers" is a puppy mill dog. Yup, even that puppy you found online, on a site with bucolic photos of dogs playing at a farm, whose owner said she bred them in her kitchen (but fails to let you meet the pup's parents).

based on current population growth [of humans]," to fill the demand for dogs. "The interesting question is, the shelters are only getting in four to five million dogs. Where are the other dogs going to come from?"

Zawistowski has an idea, himself: "'Backyard breeder' has become a pejorative term," he says—painted with the same, corrupt brush as puppy mills have been—but he thinks it ought not be. There is much to be valued in a small-scale breeder who raises a couple of litters a year, at most, "born in the basement and kitchen," cared for by hand and socialized. "I have photos of my wife, sitting around this litter of beagle puppies," he remembers, harkening back to the time when his family bred beagles in this way. "We really cared for them." Health of the animals could be the mandate, not lineage. He talks about this kind of breeder as backyard *craftspeople*, where the craft is "understanding and knowing dogs."

As I write this, California has passed a law that pet stores must sell only rescue or shelter animals. Pet-store owners fretted. The owner of a store called Puppy Heaven, specializing in teacup Yorkies and toy Maltipoos, whose website features celebrity actors and singers palming their new, tiny charges, was chagrined at the news: "It takes the freedom of choice from people who want to get a puppy," he said. Grier writes that the AKC has long fought any restriction on commercial breeding "on the grounds that additional regulation is an infringement on dog owners' property rights." The puppy-store owner adds, of his clientele: "They don't want to get someone else's unwanted dog or something of that nature."

And there it is: a perfect misunderstanding of what a dog in a shelter is, what a breed can be, and what a non-breed is. "Something of that nature." What is the nature of a mutt: the nature of impurity? No, the nature of *animal*. A dog, from this perspective, is not an animal, but a kind of product. Calling shelter dogs "someone else's unwanted dog" is a straw man: plenty of dogs in shelters are purebreds. They are there because their owners couldn't deal with the dog they had, versus the dog the pet store advertised on its celebrity-photo page.

The California law may stumble. People want puppies, and there are fewer puppies in shelters than coming out of puppy mills, unsurprisingly. Some people who are in the business of managing populations of unwanted dogs are sympathetic. People want the dog they want. I assent: if asked to make a choice among a hundred different-looking dogs, I will choose one whose looks and behavior resonates most with me. But it is flawed thinking to imagine that it should always be so, or that we would suffer without getting to adopt or buy that dog of our childhood, on whom we imprinted, or who strikes us as "cutest." Take away the hundred different dogs, and give me ten, who look more alike than different. I can still find the one with the one ear that stands up, who wags the instant I look at her. Or give me any *one*—the one who crosses my path and needs a home. I will love her, too. We can still find our dogs. Along the way, we may just find ourselves.

• • •

"Neck: The skin is supple, ample and loose . . .
Tail: Carried low, it is neither broken nor kinked
but supple . . . Feet: Toes should be tight, nails curved
and strong, and pads well developed and supple . . .
Gait: The gait is quite supple . . ."
(Dogue de Bordeaux breed standard)

We are thousands of years on from the moment that a wolf and a human crossed that invisible line between them and looked at each other differently. Let's imagine we were around then. Fourteen or so thousand years ago, when those wolves—proto-dogs—started skulking around on the outskirts of our camp, sniffing at the parts of the wild boar we could not stomach. We endure them, for a while—and they endure us, too, and look at us, and swallow their snarls. Then there are pups and you pick one up. My god, it's soft, and it gurgles and whimpers, and its eyes are trained on you and full like plump grapes. You keep it.

Or imagine yourself whisked back to pre-industrial America and England, when those wolf pups have long since become dog pups and they are ubiquitous. And you are there when von Stephanitz concocted the idea of creating a new "race" of dog for Germany out of the best example of the shepherd dogs out there, or when Dudley Coutts Marjoribanks, 1st Baron Tweedmouth, began designs on what became the golden retriever.

How were you to know that the wolf whelp was to lead to the estimated ninety million US and seven hundred million dogs around the world today? You couldn't have known that the making of the German shepherd breed line, and dozens of other so-called pure breeds, would lead to the millions of dogs registered with kennel clubs today, which breeds have an average of over thirty-two inherited disorders as a result of their inbreeding.

But you're there now. What if we could start from scratch? What if we could do it again—before artificial selection went off the rails? I've been asking myself that, and asking other people who spend a disproportionate amount of their mental life thinking about dogs.

We could leave it up to the vicissitudes of natural selection. Evolution "did a really good job of creating a dog," Amy Attas reflects. "A middle-sized, thirty- to forty-pound floppy-eared dog, with a good nose, yellow body, and curled tail. They tend to be good-natured and healthy. There is something to be said for that."

We could skip pedigree breeding. "I would probably skip everything after 1859," says Bronwen Dickey, referencing the first dog show. "Way back, dogs were doing different things based on their [body] shape; no one got all wrapped around the axle about it. And the big explosion of the AKC in the 1950s and everyone in suburbia needing to have their perfect Irish setter . . . Look what it's done to dogs."

We could breed, but breed *better*, Stephen Zawistowski suggests: "I would do a survey of the breeds. See what are the pros and cons found within each breed, and then start—thinking as a geneticist—thinking about what we can do to maintain the spirit of the breed without it being compromised . . . [making mixes like] the Labradoodle—with intention."

We could do it again exactly the same way. I asked a few of the veterinarians and staff at Maddie's Shelter Medicine Program at the University of Florida how they'd run this "re-domestication" project. Would they skip breeding? The consensus was No. "People should have whatever dog they want," one of them tells me. *What about*, I suggest, *no pugs*— that suffering brachycephalic dog. One of the vets has a pug, and everyone laughs. Okay, pugs. "Not everyone wants the medium, yellow dog of the street," they say. *Won't people just be happy with the dogs that exist, whatever they are?* I ask. Everyone says yes, begrudgingly. Maybe, I suggest, if you could do it again, you would start breeding and choosing dogs in just the way we did before. Recapitulating history. And so we'd end up in the same place: where we have a struggle but we all have choice. They all smile.

• • •

*"[A] heavy-boned, massive, awe inspiring dog . . .
characterized by loose skin, over his entire body,
abundant, hanging wrinkles and folds on the head and
a voluminous dewlap. The essence . . . is his bestial
appearance, astounding head and imposing size and
attitude. Due to his massive structure, his characteristic
movement is rolling and lumbering, not elegant or
showy . . . The absence of massiveness is to be so severely
punished as to eliminate from competition."*
(Neapolitan mastiff breed standard)

Of course, we can't go back again. But we can do it one better: we can go forward thoughtfully, mindful of where we've been and what we've done to dogs. Where the first domesticators were presumably not looking years into the future, we can. The dog of the future: what would that ideal dog be?

When asked what their ideal dog is, peoples' imaginations do not run wild. What we say we want is constrained by what we can imagine: our ideal dogs resemble our current dogs, only more so. "Loyalty" is often what we're looking for, as well as a measure of responsiveness and expression (even with an eyebrow: dogs who can raise their inner eyebrow are faster to be adopted from shelters). The Australian idea of an ideal dog, according to a large-scale survey by researcher Tammie King in 2009, is a young, medium, short-haired, de-sexed dog who comes when you call them, and who will not bite children, pee in the house, or escape. Also, it'd be nice if they didn't eat poo. Reasonable enough, in a way—although it's notable that this same group of respondents hopes to spend less than an hour a day out with the dog.

But what would be the ideal dog *for the species' sake*? It could be a dog who meets our current notions, informed by science, much as the breeders of the past who looked only to "purity" as their guide. It can—and ought—retain the spirit of doggishness as we have come to know it.

On our watch, but without our conscious assent, fashion has replaced function as the reason to have a particular dog breed. Those dogs who work with humans at specific jobs— like sheepdogs actually herding sheep and German shepherd dogs bred for police work—are beautiful and healthy breeds. For the great majority of US dogs, though, the "function" that they serve is primarily as devoted companion. Yet they are not well designed for the task, and they suffer.

Given this present, it would not be outrageous to suggest that, in the future, we breed dogs good at being companions in the way many owners are asking them to: dogs who are not only reliably loyal and delighted at your return home (as most already are), but dogs who don't get bored if you are at work for ten hours; who don't need to pee or poo but once a day; who can endure understimulation and overfeeding. Sound ridiculous? Perhaps so, but that's what so many people are asking of dogs now, and they are hardly equipped to deal with it. A bladder-holding ninja and hibernator who awakens for the ten minutes someone wants to play with them: the dog, perhaps, society deserves.

Other paths open here. One is to acknowledge the present dogs who have, of late, been shaped by nature as much as by humans: the street dogs of India; the village dogs of Ethiopia. These well-mixed dogs' lives are short, but not on their genes' account; on account of their fate. We could consider those dogs our dogs of the future, bring them into our fold, and breed them in a highly non-organized way. Alternately, we could simply embrace the strategy natural selection took there: allow breeding whereby dogs mate per *their* choices, not their breeders. Possibly still called purebred dogs, but swapping out the importance of "pure" for "health."

Healthbred dogs. This destiny highlights the conflict between our desire to have whatever dog we want and the species' best interest. I am not afraid of that conflict. I choose the dog. If humans are going to be involved, we should pay for the privilege, not be paid for the product. We could release our desire for control, for predictability—a desire that was ill-founded to begin with. Instead of "knowing" about who the dog is before we meet them, what would it mean if we didn't know all about our dogs? Where dogs are individuals who live among us, make some choices, and are still part of our families. Where dogs transcend description by form—how they look—or function—what they're *for*—and become, simply, *who they are*. They might surprise us. They might *be* us.

It is our choice, dog people. What do we want for dogs? When we look seriously at what breeding has done, there is but no question that our current posture is untenable. Dogs have been with us through many awkward, regrettable postures—from our Janus-faced use of them as nutrition alongside companion; to the morally slouching application of dogs to threaten or capture other animals or other people. Now's the time to straighten up.

The Scientific Process as Practiced at Home Watching Dogs on a Thursday Evening

The scientific process is all about hypothesis generation and testing. *Hypothesis*, I'm told, comes from a Greek word meaning "put under." As in: a guess that you should put under your hat or a large pile of papers and probably never reveal to anyone. What distinguishes a scientist is that she is constitutionally unable to do so.

It begins simply enough. You are minding your own business milling around the house, gazing out the window of a train, or staring vaguely at a data set, and suddenly your mind comes up with a brilliant piece of theory. *The heat rising in a room during the day allows dogs to sense the passage of time . . . When it appears that dogs are looking at something, they are primarily smelling at it . . . Soaring birds think dogs are legless fur missiles . . . Dogs squint their eyes in order to focus sensory attention on their noses . . .* At least, it seems brilliant at the time. If you have the wherewithal to scribble it down—a non-trivial wherewithal for the absentminded set (I've no doubt many a scientific epiphany was lost for the want of the back of a receipt to write down the thought passing through one's head)—then the next step is to design a test of the idea.

My own hypotheses usually appear after milling around the house *with dogs*, gazing out of the window of a train *at dogs outside*, or staring vaguely at a data set *of dog data*. Happily, most of the ideas are thus about dogs. While not billable hours, exactly, time walking with dogs may be the single most important tool a dog cognition researcher has. I've gone on to test—and even affirm—some of my favorite hypotheses: that dogs' "guilty look" is a response to the owner, not an expression of understanding that they've done something wrong; that in choosing a person to approach, dogs care more about whether they have lots of treats than whether they were "fair" in their treat-distribution earlier; that dogs can notice when their own odor has changed, a kind of olfactory self-awareness. Another—that your pup can tell the time of day by noticing the diminishment in your very odor through the day—even got airtime on a science program. Some of my hypotheses have led me to discover things I hadn't thought of: that dogs can smell a quantity difference; that people generally prefer canid faces with larger eyes and mouths seeming to smile, but that people who don't consider themselves "animal people" don't care; that people roughhousing with their dogs show more positive emotions than people playing fetch.

Honing the hypotheses and designing the methodologies to test ideas are the most confounding and delightful parts of any study for me. The more straightforward the hypothesis is, the more complicated the design seems to be. But in many cases simple observations do the trick to push a hypothesis from the edge of brilliance over the cliff of nonsense. The hearty scientist is not afraid of the felled hypothesis. She takes one step back, revises, and pushes on.

Such is what happens when, for example, watching dogs at home on a Thursday evening after a long day. The process, revealed here for the first time, is informative—and sometimes outright spectacular.

• • •

HYPOTHESIS: The dog is an animal. Starting strongly. All bodily evidence—the food input, the excretal output; the sleeping and waking; the eyes, ears, mouth, tailness—point at this. I feel pretty solid with this one.

But then again, we couldn't be more horrified if we found a dog in a zoo—which is, by definition, a place that houses *animals*. Also, this morning in a coffee shop I saw a Labradoodle seated on a high stool, wearing a quilted winter jacket, and gazing deep into the eyes of the person next to him. The dog's owner let him lick the froth on her cappuccino.

Revised: The dog is a person: See aforementioned puffy jacket. My dear friend knit me a lovely pair of gloves as a Christmas gift. And a full-blown angora sweater, with cable stitching, for the dog. Not only is the dog a person, she is a more worthy person than I.

On the other hand, dogs seem to be getting away with not having much of a job—a principal preoccupation for persons, if my conversations with persons at cocktail parties are any gauge. Dogs don't go to school, and few of them do anything we could really call "work." Yet it would be wrong to call them slackers. They never really watch TV or surf the web with the alacrity we'd expect of slackers. They not only don't spend the day at work, school, or watching the tube, they instead spend their walks with their nose on the ground and their idle time listening for intruders.

Second revision: The dog is a wolf. Some archaeological and genetic evidence here. But it's very, very old archaeological evidence, mostly dust. Could be planted. And genetic "evidence" is written entirely in code.

Conclusion: The dog is a spy. Why, the other day I caught Finnegan seeming to "sleep on the sofa," but actually peering at me from the corner of his eyes. And when I woke up this morning he was sitting by the bed staring at me. And the notebook I keep by my bedside had been chewed to shreds.

• • •

HYPOTHESIS: Happiness is a warm puppy. To be fair, this is Charles Schulz's hypothesis, which he posited as more of an "unsupported statement" in his *Peanuts* comic strip. But, visiting a friend with a new puppy, and having a puppy fall asleep on my lap, I feel hormones of well-being course through me, as well as a great contentedness to have *the chosen lap*. The puppy's eyes close into slender slits, fringed with fur still unsullied by life. My lap is perfect. The puppy is perfect. The world is perfect.

Revised: Melancholy is a warm puppy who has rolled in a dead squirrel. There is some kind of a scent near me. Very near me. I recall that the puppy was recently outside, and did show a lot of interest in the corner of the yard that was the site of a local hawk's dinner. Hmm, and on stroking the soft fur of the puppy I come across a bit of fur that is all matted up and a bit sticky. My contentedness adjusts a notch.

Second revision: Consternation is a warm puppy whose presence on your lap is accompanied by a warm wet feeling. The warmth has gotten pretty intense. Not only is my body coursing with good-feelingness, my lap is a full ten degrees above the temperature of the rest of my body—especially my legs, which are starting to lose circulation and cramp from sitting so long cross-legged on the floor. But the warmth is more than a normal warmth. It is a . . . wet? warmth? Am I sweating? I slip my hand under the puppy, trying to examine my legs without disturbing her sweet puppy sleep. Alas, I am not sweating.

Third revision: Exasperation is a warm puppy pinned to your chest on a warm summer's night. Do not wake the puppy. The puppy has been running like bananas all day, biting everything in sight, and has, in the hour I've been here, chewed her way through two art projects and sawn off my shoelace. Her owner's joy at her slumber is evident. I must not wake her. I manage to yoga my body into a kind of reclining position, with one arm propping up the puppy's head, the other propping up her rump, and my own head lodged at a sharp angle against the wall. While only fifteen pounds and no more than eighteen inches long, the puppy has adjusted ever-so-slightly to literally cover my entire body. It's a very warm night. There is fur in my mouth. Do not wake the puppy.

Conclusion: Puppiness is a warm happy.

• • •

HYPOTHESIS: Dogs love chew toys. Evidence for this lies around my living room, in the form of small bits of chewed-off balls, denuded tennis balls, and puffs of stuffing previously fattening up a plush animal. Upton lies with a ball grasped between his paws, gnawing off the stubby feet of a squeaky rubber creature. He is driven, intent, thoroughly engaged in his project. When I brought out the toy earlier, his eyes lit up, his tail started spinning circles, and he did a small happy leap.

And yet. I've never seen a dog who cared deeply about chew toys, if there were dogs or people available for interaction. Toys are used and loved mostly in moments of boredom, or when a human replaces their arm in the puppy's sharp-toothed mouth with a rope toy or stick. Also, if dogs do love toys, they love them to the point of actually decapitating, disemboweling, and consuming them. Dog love may be different than human love, but not that different.

Revised: Dogs feel responsible for destroying the invasive chew toys we mindlessly leave around the house. Given the careful attention my dogs pay to deconstructing the toys, I suspect that, instead of loving them, they feel an obligation to dismantle them. *My god, here's another one*, they assume, and set to work tearing it apart. One of my dogs waits until I am home and giving him my full attention, then shows off by meticulously incising the appendages off a plush toy.

On the other hand, some dogs do not chew chew-toys, but carefully hide them under a sofa cushion, or carry them around balefully, like a child's treasured lovey.

Second revision: Dogs believe chew toys are real. The vigor with which the Donald Trump chew toy was beheaded and gutted speaks loudly. Of course dogs can understand the political climate and try to use their mouths to politically protest. (I probably shouldn't be leaving NPR on during the day.) The buffalo, hedgehog, and at least the vital bits of the stuffed pig are all saved and cherished.

Conclusion: Dogs vote with their mouths.

•   •   •

HYPOTHESIS: Dog is man's best friend. So it has been said. And it seems so, to this woman, sitting astride two perfect dogs—one of whom once found my lost datebook for me; the other of whom smiles at seeing me; both of whom have no cruelty, show reliable cheer, tolerate my peculiarities and shortcomings without judgment, and are silently eloquent.

One can't help but wonder, though, as I move off the sofa to make more room for the dogs, if they are at all cunning. I do now purchase bagels specifically for the dogs, pay more for their medical care than my own, and possess pocketsful of dehydrated salmon. Our family rarely travels far because we can't bring the dogs with us. We quickly scoop their seemingly precious poop and live in a constant haze of airborne dog fur.

Revised hypothesis: Dog is a manipulative frenemy. Since adopting a cat, I have seen that there is much overlap in cat and dog behavior—only the cat doesn't wag massively when we're home, gaze at us adoringly, and promptly respond when spoken to. Without the surfeit of crazy-friendliness, it's easier to see the cat's behavior for what it is: a means to an end. Sure, she cozies up to every guest to the house, jumping on their lap and relentlessly purring and rubbing against them. But after witnessing this scene a dozen times it began to look less like affection and more like a way to control access to the warm, soft seating locations available in the house.

Now that I think about it, I noticed Finnegan making a noise suspiciously like purring when I rubbed his ears.

Second revision: Dog is a cat. Impossible. Dogs would never betray us like that.

Conclusion: Cats are really dogs who don't make it past the best-friend qualifying rounds.

• • •

HYPOTHESIS: Dogs know when you're coming home. So it's been reported. It seems possible: by habit, by smell, by some other as-yet-undiscovered sense.

And yet, if they knew in advance, would they be so bent out of shape when you leave to go down to the basement for three minutes?

Revised hypothesis: Dogs are just by the front door anyway, just in case you come home. Optimists, dogs simply figure they might as well put all their cards in the "front door" basket.

But sometimes my dogs aren't there. Or one dog is there and the other is not.

Second revision: First dog is distracting me with rambunctious greeting while the other completes their internet purchase for desired toys. Come to think of it, there are a lot of unexplained late-night Amazon purchases on my account. Mostly salmon-based.

Conclusion: On the internet, everyone is a dog.

• • •

HYPOTHESIS: Dogs know their size. When studying dog play, watching a high-speed, rich interaction slowed down into each thirtieth-of-a-second frame, I saw that large dogs seem to know when their playmate is smaller. They use less force; they roll on their backs; they slow to let the short-legged small dog catch up.

Similarly, small dogs are, research shows, more vocal than large dogs: as if by barking more, the Pomeranian and dachshund make up for their small stature.

Still, there is a dog on my lap right now. And he is eighty-five pounds, and I am only 50 percent larger than that. He does not fit.

Revised hypothesis: Dogs do not know their size. See: dog on lap. See also: dog attempting to squeeze in two-inch gap between people on the sofa; dog putting head through rails of fence and unable to extract head from between rails of fence; dog attempting to fit all eighty-five pounds onto dog bed made for fifteen-pound former self; small dog attempting escape with cooked turkey approximately the size of small dog; every Labrador retriever. (For non-Lab-owners, consider whether a felled tree could be picked up with the mouth at somewhat off the fulcrum and run off with. You have just considered a Lab at one with the stick.)

Second revision: It's less a question of dogs not knowing their size than not understanding the size of things in the world. And to be fair, the size of things in the world is hard to understand, period. To wit: my son grew four inches this year, my bank account shrank abruptly, and the ice mass at the coldest place on earth retreated precipitously.

Conclusion: Shape is inconstant, but dogs are not.

· · ·

HYPOTHESIS: Dogs do not speak. Seemingly self-evident. As our nonstop talking to dogs attests, we sure do speak to them; blissfully, they do not answer back.

On the other hand, I've been hearing from dogs all my life. There is no question but my dogs often speak to me: when I ask if they want to go out, they answer in the affirmative; when I ask if they want a treat, their answer is clear; when I ask if they're hungry or tired or want to come for a walk or would like some of my sandwich, the answer is yes.

Revision: Dogs know how to say yes, but they don't know how to say no. But: baths.

Oh. Dog is speaking to me now. He's come to tell me something. Dogs may start subtly, sitting across the room aimed in your general direction, but they know that we are pretty bad at speaking dog, and they will continue to yell at us: *HEY! HEY! HEY!* until we finally turn and look. We are so dense. Wait, he's saying something . . .

Dog has told me to stop this.

Such is the fast-and-furious nature of science.

Dog Stuff

It's a cool morning in May when he cuts me off. Smartly dressed and driven, he veers across three lanes of pedestrian traffic on the sidewalk, from the curb to the threshold of a doorway. A woman three steps behind him hurries to keep up. His head projected forward, he hesitates not a moment and charges into the building.

I follow him. He wears a tri-color Argyle sweater ringed with ribbing. I glimpse a leather cord dotted with ruby-red jewels around his neck. He glances from the floor to the walls to an invisible current of air that leads him, toenails scrambling on the floor, to a cat, hissing under a shelf. He's a Jack Russell terrier, and he's arrived at the pet store.

Should anyone claim that dogs do not know geography, we have ample evidence to the contrary. Your dog knows the way to the nearest half-dozen pet stores, by car or on foot—as well as any cafes or banks that supply a biscuit or treat on your route. Pet stores are the compass points for any urban dog, smellable from a distance, just the way the dank odor of stress emerges from a veterinary clinic. But pet stores really exist because those of us on the other end of the leash want for our pups what we want for ourselves: to buy stuff.

I watch the terrier's exploration of the space. After a moment's investigation of the cat, he neatly drools in a bin of pigs' ears, mouths a rubber ball, then runs to a high counter and stands up on his rear legs, two-stepping. For this performance he earns a small treat tossed in the air. His tags jingle as he jerks himself forward with little leaps, the retractable leash from his neck to his owner forming a tripwire that another dog, a miniature collie, neatly hurdles. Each surveys every bin along the floor filled with impossible varieties of rawhides, rubber chews, and dog-food samples, while their owners' gaze lingers at the pink, red, blue, and green toys at eye-height. Both reach for a soft toy shaped like a squirrel with a maniacal look on its face.

The clever terrier could go online. "Lifestyle for dogs: Spring is here!!! Go Shopping" greets the visitor to the website of Canine Styles, which bills itself as "New York's oldest and finest dog emporium with world-class grooming and an exclusive line of products." A testimonial from a happy customer reads "I just received your 4 legged pink fleece track suit for my shih-tzu Joey and it is by far the best coat I have bought her in 12 years!"—implying, clearly, that Joey has many, many track suits.

Canine Styles' apparel section is spectacular. Apart from the polar-fleece track suits, there are cable-knit cashmere sweaters in red, hot pink, and herringbone. There are puffer coats and both neoprene and tartan rain jackets. There are hoodies, tennis dresses, muscle tees, and Hawaiian print "vacation shirts." The ruffle-skirted, muscle-teed dog can also shop bone-shaped placemats, plaid bow ties, and a lined toy bin, reading, humbly, "Good dog."

Elsewhere in the expansive merchandise playground that is the internet, you can find a mini Leonardo Delfuoco Croc "pawbag" to be worn on the collar—matched to your Leonardo Delfuoco Croc purse—for a little south of six thousand dollars. The fashionable toy-dog owner could therewith open her purse to reveal her dog, wearing a purse. There are hundreds of colognes, perfumes, and body sprays made for dogs. Sure, some have "ear relief wash" functionality, but more aim for what Maschio, an "exciting dog fragrance that captures the essence of Quality Life for Dogs® with its powerful mix of style, excitement, and male sensuality," achieves: perfect conviction in the necessity of dog fragrance. "Made for the 'man of the house,'" Maschio creates "a feeling of relaxed sophistication and understated luxury." Note, dog parents: "spray on the withers, away from the dog's face."

While you're shopping fragrances, you can also pick up "sexy paw red dog nail polish" intended for your bitch, and a thirty-four-dollar "100% cotton dog bathrobe" with matching ninety-four-dollar "100% cotton dog mom bathrobe."

How did we evolve from being cave-dwellers to being dog-bathrobe buyers? Why are we buying the toys, food, and accessories for our pups that we are?

• • •

Despite the fact that, as property themselves, dogs can't legally own property, boy, do dogs *own property*. That blue-and-orange ball over there, for instance—no, not *that* one, the smaller one; right, the nubby, muddy one—is definitely Finnegan's. Or at least (as he snarls at a dog eyeing it) he seems very certain that it is.*

Even contemporary owners who have not outfitted their dogs in pink track suits likely have an array of dog furnishings in their homes. That ball of Finnegan's rests alongside remnants of a dozen rubberized balls formerly outfitted with feet and squeakers; soft animal toys in every stage of disembowelment; and rejected rope- and chew toys. There are dog beds in the bedroom, dog bowls in the dining room, and dog leashes, vests, and towels in the entry. While these accoutrements of dogdom feel like a modern phenomenon, the core listing of pet dog products is surprisingly unchanged from a century ago.

At the time, America, between wars, was in the throes of Prohibition, and the importing of fancy purebred dogs from overseas was a relatively new phenomenon. But culture was changing: flappers were in vogue and the first sexual revolution for woman was underway. Many of the leading reform workers were women. As the process of caring for dogs was morphing into a "pet industry," there was an opening for new business owners. Into this opening waltzed an influx of women—especially wealthy women—who played a sizeable role as breeders, importers, and salespeople, befitting their broadening role in society. These new business owners affected the landscape of dog ownership in a way that sticks with us today.

The heart of the dog trade was always a mixture of love, money—and perhaps love of money. Even while importers of

---

* Legal writers have acknowledged that dogs have a "possessory interest in certain personal property, such as a bone" (or a certain blue-and-orange ball), but the law doesn't consider this a property right.

new breeds wrote of "getting (the dogs) into perfect condition," talk reliably turned mercenary, about the commercial opportunity to be found in purebreeding. The very first pet furnishings stores, in the 1880s, seized the opportunity to "cash in," as one wholesaler stressed was possible, on owners' feeling that nothing is too good for their pups. As there have been bookstore blocks in major cities, some, such as Philadelphia's Ninth Street, had a slew of competing pet stores. Their pharmacy-like names evoked the progressive era's interest in the importance of a quality product: Cugley & Mullen and J. C. Long & Co in Philadelphia, Dr. Gardner's in New York City.

As historian Katherine Grier writes, the nineteenth-century pet store was smelly—"owing to the odors which have been gathered in from all parts of the globe, and which are intensified, usually, by chloride of lime and sulphur," a Pittsburgh paper of the time said—and noisy—"around the walls, on the counters and in the windows, in boxes and cages of all sizes and shapes, members of the furred and feathered tribes bark and yell and sing in one discordant chorus from the time the sun comes up in the morning until it drops out of sight at twilight." They were designed to be attractive to children and genteel ladies looking for a "Dear Creature to Love and Cherish." Pet-shop animals came with a guarantee, like refrigerators: your canary will sing and your dogs will guard, or they could be exchanged hassle-free. Shop owners acknowledged that lives were on the line, but looked at them practically: their trade magazines discussed "acceptable rates of mortality during transportation" and the urgency of selling puppies before they grew into "gangly looking adolescents that nobody wants."

With pet stores, expectations about what a dog is "for" were formed, firmed up—and then sold. So, too, were expectations about what else a good owner needed to buy (in the form of wares) and do (in the form of services) for their charge. The motto for the early twentieth-century *Pet Dealer* magazine—"A pet in every home"—captures the intended reach of these new businesses. Sporting-goods stores like Abercrombie & Fitch widely advertised their own lines of dog furnishings; leatherware stores branched out into dog miscellany. Soon, so did some department stores: John Wanamaker in Philadelphia and Frederick Loeser & Co. in Brooklyn. Dogs had not only become commodities, Grier writes, "they also became consumers."

As consumers, dogs were outfitted and accessorized. All of the products now at Finnegan's disposal were around in some form at the turn of the twentieth century, when pet ownership and the pet industry boomed: the collars, the beds, the toys, and the clothes. And an entire side industry of foodstuffs tailored exclusively to dogs emerged alongside the accoutrements. Each item has its own trajectory into the mouths of dogs and into our homes—and each unpacks a bit of the story of where our current practices with dogs come from.

COLLARS

The "dog collar" is prototypically doggy: not only ubiquitous, the collar has also come to stand for the dogs themselves. As I look up from my desk, a photo of Pumpernickel, my longtime companion, catches my eye. In the image, she lies with her elbows sprawled, panting toward the camera with a half-smile I remember well. I can nearly feel the softness of the fur around her velveteen ears. There is one dissonance, though: under her chin is a flurry of tags. They hang from a red corduroyed collar circling her neck. The collar, only a bit of cloth and metal, endures after her death: I finger it from time to time, and bring it to my face to remind me of her smell.

Still, it rankles that her collar now takes the place of the grace that was Pump. I never loved putting a collar on her—a flagrant sign of legal ownership, which felt at odds with our familial relationship. Collars have represented ownership and a show of control since the first collars were fitted around ancient hounds' necks. This human-animal technology is at least thousands of years old. The earliest surviving imagery of dogs—eight-thousand-year-old sandstone cliff engravings and wall-relief art three thousand years hence—show them with distinctive rope and metal collars. Peer closely at the neckline of a dog mummified in ancient Egypt over twenty-five hundred years ago and you can see a small tag poking out from the linen wrap. The dogs felled by the ashes of Pompeii wore thick leather collars, as did their representations in tile art that warned intruders of the houses' guard dogs.

Still, collars were not only blunt objects of control. From the get-go, they were decorated, adorned, even bejeweled. A Mesopotamian dog immortalized in limestone wears a collar with a bell. Collars discovered in Egyptian funerary sites are sometimes gilded and may be inscribed with a name: "Ta-en-nût," one reads—meaning, roughly, "She of the town." Other ancient artifacts feature guard dogs wearing decorated collars—such as an Egyptian white leather collar, decorated with "pink and green insets and studs, featur[ing] a frieze of horses running around it"—or spiked or nail-studded collars, intended to protect the neck from an attack by a wild animal or another dog.

Collars were commonly made of leather—or brass, for the very wealthy. And they were often worth more than the dog wearing them: Charles V's dogs wore collars of velvet, leather, and silver. Many were not intended for a specific dog but for any dog who came into the owner's house. "Jere Stebbin Esq's Dog W. Springfield," one eighteenth-century collar was inscribed, "Who Dog Be You."

Pre-war America was a time of explosion of interest in fashion, and it exploded right into pet merchandise catalogs as well. Collars, leashes, leads, and muzzles feature prominently in the earliest mail-order catalogs. You want a spiked collar? Can do. Flat lined collar with a bell? Gotcha. Flat studded collar, round-not-studded, round slip training, heavily studded round, combination round/slip, round/slip with invertible and removable spikes, double harness leather spike bull collar (for Boston, English, and French bulldogs), fancy square-studded, or jeweled? We've got you covered. "An exquisite collar," the copy for a French calf-leather studded round collar reads, "fit for choicest animals"; a bull collar is "natty, classy." Each collar is promised to "outlast the dog."

Many include designs to avoid theft (of the collar).* "The famous 'Lock Tongue' buckle is used," the copy in the 1922 Q-W Dog Remedies and Supplies catalog read, ". . . preventing loss of collar" (and possibly dog). Padlocks for the collars were listed alongside literal bells and whistles: round bells, field bells ("attach to collars of hunting dogs so that you may know their location . . . also quite the fad for use on street dogs"), "acme thunderer" whistles, "horn dog" whistles, identification tubes, and "bangles," the predecessor to dog tags.

The range of imported purebred dogs led to an important

* Today, all American states mandate that dogs be leashed in public (dog parks excepted), and most owners appear to comply. Collars or harnesses form an extension of the leash. Dogs deemed "aggressive" might be required to wear a muzzle.

development for furnishings makers: different kinds of collars for different kinds of dogs. "A dog's collar should be suited to his breed," an early catalog insisted. "Long-haired dogs should have round collars . . . short-haired dogs look better in flat collars." Pomeranians and toy poodles were expected to have dainty collars; bulldogs, sporty collars. Another catalog listed the sizing needed for popular breeds, from cocker spaniel to Irish terrier and German shepherd—including not only the collar and harness size, but also the properly sized comb, brush, dish, basket (for sleeping), raincoat, and sweater.

Some collar ideas were a bit wrongheaded in their conception, such as the Abercrombie & Fitch Blackout collar: "the radium studs on the collars glow at night." Choke collars, whose heyday is thankfully largely past, were billed to solve basically any problem, including a dog's stubbornness, timidity, foolishness, wildness, playfulness, jealousy, or maliciousness. Dog whips, and whips that doubled as leashes, were common sights in the early catalogs and stores. Given the Sanitary Code law of the time requiring muzzling dogs in public, cages of wire and leather were ubiquitous, with the one concession to dog comfort being made by a muzzle branded Happidog, which allowed an adjustment for snouts of different length.

Today, we've replaced radioactive collars with LED, but the core idea of what a collar should be remains the same. It is decoration: twenty-first-century pet catalogs still have an array of silk, nylon, chain, rope, and leather collars—with or without fake pearl studs. And it is control: there are harnesses designed to solve any perceived behavior problem; and there are such ill-conceived developments as the electronic, or e-collar. Designed to give a shock to the dog at the owner's whim, the collars are an advance from a dog whip only in technology, not in concept. A dog without any collar at all looks naked to our current eye—less like the true dog she is than like a lost one.

DOG FURNITURE

Dogs are domesticated—a word meaning "belonging to the house"—but for the lucky dog today it is increasingly more the house that belongs to them. We extend our homes to include them. Not only do my furniture choices and my rug color (to say nothing of my dog-toy collection) speak of their place in my home, the space itself is defined by how we use it with dogs. Moreover my dogs have not only furnishings, but actual furniture.

There is evidence of dogs sleeping in their masters' beds back to the fourteenth century; Henry of Lancaster was said to let his greyhound called Math into bed.* And so by the late nineteenth- and early twentieth-century pet-merchandise catalogs included a category of dog-specific furnishings, echoing products for humans: the house and the bed. Dog houses and kennels had been around for hundreds of years: the gable-roofed structure with one entrance, upon which you might expect to see Snoopy piloting his WWI fighter plane. Intended to keep a dog out of the inclement weather more than provide them with a suitable room of their own, they also were places of punishment or penance, as anyone who has been *in the dog-house* with their parent or partner knows. But by the twenties a progressively minded dog parent could buy "the perfect dog house . . . a cozy, dry, comfortable, scientific house" with

---

* Such behavior was by no means universal: Henry VIII banned dogs from court entirely.

a slanted roof, side door, and protected entrance hall. Made to endure hurricane-level weather events, it was billed as "the dog house a dog would buy for himself"; adding: "if he were buying a house."* At thirty-five dollars (the equivalent of over five hundred dollars today), it is doubtful that any dogs had the means.

Bedding, in the doghouse or out of it, began as an extension of farm-animal bedding—sanitary straw or woodchips, sold by the bale. Over time, straw was replaced by cedar shavings, and the concerns addressed by manufacturers went from economic to sanitary (keeping fleas and other nasties away), to cosmetic (keeping the coat glossy). Then kennels came inside and became, essentially, beds: mattresses on a frame or on the floor. Some were spring-upholstered; some were little more than raised cabinets on legs. Willow and rattan baskets, paired with a cushion, suited the small dog; a chaise lounge fit the more dog-sized dog. Baskets might be hooded, to protect from drafts; cushions, pneumatic. One Abercrombie & Fitch model mimicked a bunk bed, with a cushioned chair below "for day use" and a "comfortable bed" above for night. By the forties, personalization happened, and the dog's blanket or cushion or bed could be embroidered with their name, just as the owner's towels were monogrammed with their initials. Confusion about whose towels and whose bed these were was at last settled—at least for the literate. But just in case, a sub-industry of dog-repellents—"Pup Pruf" was one—appeared, promising a non-staining means of keeping a dog off *your* chair.

---

* Also notable for the early use of "he" to describe a dog, who at the time was often an "it." "She" is nowhere to be found, though.

HABERDASHERY

Dog clothing was surprisingly early on the scene. This may partly be due to the concurrent explosion of manufactured clothing options for dogs' people. By the teens and roaring into the twenties, magazines like *Vogue* were chock-full of ads for the latest coats, furs, frocks, gowns, riding habits, hats, togs, and underthings for the fashionable lady. Magazine covers were Deco masterpieces of women in extravagant couture, holding parasols and wearing fancy hats, in understated pastoral or domestic settings. Once in a while a courter or a child makes an appearance; more often, the woman's accessory is a dog. Borzois with perfect posture gaze in the distance protectively, their coats matching the women's coats' fur lining. In a striking 1922 *Vogue* cover, a woman lazily pats her long-limbed greyhound, the dog's thick jeweled collar mirroring the broad sash around the woman's waist.

That same year you might also have come across a pet-company pamphlet near *Vogue* on the newsstand—one that includes a photo of a bewildered black-and-white dog standing on two legs and dressed in a full-on tutu. Dogs not only accompanied the fashion revolution; they were unwitting participants. Nineteenth-century knitting patterns for crocheted tassel jackets, intended for Italian greyhounds, heralded an array of options for the fashionable greyhound within a few decades, from turtleneck dog sweaters "made of very fine worsted yarns" to sueded waterproof raincoats. Once the gates were open, all manufactury hell broke loose. One could soon find all-breed dog blanket coats (delicately hooked under the belly) in scotch plaid, suede leather, oil silk, and linen duster styles. The Abercrombie & Fitch catalog self-consciously reassured owners that their tweedy ulster coat was "made from the same fine imported tweeds used in our men's sports jackets." Sweaters came in angora; trench coats, gabardine. It was possible to get dog clothes with a navy insignia—for sea dogs, presumably.

Neither were the feet of these dolled-up dogs neglected: manufacturers sold dog boots of calf-skin leather and rubber dog "bootees," not unlike today's all-weather dog boots. Early versions were a little more complicated than even the most patient dog would reasonably tolerate, climbing knee high and secured with long laces, like a corset for the shin— resembling nothing more than Edwardian ladies' boots.

To model the various dog furnishings that shop owners were pitching, a dedicated wholesale dog-goods store out of Ohio, Craftsman, sent retailers a free display dog. The pup, an alert, glassy-eyed piebald terrier with a cropped tail and a bit of fringe where his penis would have been, was, the catalog touts in bold font, "modeled from a living dog and reproduced in papier mache," "exceptionally attractive," and "well proportioned." Cooperatively, like the dog after which he is modeled, the display "will wear practically every known article in Dog Haberdashery in some size or another."

Underneath their clothes, the pampered dog was groomed to a fare-thee-well. Even in the early twentieth century, shops began providing individual grooming and bathing services, promoted with images of dogs sitting in barbers' chairs, dressed in barbers' capes. High Ball pet shop in Syracuse's "Complete service for pets" included clipping, shampooing, manicuring, and "dog stripping";* Abercrombie & Fitch advertised a

---

* Used with wire-haired breeds, stripping pulls hairs directly out, instead of cutting them.

Plucking & Grooming Service at their flagship Madison and 45th store, with dedicated dog handlers. Worry not that your dog will be shipped out for plucking and grooming: "Antiseptic bathing, nail clipping, tooth scraping and trimming are done on the premises."

TOYS

The most ubiquitous possession of modern dogs was probably the last to gain traction: the dog toy. Until the blossoming of pet furnishings, dogs might make do with an old ball or even discarded skein of string. Not until dogs were being bred and kept explicitly for human amusement did it seem to occur to us that they might need some amusement themselves. While there were some curious early-dog-toy choices, the classic pet-shop standbys—balls, tugs, and chews (ideally with squeak feature)—were often tucked away in the last pages of the original pet-supply catalogs. Finnegan's favored ball would not have been out of place. Given the novelty of the idea of keeping a dog entertained, even the most obvious toy needed some explanation: owners had to be gently led to understand what these toys were about and how they operated. The "crackle-bone" made by Walter B. Stevens & Son came with biological exegesis: "when the dog bends it, the bone makes a crackling noise similar to that of a breaking bone." Abercrombie & Fitch's tug toy came with instructions: "You hold one end, dog pulls at other. Exercise for both master and dog." Sometimes, the toy design was more likely to be interesting to the purchaser than purchasee, as the various chocolate-scented Scentoy balls, bones, and rubber rings of the 1920s. Inevitably, there were Christmas stockings for dogs.

Other early designs kept the dog in mind, at least in theory. Rubber or fur-pelt toys shaped like prey a predator might reasonably want to chase—a rabbit, a mouse, a rat, a cat—soon appeared; moreover, these toys made crying or mewing sounds when shaken or squeaking sounds when bitten. So, too, though, did rubber toys of monkey faces, and, most disturbingly, a large array of rubber toys of dogs' heads—often small dogs, like Scotch terriers—with whistles inside to shriek when the head was squeezed. One hesitates to imagine what happened to any actual Scotties living in these households.

MISCELLANEOUS STUFF

Not all of the early pet-supply goods were harbingers of what would flourish in the enormous pet industry to come. Early catalogs listed such unlikely products as "tooth forceps," for removing a puppy's milk teeth—something few contemporary owners would take upon themselves. Nor do many households own a "tail shield," a kind of Elizabethan collar for the hindquarters, apparently needed to protect the tails of Great Danes and other dogs from injury when they were knocked against the side of their kennels—a physical circumstance that indicates that the life of the early twentieth-century Great Dane was quite different than today.

While the turn-of-the-century Dane might have felt shy about his tail shield, his bulldog friends fared worse: for them were products to specifically injure instead of protect. The "bulldog spreader" was designed to spread their forelimbs even wider, as per the fashion for the breed. It was a harness stabilized under the armpits and pulled up over the shoulders to steadily pull a normal stance into an abnormal one.

Happily, the spreader went the way of the trepan.* Neither have I seen the variously named "auto-stop" or "stop-chase," a contraption which clipped to a dog's collar, on any modern dog. From the clip hung two large, heavy rubber balls on leather straps, intended to train the dog not to pursue a passing car (city dog) or chicken (country dog). By dragging along the ground, they served as a ball and chain for the head: "when the dog runs, it bounces and hits him in the side, or else tangles in his forefeet."

Our outsourcing of matters of dog anatomy to veterinarians, and the gradual emergence of a modicum of common sense in welfare, led to the extinction of those products. Also fallen out of favor were more benign creations like dog goggles—"for automobile dogs." For the dog who must travel in a convertible, the sporty, dirigible-pilot headgear prevented "sore eyes." The pup's nose was left, presumably, entirely unprotected in the breeze.

THE CONCEIT OF KIBBLE

Find yourself a new dog owner and the necessity of acquiring all these furnishings—a collar, various toys, a bed—will be pressed on you. But the haphazard history of most dog "stuff" puts the lie to their necessity. As American culture turned consumer, ingenious businesses extended their wares to apply to every heartbeat in the household. Whether dogs *needed* beds or sweaters, or whether a toy amused or suited them, was not the concern of the pet shops. And nowhere was the creation of a professed need more successfully claimed than with our dogs' breakfast.

---

* A trepan was a saw used to cut a hole in a person's skull to release evil spirits.

This very morning, you fed your dog. Probably, you fed your dog from a bowl set alongside a water bowl. Depending on the degree of your involvement in dog-keeping, you likely fed your dog one of the following: a pile of dusty, single-shape kibble; fairly indistinct and very pungent canned food; or a combination of bloody raw meat and a frozen vegetable accompaniment. Maybe some homemade food or scraps made it in the bowl, but on average, the bowls of American dogs are filled with products explicitly labeled "dog food."

Let us linger here a moment, in the space where there is food—mysterious, molded food pellets, in many cases—with obscure ingredients, made just for dogs. Unlike collars, this is not an ancient practice, so when did this happen? Where did it come from, this idea of food just for dogs; the conceit of kibble; the very idea of a *bowl* of food? It, too, was a part of the explosion in the pet industry led by the world of furnishings. The same catalogs that featured double-cowhide-leather fancy spotted collars, obedience dumbbells, and cedar dog mats included distinct "Feeding" sections, first tentatively, then confidently asserting what the well-trained and -clothed dog should eat.

Early proto-dogs, living thousands of years ago, ate by scavenging on human-food remains: the gristle we couldn't chew; the fibrous stems we couldn't digest. An owned dog living in the Middle Ages likely had a diet based on bread—supplemented with "a lot of butter" if she was deemed too skinny. From this scattershot provisioning history emerged a radical transformation in the 1800s. Newspaper advertisements of the time reveal that dogs began to be lumped in with "agricultural" animals provisioned with their own food: "Cheap food for hounds and poultry," an ad from 1819 read; another, from 1810, "Good sound biscuit for dogs and hogs."

These biscuits were tough crackers made of wheat, oat, or corn, sometimes broken or damaged, and sold by the ton. Gradually, some biscuit makers turned their sights just to the hounds, and started to call their food "dogs' food." To serve your pup these delicacies, you needed instructions: biscuits were to be soaked "in warm pot liquor for about an hour," Smith Dog Biscuits cautioned in 1825—leaving no dogs drooling in anticipation.

In 1860, the dog-food business took a giant leap forward when an American gentleman named James Spratt noticed British shipyard dogs eating hardtack, a sailor's ration biscuit known less for its palatability than for its portability and longevity. Blessed with a combination of business sense and, probably, blissful ignorance about what might actually be best for dogs, Spratt soon created a company to produce more or less the same item for the landbound canine set.

Spratt took the ship biscuit a step further by creating not just one general-purpose food, but many specially designed biscuits suited to different breeds, functions, and ages of dogs—and by advertising his wares prominently in the burgeoning kennel-club, dog-fancy, and sporting-goods publications. His was a product that no one needed or even wanted, yet through Spratt's and other dog-food marketers' efforts, dog owners bought it big-time. Where the earliest dogs were recyclers of human trash, contemporary dog owners support a multibillion-dollar annual industry of food produced expressly for their charges.

Spratt's Patent, the "biscuit with an X on it," tried to distinguish itself from other fledgling biscuit brands, including Austin's Dog Bread and Young's Improved Dog Biscuit, which advertised to owners looking for "sweet breath, glossy coat and regular habits." Spratt's main products were meat fibrine dog cakes—featuring beetroot, a vegetable no one ever heard of—

and "charcoal ovals." Greyhound Cakes, Oatmeal Cakes, Patent Cod Liver Oil Old Dog Cakes, and Pepsinated Puppy meal rounded out the offerings. They gave away an accompanying book, "A guide to the choice of the correct biscuit for every known breed," which individualized diets for aging dogs, puppies, urban dogs, hunting dogs, toy dogs, and large dogs.

They succeeded fabulously. Within a few decades, advertisements for many other dog-food makers filled newspapers, among them Old Grist Mill, the unfortunately named Pard, Miller's A-1 Ration, Dr. Olding, Old Trusty All-Terrier, and Molassine. Sturdy and Purity dog foods attempted to represent the qualities of dog a purchasing owner might desire.

The now hugely common dog "treat" was slower in coming, but by the thirties one could find Chapen's dog cookies, Bow-wow bon-bons, and various dog "crackers." Maltoid Milk Bones, shaped like a child's drawing of a bone, were originally sold as meals, and only much later became treats—following a slow morph from ads touting how you should "treat your dog" with their fine food, to simply calling the food a treat.

Why would owners buy these foods? By all rights they were unwieldy and expensive: in 1876 Spratt's sold biscuits in hundred-pound parcels for seven dollars. The manufacturers worked to convince owners that these were not frivolous or luxury items, but were necessities. Most of these dog foods were not fit for or palatable to people, so were odd to buy for the pantry. Ironically, in that way, they were perfectly continuous with a history of feeding dogs our leftovers. The difference was that these were marketed as being specially formulated for dogs, at a time when dogs were beginning to be valued more for their roles as companions and show dogs than as laborers. The claims came fast and furious, well before any science or evidence could weigh in. Some foods aligned themselves with the kennel-club show winners, implicitly taking responsibility for their ribbons ("contain[s] Special Exclusive Features 'Patented' to produce Superior 'Condition' such as at once ASTONISHES THE JUDGES and secures the Highest Awards," Molassine claimed). Others reflected a growing societal conversation about "balanced" diets. Many invoked specific health improvements one could expect after eating their food: "perfect assimilation, preventing Mange, Excema, Distemper," an ad for Fish Biscuits reads; another boasted of reducing the "strong odor" of dogs, by aiding the absorption of stomach and intestinal gases. Maltoid Milk Bones were alleged to regulate the bowels, improve the coat, prevent decayed teeth, and build muscles. Spratt's had a line specifically for the "bad doer," by which was meant a dog with digestion problems who eats reluctantly. They made the case that special food for puppies could be a benefit to the newfound sport of breeding dogs, since it made it easier to rear puppies away from their mother, enabling more puppies to be sold.

Convenience was also a selling point: biscuits could more or less be dropped in a bowl with broth and soaked. By the 1880s, an owner of a puppy or sick dog could buy granulated dog food, basically biscuits-in-pieces, and a forerunner to the "kibble biscuit."* As canning foods became increasingly popular between the wars, so did tinned or canned foods for dogs. While neither kibbled food nor canning was much of a conceptual innovation, they were so popular that today *dog food* is virtually synonymous with dry kibble and wet food in cans. Eventually, celebrity dogs came in as endorsers: Ken-L-Ration (and its affiliated Pup-E-Crumbles and Rib-L-Biscuit) boasted of being Rin-Tin-Tin's food, and the original radio and screen

* Also a forerunner to flaked cereal for humans.

Lassie plugged Red Heart 3-flavor dog food. Happily, merchandise was needed for these foods, too, and dog bowls were born. Most bowls looked about the same as a modern dog dish—even to the "Good Dog" sometimes embossed on the side—with the notable exception of my favorite, the Spaniel Dish, a bowl that narrowed at the top in order to keep the breed's long ears hanging alongside the dish and out of their food. This may be the single most relevant object in any of the catalogs I've seen, though it modestly took its undistinguished place on a page of enameled dishes and whale-hide collars.

The products in those bowls were termed "food," not "feed," which was used for livestock—although the applicability of either moniker is questionable. Food might include wheat flour, oats, middlings,* various vegetables, bone meal, and unspecified meats. Many early foods were explicitly horse flesh—"solid cooked horse meat!" bragged Brooklyn's Purity dog food; this was before (and partially the cause of) modern consideration of which animals should be on our plates. (Spratt's, with their beetroot biscuits, objected to horse meat on the grounds that it caused dogs to "smell unpleasantly.") As slaughterhouses grew to large scale, manufacturers used slaughterhouse slurry—the leftover bits.

Horse meat is no longer featured in most dog foods in America; other meat choices reflect, though, culturally narrow ideas about dogs as predators (thus putting bison on the plate) or as gourmands like their owners (thus picturing prime cuts of meat or fish on the packaging). Ironically, in 2018 the

---

* Middlings, or midds, can be either a shorthand for meal or flour of medium grade (i.e., the next round after the good bits are used), or a by-product of wheat milling. Now sometimes called "floor sweepings," they are in fact of similar nutritional value as the sweepings at a wheat mill. The lowest grade of flour, called "red dog," is not usually fed to dogs.

dog-food company Wysong brought a lawsuit against other dog-food manufacturers, alleging that the packaging of its competitors' products was deceptive when they pictured, for instance, lamb chops, when no such food was inside. The court ruled against Wysong: "The Defendants' product is *dog food*. Common sense dictates that reasonable consumers are unlikely to expect that dog food is made from the same meat that people eat."

I think the court may have been overestimating the public's common sense. Early dog-food manufacturers did not: they assumed their audience was entirely without ideas. Thus, with a purchase came a free education on feeding. Catalogs of the earliest dog-food companies included many, many pages of instructions on *how* to feed your dog, a question never posed until the dog-food companies posed it. "Unfortunately," a Spratt's pamphlet began, "dogs are not always able to distinguish between what is good for them and what they like . . . It is entirely up to you—his master—to insure your dog's health and longevity by proper feeding." Thus they specified the number of meals required—usually two or three, sometimes six—and the quantity of the brand's food needed at each one. What had been a simple process of tossing the dog a bone was made out to be complicated, in order that dog-food companies could then simplify it: "why bother with a lot of fuss and muss, when Purina Dog Chow is so easy and economical to feed." Many made the claim that pampering the dog with "dainties" from the table was the reason a dog might have various feeding problems, like becoming overweight or a finicky eater. The solution? Dog biscuits. "Under no circumstances of health does any dog require other food," Spratt's explained in 1886. "Except as a change, in which case sheeps' heads, paunches, etc., boiled with them, and a little cabbage added, is all that is required." If your pup didn't take to the biscuits they recommend the owner "starve an exceptionally obstinate dog" until they ate it. That advice alone is sufficient for me to step away from the dog-biscuits aisle. Among the other foods thought to be good changes of pace were broccoli, kale, turnips, parsnips, or most well-cooked vegetables (excepting potatoes); fruits, broths, soups, gravy, milk, buttermilk, cottage cheese, onions, lettuce, or nettle. In other words, nearly anything at all.

A willing public bought it—not just the food, but the advice that came with it. The business model of posturing oneself as an authority in order to weigh in on the soundness of your product was in full force in dog-goods manufacturing. Many of the early dog-goods companies also offered information on care, training, and medicine—medicine they would be happy to sell you. They brought out purported "canine specialists," questionably credentialed doctors, anonymous "authorities," and the language of Science ("biologically tested"; "in modern research kennels") to tout not just kibble rations, but various remedies and conditioners: constipation pills, tablets for "fits" and dysentery, powders to kill fleas and give pep, lotions for ear cankers or mange, compounds for itchy dogs, general purpose healing salves, liniments, coat growers, and red blood builders. These dogs were apparently afflicted with lots of rheumatism, because there were endless tablets and liniments for this; likewise with tonics and powders for fleas and worms. There were breath-sweetening mouthwashes; a topical application called Cupid Chaser, made alternately of lemongrass or citral oil, to be slathered on a dog in heat in order to keep pesky males away; and its opposite, aphrodisiac tablets "for exciting, stimulating and strengthening sexual powers." ("Unlawful to use for human beings," it warned.)

It hadn't occurred to me. But, admittedly, I would be happy to try On-The-Nose (for coughs and huskiness, "simply put a dab on the dog's nose. He will treat himself by licking it off") or Wow pine oil shampoo. And in fact many medicines and soaps were advertised as splendid for humans. Among the pep-filled dogs pictured in the Q-W dog catalog is an image of a man happily applying Q-W mange lotion to his own head. He looks mange-free.

Feeling their oats, pet-product manufacturers also offered training advice and instructions as to proper house manners or dog education. When a twenty-first-century dog owner talks to me about a dog being "polite," I think back to the early twentieth-century dog-food-company pamphlets where this idea was invented whole cloth. Training advice relied mostly on flicking dogs in the face and pulling them by the tails if they did something you disapproved of, or setting mousetraps to keep a dog out of garbage bins and off chairs. To teach a dog to stay in the yard, a Purina Dog Care pamphlet of the time instructed, "Put light Venetian blind cord in your yard, and stretch out the kinks until it is soft and pliable. Then tie one end to the dog's collar. Wear gloves so you don't get rope burns. Then have someone call to the dog from outside the yard. When puppy reaches the yard edge, shout "no" and grab the rope end, jerking to stop the puppy abruptly."

Today, this kind of thoughtless "training" has largely been replaced by the more humane and more effective methods of positive reinforcement training—using, usually, copious numbers of the very food treats formulated by these companies to reward good behavior. Without question, a surprising lot of our view of how to take care of dogs—what to feed them, outfit them in, and entertain them with—is nearly the same as a century ago, when business interests shaped it. Even as our culture's attitude toward dogs has seen a sea change, the accoutrements of dog ownership are more or less unmoved by the tide.

• • •

The one significant strand between then and now is the bond between dogs and their people. Each little dog sketched in those early catalog pages, and the wares provided for them, banked on the owners' attachment to their dogs—and yearning to find ways to express that affection. How can we show that love? The pet industry, a recent historical development, aims to answer the question for us. The complexities of providing for an animal are reduced to buyable items—and our hunger to provide is evident in the industry's success. Just as dogs are accoutrements of the perfect life, accessories for your pup serve to advertise wealth and status the way a designer handbag or the latest sneakers might.

As I goggle at the twenty-first-century pet-store offerings, the Jack Russell has left the building. I look around me in the pet store and spy the round toys with the stumpy feet that Upton likes to chew off. I grab two. Likewise for the orange-and-blue balls with the squeaker, for Finnegan. There's a box of those peanut-butter treats shaped like small gingerbread people, and oddly satisfying-looking tough chews in earthen colors. I pick out some neoprene booties: the dogs' feet have been getting cut and stung on the salt put down on city streets to melt the ice. At the register, the shop owner and I exchange dog-related small talk. I give him $64.76, and walk home to surprise my boys.

The Dog in the Mirror

The twentieth-century French philosopher Jacques Derrida had a cat, apparently. We know this because the cat's gaze prompted considerable rumination on his part, famously resulting in many pages of prose on the topic, as well as a reflexive feeling of shame. For this cat stared at him and he found himself "*à poil*"—stark naked, or "down to one's hairs"—before her steady gaze. She stared at him "without moving, just to see," Derrida complained. He brought out a mirror, gazed at his nakedness and at her gaze at his nakedness, and declared that it is the cat that is his mirror.

Derrida may have had a perspicacious cat (no philosopher's cat gets away with much nonsense, I'd guess). But while she gazes at him, he is hardly seeing her. For Derrida, who the cat is, and what she's actually doing, doesn't matter. She is a real cat, he concedes. A "little" cat, we learn, who follows him into the bathroom in the morning, crying for breakfast, and leaves when he strips. We might wonder at the relationship between Derrida and this little mewing cat, but we don't get much to satisfy our wonder, because apart from this perfunctory description of her, there's nothing at all about her. Is she calico? Black? Fearful? Furless? Does she groom herself in the morning and chase imaginary mice at night? Is she courageous? Cautious? Destructive? Bashful? Did she ever get her tail caught in a closing door? Does she make herself comfortable on his lap, heavy-lidded and purring? Over fifty pages of cat-stare-inspired prose, he does not describe her looks, her habits, how she spends her days, or how he plays with her. Fair enough: he is not writing about cats per se. But therein lies the rub: the cat winds up just being a tool by which to consider himself—flattering himself that he is being considered by her at all.

Today, it is more often dogs, not cats, who are thought of as our mirror animals. If you live with dogs, you have seen them behind you in your mirrors. Call their name, and our dogs look at us in the glass—a quiet gaze that stops us for a moment, the mirror reflecting a scene at once familiar and new. We see our recognizable, loved dogs, but at the corners is the mystery of the mind behind their gaze. Our own habits and tendencies with them are thrown into relief; the reality of our shared presence, where neither of us is entirely known to the other, is exposed. Hold up the mirror and see what it discloses.

• • •

When writing my first book, *Inside of a Dog*, over a decade ago, I wanted to use the results of the fledgling science of dog cognition to bring a new way of thinking about dogs to dog people. After all, I recognized that my early research into dog cognition led quickly to my applying what I was learning to my under-standing of my own dog; I suspected others would be keen to as well. I also found myself on the receiving end of question marks from owners: *Why does my dog . . .* (fill in the blank: roll in things, turn circles, bark that way, lick that thing, sniff me, pee there . . .), they'd ask. The research, I quickly realized, was not actually asking and answering these questions. Though scientific results can sometimes be used to fashion a plausible response, I was interested in addressing those topics that people truly wondered about with their dogs. At the same time, the ultimate question about dogs for me was, and still is, *What is it like to be a dog?* For many others, though, the key question was more like: *What do we know about what my dog thinks about me?*

As it turns out, dog cognition research really began because of our interest in how dogs reflect back on us. It's almost a premise of comparative psychology—which field led to a great burgeoning in dog cognition science—that research about other animals is valuable *because it will tell us something about ourselves.* For instance, we worry about our place at the top of the intelligence tree. Despite Darwin's cautionary note to "never say higher or lower" when talking about the result of evolutionary change, we definitely reserve "higher" for our-selves: "Are humans special among all other animals," one comparative-cognition book opens rhetorically, "in their pro-cesses of cognition?"

The deck seems to be stacked in this endeavor, to say the least, as we are the ones doing the investigating and the defin-ing of what counts as "cognition." Indeed, there has been an ever-rising bar for non-human animals to hurdle before we concede them to be our cognitive equals.

The intellectual approach that informs science's current way of thinking about animal cognition, or mind, formed over thousands of years of experience on a continent that has no native primates other than humans. It is no wonder that Western culture has a deep-rooted sense of human unique-ness: we seemed the only ones around doing anything nota-ble on a human scale. As befits our impulse to explain and define ourselves, the question of exactly what it is that makes us unique has been tackled for just as long. Plato was among those who participated in this defining game: his defini-tion of man was "an animal, biped and featherless." To this, Diogenes, another Greek philosopher and famously cyni-cal, reputedly plucked a chicken and, presenting it, declared "Here is Plato's man!"

Plato quickly added "having broad nails" (i.e., not claws) to the list.

We've been adding qualifying statements to that list ever since. The essayist Thomas Carlyle described man as a (bipedal, featherless, broad-nailed) *tool-using* animal: as the only spe-cies who had the foresight and cleverness to extend the range of things we can do by using objects. Jane Goodall put that to rest. She observed chimpanzees using grass stems to fish for termites, a well-loved snack, in holes in clay-packed ter-mite mounds (which caused soldiers to attack the intruder— and then become a termite popsicle for the chimp). Since her studies, all manner of animals, including ants, wasps, finches, crows, and otters, have joined the club of tool-users. *Fine*, came the retort, *but what about tool*-making? For even if I do not myself know how to make a pen or a keyboard or a drill, some human did make that tool. Goodall promptly reported on chimps bending twigs and stripping them of leaves so that they would become suitable tools. "Now we must redefine tool, redefine Man, or accept chimpanzees as humans," her mentor Louis Leakey responded. He'd now have to do some radical redefining: studies have shown that ravens bend twigs into hooks to fashion the perfect grub-catching probe. There are ants—animals without a central brain to speak of—who carry leaves to be used as sponges to transport water.

The list of what might finally show humans to be distinct from animals is now long: an uneasy concatenation that is also a good historical record of the ever-changing emphases of the culture of science. It has become a list of necessary conditions for humanness that is never quite sufficient. But, ever sure we're unique, we keep adding what for a scholar's moment looks like the final distinction. We've added the ability to imitate, to teach, to use language; being self-aware; having a culture, and a dozen other criteria. None is an unqualified masterstroke. Apparent acts of imitation, teaching, and cultural transmission among animals have forced us to revise our definitions of what we meant by those skills; the plethora of elaborate communication systems in nature has forced us to be very particular about what it means to use a language.

If an interest in studying animals emerges out of an interest in ourselves, dogs didn't look like a sure bet to tell us anything of note. As a result, when I began studying dogs, there was no research field on the cognition of dogs. Researchers studied our closest Great Ape relatives—chimps, bonobos, orangutan, gorilla—and, though more distantly related, monkeys. Dogs and primates, while sharing characteristics of all mammals, seemed unlikely to share any of what were considered valuable cognitive abilities. After all, humans split from chimps and bonobos around five to seven million years ago, while our primate ancestors and the dogs' ancient carnivore ancestors parted evolutionary ways some ninety million years ago.

Happily, we did start looking at dogs, after the dogs at researchers' feet pawed us long enough to pay attention to them. And, lo and behold, dogs have some cognitive skills that non-human primates do not—such as making eye contact with us and following our gaze or point to find what we're looking at.

So much for our alleged singular expertise at being socially smart. Perhaps what dogs do indicate about us, cognitively, is that there is more than one way to build intelligence. Our human skill at reading others' intentions and interpreting their behavior is connected to social skills that mammals share going back a hundred million years, at least. We are a smart species, if we define "smart" as "doing precisely the things humans do." But other species, not at all closely related, also show some of those skills. And they can do some other things we forgot to include in our definition of intelligence, like: echolocation, electroreception, magnetoreception; detection of infrared light, ultraviolet light, electrical fields, subsonic or supersonic frequencies; flying, dam building, nest building, web spinning, structural design; cliff climbing, water walking; asexual reproduction, hermaphroditism; limb regeneration, body camouflaging, shape-shifting, sleeping while flying or swimming, smell tracking, super strength, mimicry, . . . and so on. What dogs show us is that we aren't the only way to do intelligence.

• • •

That's probably not what your dog sitting next to you right now has shown you about yourself. While dog cognition research aims at our brains, when we think about our dogs we are often considering what they do and how they look. Dogs are mirrors for our aspirational selves: we see in them what we want to see in ourselves. We admire their loyalty and rejoice in their pleasure to see us. We also have the urge to, in a tabloid-quiz kind of way, find out what our own choice of pups says about us: canine psychics, in touch with our truer selves; or astrologers, in touch with our future selves.

The dog we pick out from the rows of cages at the shelter; the profile we linger on while browsing adoptable dogs online; the dog along the roadside for whom we open our car door and drive to our home; the puppy we key in on among the squirmy new-litter balls of fluff at the breeder—these do tell us about ourselves. Our choice bespeaks whether we value predictability; are impulsive, heartstrong, unable to pass up a face in need; whether we consider the dog a companion, a replacement, therapy, or a toy.

Even more, we also match our dogs physically: we look like our dogs. Subjects in studies run from California to Venezuela to Japan are able to match a picture of a purebred dog with the dog's person at rates significantly higher than chance. Neither the subjects nor the experimenters can specify precisely what it is that leads them to match the persons and dogs. It goes deeper than a square-jawed man and his bulldog, a woman with long locks and her long-locked Afghan, or a poodle with a frou-frou haircut and an owner with same. It's not in the unnerving practice of dressing one's dog in the dog-sized version of the clothes the owner dons.* Still, sometimes there is a fuzzy but essential characteristic shared by the two that jumps out: an essential merriness; a sportiness; a seriousness-of-purpose. In one of the studies, "there was a goofy guy, smiling," according to the study's author, "and a golden retriever with a goofy smile." Everyone quickly pegged them as two peas in a pod.

I don't know if anyone would match a photo of me to the

---

* Awful. If you want to dress up to look like your dog, hey, fine; but unless your dogs are dressing themselves, leave them out of it.

curly-haired, sheep-shaped Pumpernickel with whom I lived for my entire young adulthood; or to the sleek, earnest-faced Finnegan; or to his brother, the awkward but charismatic Upton. Still, I certainly feel drawn to certain dogs' looks more than others. Expressive eyebrows make my heart leap. I'm a sucker for a shaggy beard and a soft gaze. For other people, short-nosed dogs (who make me feel uncomfortable for their faces) look button-cute. I love to meet enormous dogs but am not drawn to *own* them—nor to tiny dogs I could palm.

My urge is, very plain-spoken researchers of human choice like to say, probably attributable to "narcissism." We like that which is familiar, which resembles what we see when we look in the mirror—not the specifics (I am neither expressive-of-eyebrow nor bearded) but the gestalt. We prefer the letters of the alphabet found in our names, numbers that make up our birthdate, and we sit near people who look like us: things that remind us of ourselves. This is just what we do when choosing a mate: what researchers call "self seeking like" (but not too like*). Our practice of "assortative mating," leading us to prefer similarity and compatible genes, is an evolutionarily stable strategy. And it may have seeped into our choice of pups. It's not specifically that Finnegan's coat resembles my hair (his is shiny; mine is wavy), or that I match his earnest gaze (my expression toggles between confounded and circumspect). It's that his whole style—his enthusiasms, his concerns, his judgments—may remind me of me.

On personality tests, our temperaments match our dogs'.[†] People who score high on traits of anxiety or neuroticism are likely to have anxious or neurotic dogs; levels of extraversion

---

* —to avoid inbreeding.

† Taken by and thus relevant for people who submit themselves and their dogs to personality tests, at least . . .

and agreeableness match between person and pup. Have a friendly dog and it's likely you have a friendly way about you yourself. People who score low on scales of neuroticism have dogs with high cortisol variability, thought to be a marker of effective coping strategies—and vice versa.

Our perceived social status matches our dog. I am an unqualified mutt, and proudly so. Others would not own a dog without papers. Charlie Chaplin's tramp in *A Dog's Life* takes up with Scraps, a miserable but becoming stray. They match each other in their misery.

We like person-looking dogs: in implicit preference tests, people choose dogs who have colored irises (like humans), and whose mouths upturn at the edges, like a human smile, as their favorites. The ethologist Konrad Lorenz famously suggested that we prefer animals with baby-like, neotenous features. His idea has been borne out: animals with large pools of eyes, broad foreheads, and big heads generally, are always among people's favorites. Through consumer choice, teddy bears have, over the years, evolved to be big-browed and short-nosed. Mickey Mouse, who began his film career as a skinny, devilish fellow, has grown enormous eyes. His giant head nearly wobbles off his frame. These characters, Lorenz noted, approximate—and exaggerate—what babies look like. And many of the species humans consider appealing and worth seeing (in a zoo) or saving (in the wild) bear some of these features. The furless naked mole rat, fleshy-nosed mandrill, and small-faced funnel-eared bat get little love.

We like dogs because of the ways that they act like we do. They are more moved by the sound of babies crying than by white noise; they look where we point, not at our pointing fingers. Dogs, like children, synchronize with us: when dogs and owners share a room, dogs for the most part stay still when their people do, move when their people do, gaze where their people do, and spend time in whatever corner of the room the people do.

•   •   •

There is a usefulness in seeing ourselves when we look at dogs. We have always looked at animals to, as author Helen McDonald says, "amplify and enlarge aspects of ourselves." In myth, animals figure more as representative of human notions than as living, breathing creatures: the pelican is not pelican-like, a soaring bird searching out dinner and nest sites, but is a symbol of self-sacrifice. The viper, a venomous reptile who strikes quickly, appears instead as an object lesson in how one must put up with disagreeable husbands. In these guises, we can safely face human foibles; we can displace our own hesitancies and impulses onto the form of the animal, and watch them bloom there, unembarrassed.

Seeing humans when we see dogs is classic anthropomorphism: the projection of our own form and features onto everything around us. We see human faces in natural rock formations and sense "anger" in thunder. When directed at dogs, this approach is limiting, and can be downright wrong. But it also allows a conversation to begin between us and the dogs. It enables us to open a space in our lives for them—because we believe we know what we're looking at: we think we see ourselves. Making dogs into "pseudo-humans," animal-studies scholar Erica Fudge says, "is at the heart of the human-pet bond." By anthropomorphizing, we get to dismiss a nagging worry that, in fact, the dog might not see the world as we do (with ourselves at the center, notably). "[A]ny suggestion that the pet might be motivated by other than human feelings and desires," James Serpell writes, "instantly would devalue these relationships." And how uncomplicated it is to look at a furry, olfactory quadruped in your bed and see something less foreign. Few of us have even gotten down on all fours, nose to the ground, to meet the dogs where they dwell.

Perhaps we must always begin with that which we recognize, which feels easy to understand. It's a generous gaze we set on the dog, to grant them humanness. The farmed cow, pig, or chicken who is seen as an object, a commodity—not even seen enough to be misrepresented as humanlike—is given no consideration at all. The dog's status as object of our gaze is a considerable step up. From that vantage, we start to feel rewarded by the simple act of their gazing back at us. Emmanuel Levinas, who was interned in the camps during World War II, describes being set to hard labor in a forest with other prisoners, no longer treated or seen as humans by their captors. Yet he reveled in the friendly approach of a stray dog. For the dog, he writes, "there was no doubt that we were men."

• • •

There's a dark side to our tendency to simply see ourselves when we look at dogs. If we only like dogs because they act like we do, it can be disruptive to us when they . . . don't. In the most innocent version, we feel embarrassed at their actions. One minute we are walking our compellingly cute, social-facilitating, quadrupedal kin down the sidewalk, the next we are standing mortified beside a diarrheic dog squatting in the middle of the path. In letting our dogs reflect ourselves, we risk a reflection that is sometimes humiliating. A dog who moves from agreeably sniff-handshaking another dog to trying to hump her earns cries of protest from his owner. It is as though it were the *owner* slipping from smiling hello at a stranger to attempting to disrobe her.

As they are *dogs*, there are innumerable ways they can discomfit us. They roll in poo. They eat poo. Their nose beelines for the crotch of your new friend. They simply jump when you'd prefer they not; chase when they oughtn't, refuse to come when you call them. They sometimes pee in the house, they sometimes pee in the elevator, they may very well pee on that person picnicking on the lawn. Not for nothing, when these acts are witnessed by a non-dog other, we take the act upon ourselves, as if it were our act. To feel the dog is your mirror is one thing; to find that the mirror has a mind of its own is an alarming other.

We call it "misbehavior." Since we treat them as complicit in our ways, they are betrayers when they stray from the understanding we thought we had. We reserve a special indignation for dogs behaving "uncivilized"—like animals, using their mouths to express their feelings. Consider, by contrast, our reaction at other misbehavior. An elevator drops. A train derails. A bridge snaps, a roof collapses, a toddler picks up the gun and shoots another toddler. Lightning strikes, a river overflows its banks, rocks slide.

Devastating, all. But we know the elevator is not evil. That the toddler is not a monster. That the lightning is not aggressive, nor is the river bred to be dangerous.* While we know to avoid lightning, stay out of flooded waters, and keep toddlers from guns, we don't stop using bridges, trains, elevators; we don't stay away from nature or insist on its destruction.

Not so when the devastation is caused by a dog, biting. A

---

* . . . although ancient societies believed them to be. Projections of motives and personality onto natural phenomena—the wrath of a storm, the punishment of a flood—are among the first anthropomorphisms. A falling rock was described not as the result of a force between bodies, but as the rock acting on its desire to be on the ground.

beloved pet, living alongside a family for a decade, sleeping alongside children as they have grown, one day is startled or angry or sleepy and suddenly bites a child. In most cases, that is the end of the belovedness. Though the statistics show the frequency of a fatal injury by dog bite to be commensurate to all these other causes of death, our societal reaction to any bite, fatal or not, is hysteria. The dog is evil, irredeemably dangerous, aggressive, a monster. Typically, the dog is promptly given up on: perhaps put in the hands of animal control officers, or taken to the veterinarian to be killed—"euthanized," we say euphemistically, without eulogy.

This reaction is an unintended, unexpected result of that bond-enabling anthropomorphizing. It let the dog into our homes. We are for some reason shocked to later discover this guest has a mouth, with teeth (and may—just may— use them). While respecting the reality of the threat possibly posed by a powerful dog, and while acknowledging the horror of injuries suffered, James Serpell, who has studied dogs for nearly four decades, is among the handful of clearheaded skeptics of painting the species or particular breeds with a "dangerous" brush. "It is clear that the spasms of horror and outrage" in this reaction, he writes, "are generally out of proportion to the actual risks." In the US, where we live among some ninety million dogs, the number of deaths due to dog attacks hovers at around twenty a year. It is not nothing. But it is fewer than the annual number killed by salmonella poisoning. Everything else being equal, your risk of death by falling out of bed is over twenty-five times greater—bed breed notwithstanding. Risk of death by hot dog > risk of death by dog.

The spectacle of the bite-aggression compounds our reaction—and the singularity of these tragedies makes them feel even more profound. Just in the way that airline crashes are

noted and feared, but are far less common than ruinous accidents in the cars we confidently buckle ourselves into daily,
the dog bite feels like a "disturbance in the natural order," as
Serpell says. How could this innocent, guileless creature—
who we not only let into our homes, but perhaps even *into our
beds*—be a murderer?

•   •   •

To begin to see dogs anew, we need only look at our own
contradictory nature regarding dogs. The more I look at the
reflection of ourselves—of the person and her dog, the society and its pets—the more paradox I see. We are drawn to
dogs as animals. But we then transform our dogs into model
humans: loyal, companionable, cooperative—even willing to
be restrained by us, to be subject to the whims of our attention. Having granted dogs a special status of benign, innocent
companion, in on human notions, rules, and intents—a status
no dog asked for—we then feel angry and betrayed when they
turn out not to be precisely and only that.* When they act the
least bit "animal," our response is alarm. What their behavior
reveals, though, is our impoverished conception of them. If
suddenly transported into their heads, we might not recognize
the concerns, cares, experiences, preferences, and beliefs we
find they are having.

If seeing dogs as reflecting ourselves bolsters—if not outright creates—our feelings of love and attachment and mutual
understanding, to question these anthropomorphisms might
seem to undercut the relationship. In my own research, I think
of attributions we make to dogs as hypotheses to be tested. More

---

* Often we only realize that they aren't "exactly that" when they are pushed:
when their steely reserve is challenged by being abused, surprised, or not listened to.

often than we'd like, we turn out to be mistaken or at least premature in our conclusions. I appreciate that there is resistance to even casting a shadow of doubt. At one of my book readings years ago, an audience member, concerned at my suggestion that the statements we make about dogs should be examined, spoke up: "If my dog doesn't 'love me,'" she said, "I don't want to know." Yet there is a way to look at dogs that at least challenges our easy assumptions, without therewith concluding that dogs are "manipulating" us, in it for the food, or even, worse, playing us outright. There is a way to have sympathy for a dog without knowing exactly what their experience is; to share a space without knowing how the other is sharing it; to look at a dog and not know what they smell of you.

• • •

No dog need bite for us to see the results of our paradoxical nature. For at the same time as a dog in an American home is enjoying climate-controlled shelter, twice-daily prepared meals, treats ad lib, a doting family, and a soft place to sleep, down the street in America are millions of dogs—all of whom share the genome for attachment to humans, all of whom will gaze at your eyes and melt your heart— with minimal or no shelter or food. These include the million-plus shelter dogs euthanized for lack of family to take them in; the untold numbers of free-ranging dogs living their short lives by their wits and on our handouts. At the same time as we clone select dogs at great expense, we abandon other dogs when they are inconvenient: "put down" when an owner changes jobs, moves, or simply finds that the puppy they bought grew out of being a puppy.

We blithely create unhealthy purebreds, who will suffer from congenital disease on a daily basis, and call them cute.

Furthermore, many purebred dogs are put through one or more involuntary cosmetic surgeries: painful, entirely unnecessary mutilations just to meet breed standards. At this writing, breed standards of sixty-two dog breeds, including cocker spaniels and Rottweilers, compel tail docking (read: amputating the tail), which instantly lops off one of their means of communicating, as well as being painful. Performed during the first weeks of a dog's life, when puppies are roly-poly puddles of warmth and light, it will be the first glimpse they have of human capriciousness. The breed standards of over twenty breeds, including Dobermans and Great Danes, require or encourage "cropped ears." Cropping ears is the surgical removal of approximately two-thirds of the outer ear—the soft, lovely flap of the ear—at six to twelve weeks of age, followed by setting the cartilage erect with a splint and bandages. It is well known to cause considerable post-procedure pain. The American Kennel Club tries to sell debarking, the surgery known as ventriculocordectomy, as "bark softening." While many dog owners may find a barking dog annoying, a surgery that removes part of or all of the vocal cords is like responding to a complaining, questioning, or scared child by stapling his mouth shut.

There are thousands of dogs—most often beagles—in medical laboratories across the country, models in research hopefully but not necessarily helpful to human health. These dogs never have a home apart from a cage, and endure precisely the harms to body and mind that we protect the dogs in our home from: intentional injury, no social companionship, minimal exercise, a short life. At my college, I cannot bring owners and their well-loved dogs on to campus to run behavioral experiments during business hours, for fear of allergies or liability; but at the associated medical center researchers can breed and keep caged dogs for purposes of invasive experimentation indefinitely. The USDA makes reports of animals used in research publicly available. In 2016, nearly 61,000 dogs were used in America; as of this writing, 2017 was shaping up to be another 65,000. At Columbia University, where I teach, 154 dogs were used over the last five years, in types of "experiments, teaching, research, surgery, or tests" considered to have sufficient "accompanying pain or distress" that they needed to be reported on. I walk down the street into the nearby park with my dogs and count the pet dogs I see. There's Todos, George, Darwin. Ziggy, Bear, Ella. Django, Penny. Sixteen other dogs to whom I haven't been formally introduced. Three miles uptown, in labs, there are those dogs plus one hundred and thirty others, just as sweet, who never smelled the air or rolled in the grass of the park down the street.

The long history of dog ownership includes a not-inconsiderable period during which a sport was made of egging dogs to harass and kill other animals: bulls, most commonly, but also lions, pigs, and bears. "Dog fighting," in which dogs are tortured, starved, and prodded until they attack each other, is still very common in America. In 2007, NFL quarterback Michael Vick was tried and convicted for his part in running a long-term dog-fighting ring, wherein dogs were forced to participate in violent battles, usually to the death, and those dogs who were not suitable for fighting were summarily executed.* While now deeply underground, fighting rings like these are highly organized; laws forbidding fighting are simply flouted.

While we do not eat dogs, many cultures do. Pet keep-

---

* The USDA report said three dogs were hung, "by placing a nylon cord over a 2×4 that was nailed to two trees located next to the big shed," three were killed "by putting the dogs' heads in a five-gallon bucket of water." One died by men "slamming it to the ground several times before it died, breaking the dog's back or neck." A female dog who lost a fight was killed "by wetting the dog down with water and electrocuting the animal."

ing is increasingly popular in South Korea; in street markets, dogs to be used as pets are sold next to dogs to be used as meat. For anyone uncertain which dog to love and which to cook, the pet-dog cages are pink. Video of dog-meat farms show dogs you know—dogs whose personality you can see in an instant. The furrowed brows, expressive eyebrows, floppy ears. They are Labradors, Saint Bernards, charismatic looking mixes with dark snouts and tawny colors. They live in exceedingly close quarters, four to a cage that would fit one in transport. There is no room to move around without jumping over each other. As a camera approaches, you can see the open grate underfoot; dogs' claws reaching through the cage grating; open wounds; snouts tentatively sniffing and wagging at the visitors. Some dogs live with a dead dog lying between them. They look exactly like your dog.

Should this feel like another culture's paradox, it's not. It is unblinkingly accepted that other animals, some who are similar on tests of cognition to dogs, some who form bonds with people and come when you call them, will be food for our dogs.

. . .

If dogs are anything but reflections of ourselves—and of course they are—our way of thinking about them is woefully inadequate. As dogs were walked into comparative-psychology research because we were taken by how they remind us of ourselves, their place in the public consciousness has wound up being as small, furry humanlike animals. Their singular skill set—their very dogness—is not part of this perception.

In fact, when dogness slips through now and then, we are given an arguably more interesting vision of ourselves—if in a way other than we intended. In these moments, how we respond not only mirrors but exaggerates ourselves: fun-house mirrors that we are both the maker of and reflected within. Dogs become bearers of metaphor of a different sort: our treatment of them representative of who we are; our consideration of them a record of our biases and generosities. How we think about this other species is a measure of our species.

One risks acting too serious by half to complain about our seeing ourselves when we see dogs. At least, you might say, we are seeing them at all. Our hearts feel true—and, besides, dogs are treated so well, relatively. We do not even bother to gaze at most of the species on the earth; we spew outright scorn at countless familiar animals, from vermin to animals declared only good enough to eat. But it is because we are all looking directly at dogs that I think we must examine what we see. If we are only willing to see ourselves, how can we extend empathy to other people who are not mirror images? Step away from the mirror, fellow dog lovers. Allow dogs to be the beautiful, impressive, unknown foreigners they are.

Interlude: The Horowitz Dog Cognition Lab by the Numbers

Year founded: 2008

Number of studies run since then: 12

Student researchers involved with the lab: 40

Number of owners who have called me "Dr. Dog" to my face: 2

Number of white lab coats kept at lab: 3

Journal publications featuring the colon-enabled title phrasing Clever Title: Longer Explanatory Title Using Jargon of the Field: 9

DEMOGRAPHICS

Number of live dogs kept at the dog lab: 0

Number of life-sized plush dogs kept at the dog lab: 2

Number of life-sized plush dogs given names by experimenters: 2

Number of owned dog participants: 566

Ratio of male:female subjects: 1:.98

Tail-waggers: 565

Tail-between-the-leggers: 1

Number of studies Merlot, a sheltie, has participated in: 5

Number of different breeds: 84

Six most popular names, across studies: Charlie, Daisy, Lucy, Oliver, Oscar, Penny

Number of people who noticed that the previous list item was not a number: 0

Average number of legs of dogs in recent study: 3.97

Blind dogs: 2

Deaf dogs: 1

Smallest dog: 7 lbs.

Largest dog: 155 lbs.

EXPERIMENTAL DETAILS

Dogs injured during experiments: 0

Dogs poked with a needle during experiments: 0

Number of studies in which dog is intentionally deceived: 0

Number of studies in which owner is intentionally deceived: 1

Percentage of studies using hot dogs, freeze-dried liver or salmon, or cheese cubes: 100

Size of experimental room used at Barnard College for studies: 11 ft. × 11 ft.

Neighboring choir practices disrupted by subject vocalizations: 1

Number of months of average observational study: 14

Number of submitters of videos of dog-human play in citizen–science study: 239

Number of countries represented by submitters: 19

BEHAVIORAL TENDENCIES

Highest number of hot dogs (edible) deployed in single study: 34

Farthest distance owner traveled to participate in 30-minute study: 210 miles

Average number peeing episodes (canid) per study: 2

Dogs expressing fear at a floor fan with balloons on it: 15

Dogs happily popping balloons: 1

Number of times experimenter says "Hi puppy! What's this, puppy?" in one study: 144

Average time subjects sniffed canisters containing novel odors: 3.3 seconds

Length of time one outlier subject sniffed the canisters: 120 seconds

Percentage of dogs who would still eat a hot dog when sprayed with lavender, mint, or vinegar: 36

Of 14 dogs, number who immediately ate a forbidden treat when their owner left the room: 1

Percentage of dogs with obedience training classes who spontaneously show the guilty look upon seeing their owners: 100

OWNER BEHAVIOR

Ten most common words owners say to their dogs in a dog-human play study: you; good; it; get/getting; got, gotta; go, going, gonna; come, c'mon; (dog's name); girl; yay

Percentage of people who preferred dogs with large eyes over dogs with small eyes: 59

Percentage of owners willing to submit their smelly T-shirts for a study of dog recognition of human odor: 100

Types of human-dog play behavior suggested to Sony to be useful in design of their pet robot Aibo: 4

Number of types of human-dog play behavior Sony used: 0*

EXPERIMENTAL PARAPHERNALIA DETAILS

Video cameras destroyed in service: 4

Number of times dog-shaped robot used in study attacked by subjects: 2

Rolls of sticky tape available to remove dog hair from clothing and chairs: 7

Number of toys dogs get to choose from as reward at end of study: 25

Number of dog toys dogs usually pick: 1

Number of dog toys one subject picked: 11

BIOLOGICAL PHENOMENA

Bites suffered by experimenter during studies: 0

---

* Instead, the Aibo was programmed to spontaneously dance for you.

Poo "accidents": 0 (we don't call them accidents: we're pretty sure they were all on purpose)

Number of studies involving owner collection of their dog's urine: 2

Number of pee cups ordered, two-year period: 220

Number of studies involving dog drool collection: 1

Number of studies involving human drool collection: 1

Number of times I have written "p value" as "pee value": 3

Amount of dog saliva on plush dogs at end of study: immeasurable

Does My Dog Love Me?

Every day watching dogs I see emotion in them. At the lab, many of the scenes we create for them are inadvertent emotion provocation. I see *curiosity* directed at a small robotic "dog" toy that dances and plays a tune. I see *surprise* when a hidden person appears from behind a door. Dogs may feel anxious when I open an umbrella; disgusted when they sniff a very strong smell; delighted when their owner stops listening to me and turns to pet them again.

When I watch dogs in the "wild"—out in parks and on sidewalks among people and other dogs—I see regular displays of joy, interest, and affection; of apprehension and fear.

Still, one of the questions I am most often asked is whether dogs *really* love us, feel bored, and get angry: a testament to both the ardor of our interest in our dogs, and our uncertainty about the dog's experience. As our own days may be colored with anxiety, anticipation, or foreboding—are dogs' days so colored? As we respond to events and people with empathy, sarcasm, or incredulity—do dogs tend toward such sentiments?

Many of these questions boil down to whether dogs have feelings or emotions at all. But of course they do. Look at it adaptively: emotions are messaging to the muscles and response system to circumvent the closed-door discussions between the sensory organs and brain. I see a tiger; I know that tigers are predators and this one is coming toward me . . . and *Hey!*, chimes the brain emotively, *Be afraid! Run!*

Look at it neurologically: the areas of human brains that are active when we feel, sigh, yearn, and despair are also found in dogs' brains.

Look at it behaviorally: though we are not always great at naming which behavior indicates what emotion (as we will shortly see), the wide array of different behaviors and postures of dogs tells us about their internal states.

Look at it sensibly. The alternative to having emotions—having undifferentiated experience—defies reason, defies Darwin, defies continuity. Human emotions did not emerge mysteriously and fully formed out of unfeeling automata. Keep in mind that the last popular advocate of the latter belief, Descartes, lived in a time when bloodletting was still considered salubrious.

My own dogs, subject to my near-continuous gaze, appear to be great furry balls of emotion, sentiment, and expression: anticipation at a walk, disappointment at being left at home, grumpiness at a friendly cat's attention. I naturally see Finnegan's hoisting of an improbably large stick out of a river as pride; the dour look he gives me as I allow the cat to curl on my lap as jealousy; his look when discovered later sneaking mouthfuls of the cat's food as guilt. There is a coyness in Upton covering his face with a paw; amusement in his self-invented game of mimicking the sounds of trumpet practice; embarrassment at his own ghost-thrusting hips long after his playmate is gone.

As shorthand, it makes good sense to me to use emotional terms to describe what I'm seeing. In the lab, I would more likely say, *The dog's head extends forward, leading the body by an extra half-step; the ears are perked into their full height* (read: curiosity). *A dog jumps back, preparing the body for escape; a "rurf" sound slips out* (surprise). *Retreating, the dog's body shrinks down and back* (anxiety); *on approach, a dog pulls away her head, lifts her paw, curls her lip* (disgust); *with a high, loosely wagging tail, the dog leaps with two or four legs and attempts to lick every nearby face, dog or human* (delight).

I don't use those shorthand words as my first descriptions of what they are doing—because I hesitate to assume that a dog's experience of what looks like curiosity or delight is precisely like mine. While the similarities across mammalian brains make it highly likely that all mammals have diverse emotional experiences, we all also have very different lived experiences, based on, for humans, our cultures, where we live, and the people we meet. So, too, for dogs. My own guess is that, planted into a dog's body, we wouldn't recognize the feelings we're flooded with as being just like our own. But that there are feelings, I've no doubt.

In this way, I inhabit the territory between the presumptive granting of subjective experience just like humans—and complete denial of any experience. Not presuming to know the dog's subjective experience is not at all the same as denying them any experience at all. In fact, though, that denial has been the default model in much of science. Without definitive evidence of an animal's fear of pain, researchers say, how can we be sure that the animal feels fear—or pain—at all?

Weirdly, most of the history of medical and psychiatric research has also seemed not to doubt the reality of animals' feelings. In fact, it presumes feelings in its very premise. To prove the efficacy of an anti-anxiety drug for humans, the drug first has to be roundly vetted on an "animal model": essentially, lab animals have to be made anxious, then given the test, and have their anxiety dissipate (while no other ill effects arise). A history of this kind of thinking is written between the lines of every medical study using animals: *they are so similar to us, thus they are a good model for humans.*

Dogs—the same dogs who express alarm at a deflating balloon loping down the sidewalk; the same dogs who, having lived in your home for even only one day, gleefully greet you at the front door—have not been immune from this manner of research.

Should someone make the claim to me that a dog definitely can't be "depressed," or benefit from anti-depression medication, I'll take their hand and walk them back in time. Several decades ago, depression research took a step forward with the development of the "learned helplessness" model, made famous by Martin Seligman. He and his colleague came up with a scheme to see if helplessness could be induced by circumstance. Brace yourself: it involved dogs.

I was born at the oldest hospital in Philadelphia, about a mile from the mid-century building where Seligman's experiment was likely conducted two years before. I met my first dog, an Irish setter named Trevor—long-haired, graceful, more fluid in movement than my toddler self—at my grandparents' house a few miles to the north. Twenty years on, in the fall, I walked the same paths at Penn that Seligman did, with leaves flamboyantly littering the ground and the air scented with the new season.

His dogs never smelled that air. They lived in the laboratory, the thirty-two "adult mongrel dogs" who were his first compulsory subjects. I don't know where they came from, but if they were mongrels they might have come from the city's shelters. Like the shelter that, two years after I arrived at Penn, I walked out of with my first mongrel dog, Pumpernickel, whose soft black form and gentle pacing as we exited the building into the sunlight I still remember. Pump walked those paths and frolicked in those leaves.

One day, these thirty-two adult mongrel dogs were strapped into rubber harnesses in a small cubicle, with their legs hanging through leg holes. Their heads were yoked in a fixed position by panels restricting head and neck movement. A 70 dB noise—about the loudness of a nearby vacuum cleaner—was played in the box. Seligman, or his assistant, taped brass plate electrodes to their hind feet. Then they sent from 64 to 640 electric shocks through the plates.

The strength of the shocks, six milliamps, is described in the literature with adult humans as "painful"; "muscular control is lost" when experienced for one second. The dogs felt these shocks from five seconds to two minutes each time, dozens or hundreds of times that day. When other control dogs felt what the study describes as this "severe, pulsating shock," the researchers noted that they "barked, yelped, ran, and jumped until (they) escaped."

In some conditions, the dogs could stop the shocks by pushing their head against the panels, if they discovered this in their struggle; in another group, there was no escaping the shock. It went on and on, with no sign of ending, and despite their attempts to move, and despite their cries. Finally it did abruptly end. The next day both groups were put in a different cage with a metal grid on the floor and an obstacle separating their cage from an adjoining one. The grid was electrified. Dogs who had learned to stop the shock the previous day quickly jumped over the obstacle and escaped the shock. Those who were previously exposed to the inescapable shock sat passively, unmoving, unescaping. This is what excited the researchers. These dogs had learned that they were powerless: what the researchers called "learned helplessness."*

So, dogs were shocked, driven to depression and passivity and impotence, to prove that we could feel passivity and impotent in depression. Dogs are still widely used in medical research, make no mistake: this is happening now. Also now. And again.

For learned helplessness studies, though, subsequent researchers found it hard to stomach using dogs, and rodents have taken their place. You might not feel, on first pass, that the fact of a mouse going through the study is as dramatically upsetting as the dogs' fate. I'd hazard if you knew any mice for more than a few hours you might feel differently. Or maybe if you heard about the current test of choice, a hugely common test called the "forced swim" test—which is just as it sounds. The test is also officially called the "despair" test. It is, as one paper writes, "probably the most widely used screening test of antidepressant potential of novel compounds": a good way

---

* It took me three sittings to read their study through. After one, I slammed shut the computer and left the room. The second time I had to lie down and close my eyes. By the time I finished it, my jaw was completely clenched. I carefully dragged the pdf to the trash icon, turned the volume of the computer to eleven, and emptied the trash.

to test if antidepressants work at "rendering or preventing depressive-like states" in rodents. A mouse (or a rat) is placed in a tank or bucket filled with water, from which they cannot escape. Researchers watch them, for many minutes. The amount of what is described as the animals' "struggling" is measured. After a while, the mice lose their wills, they lose energy, and they become passive. Their feet still stir the water, but their heads are barely above the surface, just holding on to life. But, hey, tested antidepressants "reduce the immobility time," that is, cause the mouse to *keep struggling*.

To watch struggling animals without working to relieve their struggle demonstrates the great dissociation we condone with animals. Our society's attitude toward animals is thus mismatched. We grant them feelings when it suits our testing needs, but grant them no feelings when it would not suit our testing needs. The human behavior in these test settings—electrocuting; near-drowning—is considered animal cruelty anywhere outside of the test setting.

So why is the question of animal emotions still posed? We are trapped on the far reaches of the pendulum's swing: either assuming dogs are entirely unlike us or assuming dogs are just like us. As wrongheaded as it is to presume dogs to be unfeeling, it is no more correct to presumptively grant them a humanlike emotional life. (Nor must it be somewhere in-between: for all we know, dogs' emotional experience is far more elaborate than ours.) We glance at dogs and conclude we know what they're feeling, but our haste to make such conjecture on little evidence—and inability to read a dog's emotions when they are displayed—is profound.

There is little place better to see this than in the movies. Dogs are in films not because they are great actors but because they are part of our lives. The actual dogs who trot through most films* are methodically managed, like everything that appears on screen. They are situated as companions, caring about what happens. But their body language easily betrays their indifference. If you zoom in on the dogs at the side of the shot, they are often doing something quite unlike what the scene requires. Dorothy arrives in Oz with Toto, a cairn terrier. As she gazes around her at the colorful, fantastic new world, a radiant bubble appears in the sky: Glinda the Good Witch is about to make her appearance. Dorothy is struck with apprehension and amazement, staring at the approaching bubble. Indeed, even after a trip in a tornado, one would be surprised at this new weather phenomenon. But look at the little dog at her feet. Toto, apparently not sharing her anticipation, is the picture of insouciance. She gives a small shake, turns away, and casually exits the scene.

"What is happening" for the dog (for Terry, as she was known) is defined by the presence of a trainer off-screen. A keen-eyed movie viewer can readily spot the dog's participation in a parallel experience, their attention directed toward an unseen presence. They are, of course, unwitting actors: their performance is only training to "act" in a certain way on cue. What film directors know, though, is that the audience's willingness to read, say, a dog's covering her eyes with a paw (a behavior not particularly common in the species) as modesty or apprehension will trump our interest in seeing what the dog is really doing (performing a behavior for a reward). The dog is acting—for the trainer; the actors are acting—for the director; and we are acting—like humans, who will suspend not just disbelief but all common sense. Movie dogs are meant

---

* And they are in most films, weirdly: next time you're at the movies keep an eye out for the dog wandering down the street, hanging out on the sofa, or barking in the distance.

to be shy of their nakedness, to be covetous, to be uncertain—in short, they are meant to be quadrupedal versions of us. They are not meant to be honest-to-goodness dogs. Movies with talking dogs are beyond the pale: dogs nearly stop being canid at all. While they are still dog-shaped, and do a handful of banal doglike things (bark, sniff butts, scratch an ear), they are just furry mannequins on which to drape our own concerns and feelings. We willfully disregard what a dog's posture or expression might indicate about what they are actually saying or feeling.

Our indifference to trying to puzzle out what a dog is actually doing is legendary. In fact, there is a legend, rendered in everything from ancient Greek stories to Arabic text, Medieval French to Welsh tales, about a man who returns home to find his baby and his dog—usually described as a greyhound—covered in blood. The greyhound excitedly greets the owner at the door. The owner takes one look at the bloody mouth and slays the pup, assuming that it is his baby's blood on the dog. Only afterwards does he discover a snake in the baby's crib, killed by the dog before it harmed the baby (who is unharmed).

Or consider all the portraits painted or photographed with a dog sitting at a person's feet, or submitting to a hug. The pose reads "affection" to us, but anyone who's had a portrait taken with a dog might observe that the dog's experience is closer to "patient tolerance" and, usually, "willingness to endure drudgery for prospect of liver treats."

Our interpretation of an emotional state of a dog, based on extrapolation from our own behavior, is necessarily parochial. What we see depends on what is in the air at the time. In the context of the movie, Toto is assumed to be doing the thing that Dorothy is doing; feeling what she is feeling. Look at Darwin, alluding to one of his contemporaries' suggestion that dogs' behavior on reunion with their owners after an absence is evidence that "a dog looks on his master as a god." Darwin himself was concerned with the origins of religious thought in non-humans—consistent with the quite profound notion he popularized of continuity between humans and non-humans. The argument from religion was one, in that religious climate, which was "in the air." So they see quasi-religious devotion.

In the air now, in twenty-first-century America, is the idea that dogs accompany us not only physically but also psychically.* We—this dog scientist included—naturally read a dog's attention as caring; their gaze as understanding; their silent presence as commiseration. As we feel pride, jealousy, embarrassment, shame, so, too, we reason, must they.

As a scientist, I don't yet see a way to definitively test another animal's emotional experience. What I can test is whether the behaviors that prompt us to make the attribution—*she's next to me when I'm sad (so she's commiserating); he's paying attention (so he loves me)*—in fact appear more often in commiserating, loving contexts, or not. If a dog is *regularly* by your side, that looks less like commiseration than simple desire for proximity; if you keep pocketsful of cheese, their attention may have other explanations.

In this way, our lab has shown that the behaviors of the so-called "guilty look"—the head-down, tail-tucked, contrite-looking pose we might find our dogs in—don't actually appear more often when dogs have done something to feel guilty about—overturning the trash, mauling your best shoes,

---

* The notion of dogs as emotionally connected to us has reached its peak in the proliferation of "emotional support" dogs, whose simple presence is steadying. Interestingly, there is not much research to support the idea that it is the dog's behavior that is a palliative; instead, dogs may be the furriest placebos we have ever invented.

de-feathering your feather pillow. Instead, dogs show more of the guilty look when we're angry or about to be angry with them (dogs are terrific readers of what we're about to do)—whether they've done something wrong or not. Rather than being evidence about a dog's ability to feel guilt, the studies show that what we read as guilt, simply isn't.

To design these studies is tricky, though: what does emotion look like? Our own feelings of guilt, shame, jealousy—even affection or fear—may or may not be accompanied by any overt expression or act. One can only attempt to create a context that is more likely to prompt any expression. In that, science has had mixed luck.

For instance, "jealousy" seems to be rooted in appreciating that someone else has something that you'd like to have, but do not. In one study, dogs stop performing a trick if they see someone else getting a treat for doing the trick, when they are getting no treat. But on examination, this looks less like jealousy than a reasonable refusal to work for nothing. Our lab ran an experiment looking at dogs' feelings about a person who always gave another dog more treats (*unfair!*) compared to one who dispensed treats fairly. Against expectation, they preferred to hang out with the unfair person. Again, it seems like they are motivated less by the kinds of feelings of unfairness or jealousy that humans have than by pure optimism that maybe *this* time, some of those treats will be tossed their way . . .

Research designed to test a dog's inherent empathy finds them more likely to approach an owner who is crying than one who is humming a tune. This turns out to be less proof of empathy than evidence of their complete lack of interest in humming. In another study, dogs trained to pull on a tray to give sausage or cheese to someone *else* will do so with a famil-

iar dog, but not with a person—including their owner—as
though they might feel empathetic, but just not to you.

So not only owners but researchers, too, have trouble pinning the right emotion to a behavior.

Our inability to read dogs' emotions well probably begins
with our inability to understand our own emotions well.
Though perfectly accessible to us—and only to us, truly—
our society is constantly putting us to work to "get in touch
with" our emotions. And that's when they are right there for
the touching. Given our difficulty, it's no wonder we are ill-
equipped to figure out the emotions of the four-legged creature beside us. So we default to granting dogs emotions, but
of the most human sort. We assume dogs are not only in the
room with us, but sharing a kind of hive mind with humans.

Indeed, Darwin seems to suggest that it is humans who
are less empowered in emotional expression than dogs: "man
himself cannot express love and humility by external signs, so
plainly as does a dog, when with drooping ears, hanging lips,
flexuous body, and wagging tail, he meets his beloved master."
We use language to make up for our lack of ears that droop
and tails that wag.

Despite our widespread anthropomorphisms, what I see
less often are attributions of the kinds of characteristic traits
we recognize in each other: of a sarcastic manner, chronic self-
doubt, or a morbid temperament. I wonder why we don't
describe our dogs as ironic or deliberate or serene. It seems as
likely that dogs feel awe and gratitude as that they are jealous
and full of shame. But it's not currently in the air.

I'd relish trying to test such attributions, where at risk is
not whether the dog has any emotional experience but instead
how ably we can describe it. The dog carefully trained to do
the servile task of bringing you your newspaper who then

carefully retrieves you your angry neighbor's: *mocking*. The *pedantic* dog might be one who sits just-so when requested, or who snipes at another dog who doesn't come when called (Finnegan, I'm looking at you). *Pragmatic* might be the dog who carefully carries one ball to her bed at a time; *ostentatious*, the Labrador whose jowls are stuffed with three.

Neither rampant anthropomorphism nor complete denial of experience is right. One is too simple, too pat; the other defies logic, defies science. There is considerable territory between the poles yet to examine, though. Darwin—and all of modern animal behavior—suggests that dogs are showing us what they feel all the time, if we only look. Start by looking, and being willing to wade in the knottiness of phenomenal experience. We've been led to believe that emotion in a dog is a matter of a simple movement of a body part: tail up, happy; tail down, sad. But what of the tail wagging horizontally; or wagging low, combined with flattened ears and a crouched posture; or stiffly wagging with ears forward? They are neither precisely happy nor sad. If we acknowledge the complexity there, we get closer to what the bearers of those tails might be feeling.

Does your dog love you? Watch them, and you tell me.

Against Sex

Here's why. Say you live in a city with a dog or two. You walk the dogs maybe twice a day, for, on average, an hour outside. You encounter other dogs. Smiling golden retrievers; a smattering of small furry white dogs wearing hand-knit sweaters; a brindle mongrel, just the right size; dogs who turn and bark at you and whose owners pull them to the curb scoldingly; a beagle with an appealing gaze; a pair of Frenchies, tongues wagging, looking starry-eyed; a black-and-white, medium, with a spot like a saddle on his back; a black-and-white, small, a spot like a patch over one eye; a Rottie with a prong collar held by a stern-looking gentleman; a wiggling, whimpering, nearly ecstatic pit mix who you must greet in kind. Maybe on a sunny day that invites walking you see, oh, a hundred dogs when you're out.

On that very day, for every one of the hundred dogs you see, eighteen healthy dogs are euthanized in the US. Your hundred dogs, lined up nose to tail down a city block, is followed by a queue of recently smiling, barking, wiggling but now dead dogs, laid out ghost nose to ghost tail, for a full mile.

The fault is ours. Our species' fault. When we began, some tens of thousands of years ago, to carve dogs out of wolves, we brought them into our fold. We took a resourceful carnivore and bent and molded it into an animal critically dependent on humans for survival. Even the hundreds of millions of stray dogs who now wander the globe are wandering alongside humans—living on the periphery of cities, scavenging in villages, living off human spoils, kindnesses, waste, and excesses. But while we made dogs dependents, we did not hold ourselves accountable. We lose dogs. We let them run unchecked. If they are a nuisance or misbehaving or we have simply lost interest, we "release" them. Maybe it was only that cute puppy or helpful guard dog that was wanted; the full dog was not. Our perfectly admirable aims of bringing dogs into our families has careered off course and we have unleashed a monster—a reproducing monster, unchecked by our intervention.

That is why in the United States, there is a highly popular secular religion. Its leaders are the people who are employed and tasked with caring for animals: they are the humane societies, shelters, veterinarians. Its adherents are devout, unwavering, and willing proselytizers. Its tenets are clear: there is one way to be saved. And it is this way.

The religion is called "spay or neuter." To spay (a female dog) or neuter (a male dog) is to surgically de-sex them: to remove their gonads—testicles or ovaries—to prevent that female and male dog from getting together and making puppies.* To solve the problem of our own unwillingness to keep track of our dogs, we do not address our unwillingness. To address the overpopulation of unwanted dogs, we do not address the overpopulation. Instead, we non sequitur: we take brand-new dogs and introduce them into our homes by first putting them through a surgery at six, four, or even three months of age. These new, sexless puppies are at once our projections into the future and our ducking of the past: *Here!* we say, *In the future there will be fewer unwanted dogs!* As for our past misdeeds, we are quiet.

To de-sex is to effect two things: the surgery it describes, and the blunting of sex. It is also convenient. The contemporary dog isn't meant to be sexy. In no breed description will you find reference to the breed's sexual drive or future sexual performance. Dog-dog sex is undesired and unimagined by the great majority of Western dog owners, whose dogs come to them already without ovaries or testicles. De-sexing is a given. For the most part, outside of the shelter world, we have ducked any conversations or personal decisions about de-sexing dogs. We don't even want to use the "s" word. There are a humorous handful of ways to talk about de-sexing without referencing anything remotely graphic: we "alter" dogs; we "sterilize" them, as though disinfecting our sink; we "fix" them. If you have ever met eight-week-old puppies, still mere wiggly grubs, their skin soft and folded, their newly blinking eyes having yet to see much of this world, you know there is nothing that needs to be fixed about them. They are perfection.

"For the urban dog at any rate expectation of sex is slender in the extreme," J. R. Ackerley wrote in *My Dog Tulip* (a mem-

---

* In fact, in the US it is more common to remove a female dog's uterus and fallopian tubes, too, while they're at it: an ovariohysterectomy.

oir of the life of—and his life with—his dog Queenie). "He is equipped for it, but the equipment is not used." Ackerley puts this down to a "human conspiracy" against the dog—and he's not wrong: it is the conspiracy to put sex in the hands of a few (breeders) and out of the loins of the many. Ackerley himself aims to "marry" the female German shepherd Tulip, but in his telling, at least, she won't have it.

Published in mid-century Britain, Ackerley's book, full of ruminations on the biology of dogdom, including defecation, menses, urination styles, and sex, must have raised some human eyebrows. Search the indices of your dog-book library: how many even mention the sex organs, or sex itself, at all?* But how extraordinary is this sex blunting. Sex, the reproductive method of choice for every mammal (and most non-mammals)—a defining feature of human adult social life—is quietly extracted from books and the lives of dogs.

Spay-neuter is so widely accepted in our country in this time, that those who take exception to it are roundly chastised. Each year, when I ask the undergraduate students in my canine cognition seminar what they thought when they last saw an intact—non-neutered—male dog, few can recall ever seeing such a dog. Last year, of those who could, two responded in near-chorus, "irresponsible." Not the dog: the owner, for not removing the dog's testicles as a matter of course. The chorus is much larger than their two voices: rare is the humane society or veterinary group that does not turn the phrase "responsible pet owners" to describe those who de-sex their animals. The opposite, of course, is irresponsible, derelict, criminal. The author Ted Kerasote, who wrote of his interest in keep-

---

* And so I checked the index of my last book, *Being a Dog*. Nope. From "septum, nasal" to "shampoos, smell of" with no sex in between.

ing his dog Pukka intact, found himself compared unfavorably by an acquaintance to Michael Vick, convicted for his role
in a brutal dog-fighting ring. To compare an owner's decision
not to remove his dog's testicles to the willful and giddy elec-
trocution and methodical torture of dogs is to feel very, very
sure about the importance of universal de-sexing.

Dog owners who have intact animals may find that efforts
to be "responsible" in other ways—by socializing their dogs,
or by finding a doggie day care for long days at work—will be
rebuffed. Intact dogs over six months of age are often forbidden to come to doggie day cares at all. Some city parks and dog
runs similarly forbid dogs who are not de-sexed. Many people
will cross the street to avoid interaction with a clearly unneutered male dog (or his person).

For me simply to bring up the topic of de-sexing for discussion will be, in the eyes of some, impermissible. So sacred
is the policy—so heartfelt (and good-hearted) is the intent
behind it—that one is almost not allowed to talk about it. But
there's the rub. If there's a topic we can't talk about with dogs,
then that's one we should be talking about.

•   •   •

The doctrine of sexlessness has been affirmed, in our secular
way, into law. "Spay-neuter" is the straightforward name of
the law now on the books in nearly two-thirds of states, requiring all dogs adopted from animal shelters or rescue groups to
be de-sexed. Should you go to a local ASPCA, no-kill shelter, or rescue organization, you will meet a great variety of
possible pet futures who all share one feature: their infertility.
There may be a few animals still intact, for age (too young) or
medical (too sick) reasons, but adoption is then conditioned on
a promise to sterilize the animal when they are of age or well.

Ascent into the legal system happened quickly. The phrase "spay-neuter" wasn't often uttered until the 1970s. It begins appearing in newspapers the decade prior, as when the vice-president of the Cincinnati SPCA responded to an irate letter writer (who was surprised to find the twelve cats she had dropped off the previous day all destroyed) by saying that irresponsible breeding had forced them to euthanize animals, using "the completely painless high altitude method." He urged "all pet owners to SPAY, neuter and control pets to stop this cruel overbreeding." The surgery itself was rarely performed on dogs at all before the 1930s. Early twentieth-century veterinary texts include mention of castration of the dog, but as an afterthought to the more common castration of boars, bulls, rams, and stallions. Dogs and cats were newcomers to the sterilization game. For dogs, the procedure—performed with the aid of a tape muzzle, assistants to hold the dog down, and a scissorlike tool called an "emasculator"—was performed to stop nighttime roaming (and visitations of the "female society members" of the species). De-sexing only became a large part of the veterinary practice after World War II, as more veterinarians transitioned from livestock and large animals to exclusively treating dogs and cats, and they were schooled in the procedure.

By the 1970s growing concern over rampant overpopulation of seemingly homeless dogs (and cats) led to a few cities, all in California, opening spay-neuter clinics. The first low-cost dedicated spay-neuter clinic opened in North Hollywood in 1973. Concerns revolved around a few points: the startling increase in stray dogs—as well as the fear of the (unarticulated) danger they posed—and the cost it took to kill all those dogs, once captured, in the pound. One reporter put the cost of killing the thirteen million strays the previous year at one hundred million dollars. On the other coast, after reports of "packs" of stray dogs in Brooklyn, the local City Council formed a spay-neuter clinic. Though the ASPCA was against the plan, by the mid-seventies they had become a leader in de-sexing, and began requiring spay-neuter before adoption. As their science counsel Stephen Zawistowski describes it to me, the policy was "incredibly controversial. [The ASPCA] was worried that people wouldn't want to adopt" fixed dogs and cats. One of their board members, the Broadway musical actress Gretchen Wyler, went on the TV talk show *The Mike Douglas Show* to explain the requirement. At the time, it was exceedingly common to let dogs roam by themselves—and not at all common to routinely de-sex. A veterinarians' group expressed concern that if spay-neuter clinics become widespread, owners will feel even less responsibility to mind their dogs—and perhaps, as some have suggested, the vets were concerned that *they* wouldn't get the business.

In fact, euthanasia rates did go down initially; over time, so did the numbers of "intakes"—a proxy for how many unwanted dogs (mostly strays or animals relinquished by owners) were out there. Eventually, it was shelters that made spay-neuter ubiquitous. In the years before there were shelters, there were "impounds," primarily responsible for gathering up errant animals. While until the nineteenth century these animals were mostly pigs and horses, eventually there were dedicated "dog pounds." In 1851, in New York City, a summertime pound was formed partly out of fear of the increase of dogs on the street, and thus the fear of rabies, in the dog days. The NYC pound was also a response to a city council resolution paying fifty cents for each dead dog delivered, which resulted in wanton slaughter. The early pounds subsisted off of redemption fees, and thus paid people for bringing in (live) dogs. This policy quickly led to various other nefarious means for finding dogs: raising puppies simply for the collection fee, and outright stealing of owned dogs. Those dogs not redeemed by their owners were quickly killed—and that usually meant death by clubbing or shooting, and eventually by mass drownings: up to forty-eight dogs at a time, crowded into a 4 × 7 × 5 foot crate, into the East River. One day, that crate dipped into the river sixteen times, until 762 dogs had been dispatched. Their bodies were made into fertilizer. Eventually, the ostensibly more humane method of killing via a literal gas chamber—an airtight tank filled with carbon dioxide—was developed. However, this method often took at least twenty minutes, and sometimes had not killed its contents even after an hour. Early humane societies helped oversee the eventual transition to the vastly improved injectable form of killing that continues today.

Enthusiasm for spay-neuter has reached such a fevered pitch in some parts of the country, such as unincorporated Los Angeles county,* that these areas have enacted *mandatory* spay-neuter laws—in LA, for any dog over four months of age. The fine for transgressions is $500 or forty hours of community service—a modest if not negligible cost. For if it makes sense to de-sex the shelter animals to control the population, why not de-sex all the animals? That would do some population control. Los Angeles in 1970 was picking up and later killing over one hundred thousand animals a year. That's too much death.

"Population control" is usually the first explanation for the laws on the books. The legal-code writers often then make a rhetorical move—one common in the discussion

---

* About an eighth of LA county proper, though excluding the cities.

of de-sexing—to lend an air of inevitability, and indisput-
ability, to the policy. Typically, this involves invoking the
health and behavioral improvements to the dog. LA's law
asserts, for instance, that:

"Certain types of cancers are eliminated by spaying or
neutering."

Not only that, but the animal is safer if neutered:

"Sterilized animals are less likely to roam and therefore
less likely to be lost, hit by a car, injured in a fight, or abused."

And if lost, the animal becomes classified as a "stray." Once
in this category, the animal is a no longer a pet; it is a risk to
the public:

"Stray animals are public safety hazards and unsterilized
animals are more likely to stray. Stray animals can bite or
attack people or other animals, cause traffic accidents, spread
disease, damage property, and harm the quality of life for res-
idents in a community."

Besides which, sex—the desire for sex, and the searching
for sex—is presented as deeply problematic:

"Unneutered male dogs and cats search for mates and
are attracted in packs when female dogs and cats come into
heat. One female in heat, even if confined, can make an entire
neighborhood unstable by attracting packs of male dogs intent
on breeding. These situations often become dangerous."

In a few sentences, de-sexing has gone from a question of
dog reproduction to the thread that holds civil society together.

New York State, which includes consideration of pets' sex
status among their laws regarding "agriculture," also invokes
the "overabundance" of dogs and cats in their explanation of
the need for de-sexing. Such overpopulation leads them to
"suffering privation and death" as strays, as they describe it.
The laws also invoke the "great expense to the community"

of impounding and destroying these strays, who are an unde-scribed health hazard and an unelaborated "public nuisance." In New York City, which has shelter spay-neuter laws, the Mayor's Alliance leads with the health claim: that a de-sexed animal will "live a longer, healthier life," and that males will be "better behaved" if they don't have testicles. Spaying females "helps prevent breast cancer and uterine infections," they announce, adding, it "keeps your female pet from going into heat." Especially if de-sexed "before 6 months for a male and before a female's first heat." Animal Care Centers of NYC (ACC) appears to believe that this is helpful information: "Spaying also prevents unwanted animals from being born," their "About Your New Dog" guide reads.

A number of US cities have passed de-sexing ordinances specific to breeds—usually targeting one specific "breed": pit bulls. Invoking the danger of dog attacks on people, rather than the concern for the species (or the dogs themselves), the laws require that pit bulls be spayed or neutered. Put-ting aside for a moment the fact that, as we now know, there is no "pit bull" breed of dog, and the difficulty that even experienced dog handlers have reliably identifying the breed(s) of a dog that they see—even so, de-sexing these dogs does nothing to reduce dog attacks. It only makes it less likely that the owned dogs identified as pits will have puppies. Hav-ing testicles or ovaries is not the cause of bites.

•   •   •

Every dog I've lived with has been neutered or spayed. Until a half dozen years ago, I never gave this a thought. My pups all came from shelters, whose practices, even before the laws, have often been to de-sex a dog before adoption if possible. I never knew Pumpernickel as a fertile young thing, or Finnegan: The Virile Version. This is by design, and the design had its desired effect. I did not need to make a choice about the future of my dogs reproductively; and I did not mourn what I had never known.

At first glance, insofar as spay-neuter has been aimed at overpopulation, it appears to have been an undeniable success. The number of animals coming into shelters has decreased dramatically. As the intake numbers have plummeted, so too has the number of euthanasias. From estimates of over twenty million animals (cats and dogs) euthanized every year in 1970, as of this writing the number of euthanized animals last year was down to two to four million. Imagine the great relief of the people who work at shelters, who are charged with over-seeing the choice of which dogs to kill, and dispatching them to be killed—or being the person who spends their days end-ing a dog's potential life of backyards, tug toys, and hikes, and closes their eyes for good.

While this seems like a triumph, it is asterisked. The imprecision of the numbers of euthanized dogs reflects a gen-uine inability to pin down the specific facts of the matter.* "The struggle is in the reporting of the numbers," Stephen Zawistowski tells me. There is no central organizing struc-ture for animal shelters, and it has been difficult for research-ers looking into the question to get reliable reporting about the intake and "outcome" numbers. Some "no-kill" shelters, philosophically opposed to euthanizing animals, are, Zaw-istowski says, "queasy" about releasing numbers. And now, with the explosion in popularity of these shelters, "it becomes

---

* Specific numbers are terrifically hard to come by, given the vagaries of reporting and data collection by the shelters nationwide. An extensive 2018 report by the Chief Scientific Officer of the Humane Society suggests that the 1973 figure was closer to 13.5 million, for instance.

tricky. Because the new part that's happening with shelters is the moving of animals," he says: adoption programs have been so successful that no-kill shelters in one location need to bring in animals plucked from elsewhere. What has been called the "overground pet railroad" uses cars, buses, trucks, and planes to bring animals from areas with overabundance—such as Los Angeles and the southeastern US—to places where the shelters have only pit bull mixes on offer—such as Portland, Oregon, and the northeastern US. "It used to be if a dog came into Baltimore, it stayed in Baltimore—and was adopted or killed. Now, it's difficult to track," he adds.

The advent of no-kill shelters is one reflection of the significant changes in the shelter system since 1970—whose influence on welfare improvements for dogs should not be discounted. Other profound societal changes in our attitude toward animals, and domestic animals in particular, have also affected euthanization rates, such as increased popularity of dog adoption, better "containment" (more pet dogs live indoors, instead of being let loose to run around), and better pet identification methods (such as microchipping), which allow for reunion of lost dogs with their owners.

On examination, the causal story told between a decrease in euthanasia of unwanted dogs and the advent of spay-neuter policies has other holes. Zawistowski, who has looked at the intake rates in the ASPCA in New York City since it was founded in the nineteenth century, tells me that "the largest decrease in dogs and cats coming into the city happened in the '40s, '50s, and '60s"—before spay-neuter became common, and well before it ever became law. In some areas, studies have found that there was no effect of opening a subsidized spay-neuter clinic on the rate of euthanasia.

I have not spoken to, heard about, or visited a shelter or

humane society that thinks spay-neuter is the exclusive solution to pet overpopulation. But it is such a pithy, uncomplicated solution that it stands in for dedicating resources to a more multifaceted approach that gives, perhaps, owners the decision about the reproductive (or just gonadal) future of their dogs. Funding for education departments at shelters, which might help owners understand the responsibility of taking home that puppy that they are possibly impulsively adopting, is being slashed. Instead, shelters are aiming for outreach programs outreaching to less well-served communities, and subsidizing veterinary care, especially de-sexing. Incentive programs sometimes waive an adoption fee if the owner will de-sex; "litter abatement" programs take in puppies and offer to de-sex the parents.

Perhaps worst of all, the notion of spay-neuter as a solution has been imprinted in the public's mind. Having been handed a simple solution, the citizenry takes it, runs, and proceeds to make the initial problem worse. "By having your dog or cat sterilized," the American Veterinary Medical Association tells us, "you will do your part to prevent the birth of unwanted puppies and kittens." *You will do your part.* After that, "our part" seems to be over, and we can get on to the business of being indignant that others didn't do their part. But if the responsibility for overpopulation is discharged by having a de-sexed pet (whose surgery came prior to ownership), then the complexities of managing thoughtful ownership—of learning the dog's behavior and communicative signals, to understand her more clearly; of appreciating the monetary investment and time demands of living with a dog; of appreciating the complexities of letting a dog impregnate or become pregnant—are evaded. One can get away with abandoning the dog when his "misbehavior" (often due to mutual misunderstandings) causes the owner to give him back to the shelter. And one may be excused for thinking that dogs come without complicated and messy bodily functions—because after all, that was *fixed*.

• • •

When I met with French veterinarian and fellow dog researcher Thierry Bedossa in New York City a decade ago, we headed straight to Central Park—to observe dogs, naturally. Sitting on a bench by a park entrance, watching the parade of dogs and people entering for early-morning off-leash hours, he commented offhandedly about how fat American dogs are. I hadn't thought much about it, but his remark prompted me to look again at the rumps and tails disappearing down the path. A yellow Lab waddled; a pair of dachshunds nearly folded in their middles under their own weight. No dog looked underfed, and many looked plump. I had gotten accustomed to seeing well-fed dogs; in point of fact, the only dog that had recently provoked my concern was a wildly underfed one, his skin corduroyed where his ribs pressed.

While I wanted to defend my fellow American dog people, in fact Bedossa was right: the obesity crisis of the American citizenry has been contagious. Studies report up to 56 percent of owned dogs as overweight or obese. And one contributor is their reproductive status: the metabolism of de-sexed dogs slows, and thus they have a tendency to become overweight. While there is truth in the suggestion that the loss of gonads alone does not oblige obesity—"Lake [*sic*] of exercise or over-feeding will make your pet fat, not spaying or neutering," the NYC Mayor's Alliance site informs us—it is contributory. In a world where we like to show our love for our dogs with food treats and there is a multibillion-dollar industry devoted to pet meals, the advice given to simply feed your dog "around 25 per cent less" if neutered is comical. Not only that, but this feeding advice is rarely given to the potential adopter at the time of adoption, and so is unwittingly ignored. Compounding the problem, the premise of the best training out there—positive reinforcement—most often uses *food* as a reward. Even if I fed my dog less, on every walk in the city we run into well-meaning owners with pocketsful of love to dole out to the neighborhood dogs.

One reason that Bedossa had noticed our unmuscled, roly-poly dogs is that he is French. Far from a perceptual prescience, his citizenship simply exposed him to a different range of dog body types. For in much of Europe, until recently, spay-neuter was not widely performed. Unneutered dogs in France, he said, are not only leaner, but are more muscular—a natural result of having more testosterone, for both males and females. This has not just aesthetic but anatomical benefit, giving them stronger backs and legs, and less likelihood of torn ligaments and ruptured disks.

Across the ocean from us, de-sexing has not been routine, and is far from a religion. Indeed, until recently, it was illegal *to* de-sex a dog in Norway. Formalized in the country's Animal Welfare Act is the startling statement that animals "have an intrinsic value which is irrespective of the usable value they may have for man." On the question of de-sexing, the act specifies, simply, that any surgery or "removal of body parts" is only permissible when "there is a justifiable reason to do so out of consideration for the animal's health." When the welfare of the specific animal is put first, as well as "the animal's ability to function and its quality of life," de-sexing is out.

In Oslo, the professional dog trainer Anne Lill Kvam told me neutering was still forbidden, but that the city was "becoming more open-minded about it." In the rest of Scandinavia, spay-neuter was not always, but is now legal, though it is still not widely performed. Seven percent of Swedish dogs are de-sexed (compared to the over 80 percent in the US*). Nearby Switzerland has a clause in their Animal Protection Act that appeals to the "dignity" of animals: "its inherent worth, which must be respected when handling it." Any pain, suffering, or harm to the animal, such as would be incurred by de-sexing, any "major interference with its appearance or abilities," is said to cause "anxiety or humiliation," disrespects the animal's dignity, and is forbidden.

"Dog ownership in Europe is a different concept," Stephen Zawistowski tells me. "If you own a GSD [German shepherd dog] there, you probably belong to the GSD club. They are serious." Anne Lill Kvam tells me that stray dogs are "not a problem"—in fact, there are almost no strays—because everyone "takes care" of their dogs. In other words, they keep their animals close, attend to them, and train them not to behave in such a way that would lead to unwanted animals. As a Norwegian animal-welfare official was quoted as saying, "Neutering can never be a substitute for proper training of a dog." What if a dog is unwanted? I ask Kvam. It's rare, she says. But, "they are simply killed," she shrugs.

•   •   •

If spay-neuter is going to be our religion, despite the fog of uncertainty over what precisely its effect has been on overpopulation, we should ask what the consequences of our faith are for the dogs. Despite the unambiguous statements made by

---

* Though the Humane Society points out that 87 percent of dogs in "underserved communities" are *not* de-sexed.

advocates of the salutary effects of de-sexing on dogs, results from a series of long-term research programs have bubbled up showing that the effects are far more subtle—and sometimes outright damaging.

After all, Benjamin Hart, professor emeritus and researcher at the UC Davis Veterinary school, has said, "basic biology suggests that removal of gonadal hormones can lead to adverse effect." Bodies are integrated, highly interconnected designs. If one part stops functioning, because of damage or outright removal, there will be repercussions—gentle or profound— in other parts. Slightly injure a leg, and in an effort to maintain steady balance and momentum, you will implicate not just the other leg, but the torso, back, neck. If a lung is damaged, not just the other lung, but the heart, and eventually other organs are affected. Remove the gonads, and you've removed the main producer of estrogen, testosterone, and progesterone. These are sex hormones, crucial to any reproductive system, but their effects in the body range far from the genitals. Estrogen is involved in bone growth and maturation by triggering the closure of bone plates. Testosterone improves muscle mass by increasing protein synthesis at the muscles. Progesterone is an important protector if the brain suffers traumatic injury, partly by managing levels of inflammation; estrogen also works in the brain, affecting learning, memory, and emotion. People who work with dogs professionally know this. The dogs at the Penn Vet Working Dog Center are not neutered until they are fourteen months old, director Cindy Otto tells me, in order to let the growth plates finish developing and close. Ted Kerasote writes about a veterinarian who stopped de-sexing dogs altogether after she noticed an uptick in dogs with adrenal dysfunction in her practice. The vet, Karen Becker, reasoned that without the gonads to produce the needed sex hormones for normal bodily functioning, the adrenal gland, which produces small amounts of the hormones, is overtaxed. Benjamin Hart has suggested that gonadal hormones may have a protective function for the body, and that removal of estrogen "might trigger metastatic cells."

Hart has led the biggest effort to date to see exactly what the repercussions of the lack of these hormones might be in the long term. Using the database from his university's vet hospital, he and his team are looking at the prognosis for specific breeds, particularly at rates of diseases that are claimed to decrease with de-sexing: cancers and certain reproductive tract disorders, such as pyometra, a critical uterine infection. They are also looking at rates of joint disorders and urinary incontinence, which might be suspected to rise post-surgery.

What he has found complicates the simple solution that spay-neuter is held out to be. The group's first publication on the topic, in 2013, reported that de-sexing golden retrievers, especially before six months of age, *increases* their risk of serious joint diseases four (females) to five (males) times over the risk intact dogs face. This result did not sit well with spay-neuter advocates. "We raised all kinds of hell with this thing," Hart says at a conference about spay-neuter held in Davis, California, in 2017. People were saying, "why did you do this? It's irresponsible." Besides which, "we can't believe your data."

He has since followed up with studies that revealed an increased rate of joint diseases among Labrador retrievers, German shepherds, and Doberman pinschers, and alarming rises to a quarter or a third of Bernese mountain dogs and Saint Bernards. With cancer, the alarm is increased: spaying female goldens at any age increases the dogs' risk of cancer fourfold. Other breeds have their own, depressing trajectories: neutering male boxers at one to two years old increases their cancer risk to 30 percent; de-sexing Bernese increases their risk, to nearly a fifth of both male and female dogs. One of the most touted claims of spay-neuter, that it increases an animal's life span, may be tempered by the finding that with an increased life span comes an increased rate of cancers. Moreover, rates of age-related cognitive impairment are higher in de-sexed dogs.

Not all breeds are so afflicted, though. From what Hart has so far seen, many smaller dogs who are de-sexed don't seem to have increased rates of joint disease; rates of cancers in mixed breeds appears to be the same irrespective of sexual status. And de-sexing at later ages may, at times, eliminate the increased risks of disease seen. Problematically, shelters like to de-sex at an earlier age—because that's often when they have possession of the puppies.

The upshot? The veracity of nearly every one of the stated health benefits is imperiled by the emerging results. Rates of pyometra do decline if the uterus is removed, as pyometra is an infection of the uterus. But rates of urinary incontinence in females go up with de-sexing. Most critically, risks are wildly different for different breeds, sizes, sexes, and age of de-sexing. Such a result lends itself to a considered approach to spay-neuter—one that takes into account the particulars of the dog.

Similarly, the oft-cited behavioral improvements of de-sexed dogs are in some cases overstated; in other cases the behavioral change may be for the worse. Owners of male dogs de-sexed specifically to address their aggression to dogs or people may see the unwanted behaviors diminish after de-sexing—but only in about one in four dogs. The same holds for other perceived misbehaviors: mounting and excessive urine-marking. In the other 75 percent of male dogs, no meaningful change is seen. In females, there is evidence of an *increase* in aggressive behaviors, if spayed before the age of one.

The more of a handle we get on the medical consequences of de-sexing, the muddier the choice appears to be.

• • •

Forgotten in much of the conversation about spay-neuter is that it is also a medical procedure, a surgery. While it rises to the level of "routine" surgery, every surgery requires compromises and risks to the individual. Peter Sandøe, a bioethics professor at the University of Copenhagen, has enumerated a few of them: from being left in an unfamiliar place with unfamiliar people, to the pain of an incision and other surgical insults to the body; later risk of inflammation or infection at the incision; and sometimes fatal complications during the procedure. Finally, as with any surgery, there is the risk, including of death, of using general anesthesia.

Risk of death. One must risk death in order to avoid making more young lives—to avoid then being put to death. So spay-neuter seems to require. Now, I stand among the many of us who have been asked to sign a sheet of paper acknowledging the risk of death by anesthesia when someone—our human family, our animals, or ourselves—awaits surgery. *It is a slight risk*, we are told. And we *need* the surgery, surely, so any on-the-fly calculations about the "slight risk" versus the possible benefits from a surgery we have already decided to do, and are moments from submitting to, lead to our signing the paper.

I've signed the paper. When our son was five he was into his sixth year of admiring, waiting for, and petting any cat (cat willing) he came across. The bodega cat, the pet-store cat. The bookstore cat, the library cat, the street cat. Friends' cats, shelter cats, a cat on a tractor. In a house of dogs, my son pined for a cat to join them, and in this year he formulated that interest into a plea. I was reluctant—generally hesitant about adding new animals to the family on the basis of the fleeting impulses of children—but I told him that "if we ran across a cat who needed a home, we could take her in."

Of course the next week I ran across a cat. A beautiful brown, brindly cat, skinny and long, barely out of kittenhood, prowling the streets of Bensonhurst, Brooklyn. I was on a miles-long meditative walk, mourning the recent loss of my own father, when this small sprig of a cat crossed my path. She paused as I approached her. From above her back her tail curved into a question mark. I greeted her, then kept walking—and she pursued me, for blocks, darting under cars and along the sides of buildings, keeping close but not too. Concerned that I might be leading her away from her home, I doubled back, shadowed by her quiet form. I ducked into a bodega and purchased some milk and a makeshift bowl for her. She skirted under the hedges lining a modest funeral parlor just as a man walked out of the building.

"Is this your cat?" I asked.

"Yeah," he said. "No. She lives here. She's not my cat."

"Is she a stray?"

He nodded. "She had kittens. I think they all died. She lives around here," he said, gesturing around the funeral parlor. Hedges lined the building as well, and I tried to imagine this little wisp of a mother cat with kittens, huddling under a hedge. I held out the canister of milk toward him.

"Will you give this to her?"

He recoiled, "No way. I'm not going to feed her." As he walked away, he said, "Take her—if you can catch her."

I ran across a cat. The next day I solicited the help of a friend who lived nearby and she found the cat, skillfully lured her into a box, and by that evening we had a cat.

"Beezelbub Jehoshaphat!" my son called out.* The name didn't quite suit her, as she was a sweetheart of a cat, but it reflected the exclamatory pleasure we felt with new animal energy in the house. (And she was a jumper.) She was a willing playmate, pursuing every small item on the floor and kicking it down the hall; madly racing around corners and up shelves and the library ladder. Dangling cords thrilled her, and she quickly dispatched with our home phone cord (which relieved us at last of maintaining a landline: thank you, Beezelbub). Within a few weeks she had taken to joining me in my office and depositing herself squarely on my hands on my computer keyboard. The dogs were alert and excited about her presence, and she was guarded and attentive to theirs, but they were forming an easy friendship. As is always the case, we soon couldn't imagine not knowing her.

I took her to the vet for shots and a checkup, and he recommended spaying her. My inclination was to follow the advice. It was the first time I had been asked whether I wanted to de-sex one of my animals. In general, I am predisposed to follow a medical professional's advice; I am pleased to be the recipient of their experience, in their advice to me, as patient or as patient's proxy. Certainly I had no reason to believe that this or any vet would give me poor advice.

Still, I knew she would be an indoor cat, and in New York City, indoors is indoors. There is no back door to accidentally slip out of. The windows are screened and guarded when open. She would not be going out. Instead, she would be continuing to sleep with my son, who adored her, play with the dogs, and quietly disenable me from typing on the computer.

The vet was persistent. He called me repeatedly, in one

* Fanciful transliteration of Beelzebub by five-year-old mind and tongue.

234

case leaving a three-minute message about my responsibility to spay her. Even while I was put off at his complete disinterest in our individual circumstance, I was also attentive to his voice as the experienced one, as medical decisions go. My years of observing dog behavior weren't necessarily relevant here. We brought in Beezelbub to be spayed, about a month after she entered our home. My son gave her a casual wave in the carrier we'd acquired for her, and we assured him he'd see her that night after school.

He didn't. Instead, I got a call from the vet while at work that Beezelbub had died during the administration of the morphine, prior to anesthesia. Six months out from my father's protracted death, I sat outside on the sidewalk and bawled. I had scooped this cat up from her life, "rescuing" her, only to send her to her early death. And, I realized at once, in the way that in moments of great and sudden loss one's mind spins through every related notion, I would have to tell my son. She is gone for my son.

The vet was sorry, of course. "It happens only about one percent of the time," he told me. Between sobs, I could not respond, and only later did I reflect on this. If I had realized the chances of her dying in what I considered to be an unnecessary surgery were *one in a hundred*, there is no question that I would not have sent her there.

• • •

I've only received equivocal responses when I ask veterinarians about the rate of death by anesthesia. But what has stayed with me was not the statistics of the risk. It was that the *particulars* of our family—of this cat, of these people—had not been of interest to the vet in making his recommendation. She was not an individual cat, living with specific people, who know a

235

certain amount about the lives of animals . . . to him, she was just "a cat." And a cat with ovaries. And that was the beginning and the end for him.

Why did Benjamin Hart's results raise "all kinds of hell," as he puts it? Because the stakes are high. Should spay-neuter policies disappear overnight, the numbers of stray and unwanted dogs would almost certainly increase. Nobody wants that. Thus, it is deeply troubling to see that one's solution is not simple—and sometimes may be unwittingly deleterious.

What the research into the health of de-sexed dogs serves to do is to shift the focus from the species to the breed—and even to the individual. "There are major individual differences," Hart says, summarily, in the rates of success and damage caused by de-sexing. And there are individual differences in families. The indoor cat, who will not meet other cats, is different from the neighborhood cat, is different from the barn cat. The Norwegian dog is kept on a tight leash, responds to their owner—or, perhaps, it is that the Norwegian dog owner simply knows not to, say, expose a female dog in heat to male dogs. By considering the individual, some European countries change the terms, from "how can we control the numbers of dogs" to "what is right for the dog."

There are, plainly, alternative ways to treat our animals. Should "sterilization" still be the mantra we want to chant in the US, there are non-surgical options. Injectable sterilants are on the market internationally—including one in the US—and many are in development. One wealthy surgeon, Gary Michelson, interested in the fate of animals, began offering grants for research leading to development of an affordable chemical sterilant, and twenty-five million dollars (since upped to seventy-five) for whoever gets there fastest. The products now on the market have names like "Infertile," which cuts to the chase: these are intended as permanent sterilizing products. Instead of a surgical procedure, though, they are shots, administered with light sedation. Since the dog's gonads remain intact, some sex hormone production is maintained—possibly staving off the health problems that Hart and his team have been uncovering. Implant contraception, minimally invasive, is available in some parts of the world. Or, if the risks of surgery are of less concern than the loss of the hormones, some of the same procedures that we humans have—vasectomy, tubal ligation, and hysterectomy—are options—if much less frequently done by your local vet.

Or: we could turn the notion on its head. What if we addressed overpopulation by dealing with the overpopulators? In this case, the overpopulation is not created by dogs. Though dogs have the equipment and the biological inclination to populate, it is humans who have created the overpopulation.

In the early days of spay-neuter, guidelines advised veterinarians not to de-sex animals before they turned six months. Though Hart and others' research indicates that this might be beneficial for many dogs, and it is ill-advised to give a very young animal anesthesia (their bodies cannot maintain core temperature under anesthesia, for one thing), this guideline was "a hindrance to population control," as a history of shelter medicine describes it. For when animals were adopted before turning six months, they were intact. "Many of these animals were subsequently allowed to breed by irresponsible and unknowledgeable owners who added to the shelter's problems by bringing the unwanted offspring back to the shelter."

Ah, now we have found the culprits. "Irresponsible and unknowledgeable owners." It is not only this paper's authors who turn this phrase. Responsibility can be taught, and required. And knowledge is communicable. Some shelters have developed outreach programs, with mobile vans, pet events, or home visits, which provide a means for people who are having enough difficulty with their animals to consider relinquishing them to get back on track. In other words, to financially support and to educate these owners. One shelter worker I speak with cites research showing a correlation between stress in the home, financial or otherwise, and relinquishment. "The animals dropped off in the shelter are coming from very focal areas," the lead shelter veterinarian adds, "In my mind, the 'spay problem' is that the people who need to spay aren't. And the people who are spaying are not the ones who would be causing the problem."

If education alone might suffice to change behavior, why not put down the scalpels and focus on education? Surely an approach that doesn't involve opening up dogs is preferable to one that does. The American Veterinary Medical Association, a vocal proponent of shelter spay-neuter, also encourages education programs—though they define that as including "consulting with veterinarians for information" on responsible pet ownership. No state or local government has passed nor suggested any law about mandating education for pet owners, though, nor would any restriction to pet ownership be easy for legislatures to swallow. Instead, the preference for de-sexing programs over education programs reveals that the procedure is more about relieving shelters of their impressive burden than concern for the best solution for the species *Canis familiaris*. "We have to drop the idea that 'oh, shelters'll take care of it,'" the shelter veterinarian told me. They've been handed the problem and they are simply trying to find the solution.

• • •

We adopted Finnegan, our earnest-faced, bag-sniffing, black-Lab-mixy dog, from a shelter eleven years ago. It is a large New York no-kill shelter, the air filled with barks and redolent of wet dogs and veterinary medicines. Cages stacked on cages, nearly every one was filled; friendly employees stood by to arrange brief meetings with whichever doggie in the window caught your eye. I waited to come here for a year after losing Pumpernickel, the sweet, smart curly-haired dog who had accompanied me through early adulthood and all of her nearly seventeen years. Knowing that "seventeen years" is a real (if lucky) possibility, but also deeply susceptible to falling in love with every dog I see at a shelter, I came prepared. I knew we would be leaving with a dog. But I wanted to know the dog as much as we could before we left. We poked our fingers through the cage of an impossibly cute young puppy who had already learned to bark, smiled at a pair of siblings curled around each other in sleep, lingered at a doleful two-year-old who had been returned to the shelter. When we met Finn, we were excited but guarded.

We asked to see him, and after lingering with him in the kennels for a while were allowed to take him to a gated area with a fake tree near the shelter entrance. There we watched him, for hours. He took a nap. We filled out paperwork asking for our employment, the rules of our apartment building regarding pets, our past ownership details, and two references. Neither reference reported being called, and we were quickly approved. Still we lingered and watched him: How did he respond to people, to noises, to being tickled on the ear or chin or rump? What caught his attention and what raised his hackles? What did he mouth and when did he vocalize? Who was he?

While we considered who this cheery but calm puppy

was, at least a dozen people came in the shelter, chose a dog or cat, and left with the animal. With each person, I grew more astonished. Theirs seemed a very brief introduction for a relationship that might last them seventeen years. The seven-year-old getting a roly-poly puppy would enter and graduate high school—and college—before this dog left the home; the young couple, just starting out, would be approaching middle age with this same dog. How could it be that we took more time to find the perfect jeans at the store than to find the perfect dog companion?

From the shelter's view, though, they can't get the dogs adopted fast enough. When I visit Maddie's Shelter Medicine Program in Florida, professor Cynda Crawford, a longtime researcher of shelter medicine, who discovered the canine flu vaccine, listens to my suggestion that it would be great to have some pre-adoption education for prospective owners, and shakes her head. "We need to *drop* the obstacles to getting animals adopted. It's easier to get a credit card" than to adopt a dog. I'm not sure why getting a dog *should* be easy. But for her it's about moving the animals out, because there are so many coming in from the streets, on the overground railroad, every day. She echoes a complaint I've heard many times about onerous application procedures at shelters, which turned down eager adopters who were nonetheless deemed imperfect by protective shelter administration.

Let's turn the notion on its head again. What if instead of seeing dogs as animals to be managed through surgical sterilization, we saw dogs as animals to be considered as individuals? What if we thought about each dog as some*one*, who we are doing some*thing* to?

"The thought's obvious if you think about someone wanting to spay *you*," Shelly Kagan, moral philosopher at Yale University, said at a roundtable discussion on the fates of animals. If we acknowledge that dogs are conscious and sentient, what their experience at the time is, and what their later health and experience might be, have bearing. Kagan is not convinced that the cliff that shelters feel backed up against is sufficient to justify compromises to the individual. Even if universal spay-neuter were "better" for dogs, "it doesn't mean the better option is *permissible*."

And what of sex? Norway's mandate to treat dogs as having intrinsic value, and Sweden's concern for the "dignity" of the animal, require that their citizens consider dogs as individuals, not property to be managed. And individuals have not only sentience, but, perhaps, desires—to have sex. We owe animals a sex life, these countries' approaches seem to be saying. They want dogs to be able to lead the life they want to lead, within reason. "The ideal," Peter Sandøe has said, "is that we really start to look at every animal as an animal"—treating each with respect and with an attention to the needs of the species and individual.

Talking about dogs' biological *needs*—whether dogs deserve to have sex, or sexual urges—is sure to prompt some guffaws. I suspect that the reason we might be reluctant to consider the dog sex life is that our dogs (again) reflect ourselves. Just as our society, despite radical liberalization over the last sixty years, considers the particulars of sex mostly private, undiscussable in professional company, as though no one had sex at all, we are pleased as punch to pretend that dogs have nothing sexual about them. Our spay-neuter policies and acceptance reveal a profoundly ambivalent feeling about our dogs having sex.

The US has a downright aversion to dog sexual practices. The topic of dog sex has all but disappeared from dog-training and dog-owning manuals: it is assumed that dogs will not be mating or, heaven forbid, having salacious thoughts. While a restriction on mating is responsible pet ownership, as defined by spay-neuter advocates, it is a profound circumscription of what is, for all animals, an ordinary part of life and a significant part of social interaction with other dogs.

It is not only sex. The dogs at the ends of our leashes are expected to be *civilized*: we demand they be our proxies and abide by our culture's terms to a surprising degree. That means urinating and defecating in specific places, not willy-nilly; no poking their noses in others' private parts (human or dog); and no public intimations of sex with casual acquaintances. It is the mark of an ill-bred dog indeed to follow a short sniff of a new acquaintance with a vigorous attempt to mount her backside.

The mere act of mounting, or humping, is given its own section in books promising to cure your dog of various so-called misbehaviors (that can all be explained by a combination of dogs' natural inclinations, and an inability of humans to clearly show dogs what they would like to have happen): jumping up, barking, gnawing the owner's shoes or underwear or pillows. Many dog owners will recognize the humiliation of being the person (or leg) to which a dog directs such amorous intention. But mounting is a perfectly reasonable behavior in dogs' toolboxes, and some dogs like to use it with each other during social play. Still, the discomfort that owners feel when their (de-sexed) dog mounts another (de-sexed) dog is only matched by the discomfort that the owners of the mountee feel. Even I have been so well inculcated in the culture of "polite" behavior among dogs that, though I feel it is perfectly polite for a dog to sniff deeply into the rump of another dog (dog willing), I will move to unhump my humping dog, to save us owners the embarrassment.

We recoil from that most overt display of a dog's urges. But what are we embarrassed of—that the dog's mounting serves to express a latent desire that *I* mount that other owner? Some other, unknown lascivious feelings in the air? Or that our dogs are, like us, animals, who occasionally or regularly would like to be sexual—and may act before receiving "consent." It may be all three—but we never get to that point, because the owners of the two dogs inevitably part, leaving the dogs to sniff the air left in their wake.

Do dogs want to have sex? Biologically, yes. Individually, differences likely occur. The sex act for dogs ends, for instance, in a copulatory tie, in which dogs are attached by their genitals for many minutes or up to an hour, rump to rump. Dogs can appear to be quite distressed at being so tethered, and their genitals can remain swollen post-coitus. But dogs hardly show evidence of forethought about this surprising coital conclusion. Female dogs in heat certainly act as if they want to have sex, trying to make themselves available, presenting their rumps for examination, moving their tails aside. This behavior is of course obliged by the hormones that prompt the heat. Male dogs I have known make terrific efforts to sow their wild oats. Might the de-sexed dog still want to copulate? Animal frustration is well acknowledged in the scientific literature. As Sandøe has described, even the British government assented, way back in 1965, that animals feel not only pain, but frustration: "then, officially, it was recognised that animals can be frustrated if their behavioural needs are not satisfied"—and thus, any act that blocks their needs would be hurtful, and was forbidden.

And yet, dogs' needs are not identical to ours. A male dog having an urge to mount can be, and is, in some circles, confused with a person's having an urge to be considered virile. That a testicular implant named "Neuticles" exists attests to this confusion. "Neuticles allows your precious pet to retain his natural look, self esteem and aids the pet and pet's owner with trauma associated with altering," their advertising copy proclaims. The scientific literature on dogs gives us no help in explicating how de-sexed dogs might be missing the "self-esteem" typical of an intact dog—because it's nonsense.* The product, which aims to "replicate the pet's testicles in size, shape weight and feel" (feel—to whom?), is aimed at the owner who is concerned about his own self-esteem and "natural look." The *New York Post* cited one man's hesitation in getting his fifteen-pound miniature pinscher neutered: "I thought, 'He'll be smaller, or not muscular, more girly.'" Some humane societies, ignoring the specific cluelessness of this kind of commentary, have supported the product, insofar as it might get an individual to de-sex his dog.

Owners' sensibilities are more on display than the dog's needs, where spay-neuter is concerned. "Convenience" is often cited as a reason an owner should de-sex her dog. "A bitch in estrus is very messy and owners don't like that," Anita Oberbauer, a researcher of Animal Science at UC Davis, says at the spay-neuter conference. She says this as a dog breeder. "It's messy: I had to confine her to the kitchen," another vet tells me.† A female dog may urinate in the house and will spread bloody vaginal discharge where she rests and walks;

---

* The product website excitedly cites a 2009 study in which researchers implanted neuticles in castrated adolescent monkeys to control for visual similarity with the intact monkeys, then looked at the effect of gonadectomy on the monkeys' social development. Alas, the company must've misread the results: the castrated monkeys were socially impaired in their development—the researchers suggest that it was a lack of hormones that impaired the monkeys' sociality—and having neuticles did not improve their skills. The study's finding is also consistent with the interpretation that neuticles may have contributed to the social impairment.

† "Messy," in fact, is the word regularly used to describe this very ordinary biological phenomenon—one that, incidentally, is part of the system responsible for bringing you your puppy.

her heat lasts for a few weeks. Oberbauer cites the alleged improvement in "undesirable characteristics"—that is, behaviors like nighttime male roaming and sexually related aggression—as advantages of de-sexing. Because we own dogs, we are able to set up their lives so that it is more convenient for *us*—less messy, more controlled.

•   •   •

Viewed from another angle, the most mysterious feature of the spay-neuter laws is the existence of so many exceptions to the law. In Los Angeles, for instance, exempted from the mandatory de-sexing policy are not only dogs whose health might be compromised by the surgery, but dogs used "by law enforcement agencies for law enforcement purposes," "service or assistance dogs that assist disabled persons," and "competition dogs." Why law enforcement personnel need unneutered male dogs (and males are resoundingly preferred in this role, although female dogs can outperform them) is unarticulated—likely because there is no scientific reason to articulate. In fact, for search-and-rescue and other working dogs, working-dog veterinarians recommend spaying females, "because dogs in estrus searching with other dogs create a distraction," and "bitches will lose several months of training and service if they are bred." But "for males the neutering or lack of is more psyche than data," Cindy Otto of the Working Dog Center tells me. "People think [males] have more 'aggression'" if they are intact, "but it is really not substantiated—and in my opinion, based on our dogs, they actually may be more focused once neutered," she says. There is exactly zero evidence that lack of testicles reduces skill at detection, guarding, or even bite work. A need for testicles or ovaries on a guide or service dog is equally puzzling.

"Competition dogs" is the third exception, and refers to dogs registered with the American Kennel Club or other purebred dog club, who may or may not compete in any sport or show. Let us linger on this point. To qualify in this category, one must be a purebred dog, produced by other purebred dogs, via a breeder of purebred dogs. That is to say, breeders of purebred dogs are entirely, unequivocally exempt from the requirement to de-sex their dogs. The puppies produced and purchased by others are also exempt. Putting aside for a moment anything you know about breeders (good or bad, responsible or backyard), this is a law that forbids puppy-making except by puppy-makers. That's a bit like forbidding killing except by the killers. There is a class of people, "breeders," who are considered acceptable puppy-makers, though there are no qualifications to be a breeder except saying that you are one, and paying dues to a dog club.

Breeding purebred dogs, we will remember, is a process of inbreeding. It has produced many terrific individuals and it has also produced genetic nightmares. But not only does our current culture accept inbreeding, our laws ensure that the perpetuation of purebreds—to the specific exclusion of non-purebreds—is inevitable. Should spay-neuter be universally successful, what we'd have done is not only curb unwanted populations. We would have inadvertently changed dogs: the mixed-breed dog would be extinct.

• • •

How can we do right by dogs? Any thoughtful dog person wonders this. The answer has been hijacked by the story of overpopulation, itself a powerful story, and its posited solution, spay-neuter. But what would happen if what it meant to be a responsible pet owner meant having to understand the dog *qua* dog, its biology and behavior? If one's own preference or convenience could not outrank the dog's preference?

With spay-neuter, we are treating the dog as the responsible party for a problem that we created and we maintain. Overpopulation, one animal enforcement officer is quoted as saying at the beginning of acknowledgment of the crisis, "is not a dog problem, it's a human problem." Dogs are being asked to undergo a surgical procedure on behalf of us—to address the overpopulation that our actions have caused. Dogs are being asked to undergo the procedure on behalf of the other members of the species, assuming that the fate of dogs will be improved by having fewer of them. Why is this a burden the dogs must take on? Why is this not the human's problem, who has, through millennia of domestication, taken on the dog?

It *is* our problem. It is society's problem, and it is a problem for society. Just as it should not be the shelter worker's duty to shoulder all of overpopulation for society, it is not the dog's duty to be de-sexed to save his species. A shelter, the bioethicist Bernard Rollin once wrote, does not truly shelter animals: it shelters irresponsible people; it shelters our society from having to deal with the consequences of our impulses. Though it is the dogs doing the overpopulating, we made dogs, and we are responsible for them. We have acted as though it is perfectly acceptable to choose the specs of our animals because of fleeting fancy or local popularity—dog breeds that appear in movies prompt floods of imprudent puppy purchases—then discarding them as they grow older, unruly, or simply lose their early shine. As the authors of dogs, as the ones who shepherded them from ancient proto-wolves into our villages and homes, who sculpted bizarrely small-nosed, short-legged, furry-faced dogs out of the well-adapted wolf, we humans have a moral duty to see to it that they do not lose all of their animalness. The wanton designing of dogs indulges our desire and ignores their desires and their dignity.

Our love for the designer dog extends to surprising quarters: some shelter workers I have spoken to, eyewitnesses to the devastation of inbreeding and the continued strain caused by overbreeding, tell me they'd like a dog who looks a certain way, or is a breed they'd owned before— even if this is a dog genetically damaged by breeding, like the pug.

To a lesser degree, people who adopt dogs are also weirdly singled out to be the solvers of society's problem. "Responsible" people. Here it becomes relevant that those who choose to breed dogs as "breeders" are exempt, by law, from bearing the brunt of having their dogs de-sexed; for love or money, they are allowed to continue to produce dogs. Also exempt, in point of fact, are those who spurn the burden and breed dogs through recklessness or neglect, creating more problems for all. There is no punishment nor even discouragement of this practice. Whatever the best path is for humans and dogs, this is not it.

Do we owe an individual dog—the devoted pup by your side, the hopeful dog at the shelter, the future dog waiting to be born—moral consideration? The philosopher Shelly Kagan argues that all animals have moral standing—that how we act toward them is not "morally irrelevant." Certainly most owners treat their dogs with consummate care and consideration: owned dogs are subject to all manner of affection and attention. That we sometimes err in our judgment about what the dog needs or wants is here beside the point: the point is that we are considering our dogs' needs at all.

De-sexing is a notable exception. The proliferation of veterinary options attests to the diversity of ways that we treat dogs as we would like to be treated. Today, as I write this, I am just off the phone with a veterinarian who, on the basis of the results of an MRI and X-ray of my limping dog, suggested we next try an ultrasound, a steroidal injection, and aquatic physical therapy. We consider this full menu of options. Somehow, spay-neuter has slipped under the radar: that same dog had a major operation before we knew him, and we simply accept that, head-noddingly agreeing that overpopulation of dogs is a horrible problem. With that act of neutering, though, we are asking my dog, and all dogs, to bear all of the weight of the moral burden for our own immoral act: overbreeding and outright irresponsibility to the species.

Why do we do it? Dogs are animals to whom we can do these things. We "can," in that we largely control their fates. As dogs cannot protest their treatment, though, it is up to us to consider it for them. If it is a harm to dogs, and we consider dogs worthy of individual attention, then we have to be able to justify that harm—and not just to the species, but to the individual: to Finn. To Beezelbub. Isn't the reason we live with dogs that we like having that animal—their animalness—alongside us? Should we not be able to justify our own behavior, we should question whether future generations of humans should be allowed to keep dogs. Are we up to it?

Humorless

At first, I blamed myself. As I walked out of the movie theater into the bright skies of midday, I was silently fuming. I'd
just seen the Wes Anderson movie *Isle of Dogs*, an animated
tale of a dystopian Japan in which dogs are exiled to an island
of trash, in seat-vibrating Dolby sound. I flinched at the high
sun, and quickly surmised what caused my ire: I should never
see a movie during the day. Emerging from two hours of the
dark embrace of a fictional world into the middle of an ordinary day always sets me on edge.

After walking a few blocks, my pique adjusted a notch. It
wasn't the daylight furrowing my brow; it was the dogs. The
dogs in the movie I'd just seen: stop-motion creations, expertly
figured, who were the backbone of the film.

I sit down to films featuring dogs with a mixture of trepidation and thrill. While there is much that I hope to know about what dogs experience, understand, sense, and feel, the science of dog cognition is in its infancy. We don't know more than we do know: and I always hope that a fictionalized account of dogs will give me a novel glimpse of dogs as they are—even see something that we scientists don't.

Alas, that was not to be in this movie. The dogs were recognizable figments of our imagination: with human voices and human concerns, they served mostly as vessels for a human storyline. This is certainly not the first time that the dogs' role in films has been as furry, button-cute human-replacements. As with all animals, they find ample employment in animated movies—as everything from genius professor (Mr. Peabody in *The Adventures of Rocky and Bullwinkle*) to loveable dolt (*Scooby-Doo*) to conscientious and loyal partner (Gromit in *Wallace and Gromit*). Through a misuse of film technology, dogs' mouths are seen to move in live-action movies like *Beethoven* and *Marmaduke* and *Beverly Hills Chihuahua*, to eliminate any concerns that a dog might actually be . . . simply a dog. Even having a dog wandering through a scene in a movie—accompanying a child, walking through a town, or waiting by the Christmas tree—is well known for lending a sense of reality to a scene. Reality is not only effected but improved upon by writing a dog into your film. Alas, many directors overdo this, displacing reality with dogs. Fictive dogs become the motif and the subjects. And it is apparently crowd-pleasing to see, say, a well-groomed Scarlett Johansson–voiced purebred flirt with a scruffy Bryan Cranston–toned mutt. The audience around me laughed heartily at the foibles of these *Isle of Dog* characters: so recognizable! Because they were human foibles, transplanted onto dogs.

As I squinted in the sun and silently stewed, I realized

with a start that I have become humorless about dogs. About the Hilarious YouTube videos and Must-See photos of ridiculous getups (hats, small tuxedos, pantyhose) that owners put their dogs in. About the GIFs of grimacing, stoic dogs forced to wear a crown of balloons; the memes that represent dogs as clueless, unable to control their bowels, or responsible for their overeating.

On reflection, I think that I've actually been humorless for quite a while. In the decade since I performed a study on what prompted the "guilty look" of dogs, the sharing of "dog-shaming" photos has mushroomed into a massive fungal accretion. The apparent hilarity of writing a note representing what your dog definitely does not feel or say ("I'm sorry I ate the chicken wings"; "I humped the pillow"; "I eat panties"), pinning it around their neck, and sharing it online, is completely lost on me.

Humans have long known the power of public humiliation of violators of the norms of a culture. One has only to turn the clock back a few hundred years to find criminal punishment meted out by shaving heads, branding foreheads, confessional-sign-wearing, and public pillories. She with a scarlet *A* sewn on her dress was a disgrace to her sex and a social outcast. Or keep the clock where it is: the twenty-first-century American judiciary still convicts a man, guilty of mail theft, to "stand outside of a post office with a sandwich board sign containing the following message: 'I stole mail. This is my punishment'" for one hundred hours.

Humiliation's effectiveness as a punishment depends both on being seen and on knowing that one is being seen. While dogs might be exempt from a feeling of shame that their alleged transgression is being broadcast across the world, the "guilty look" is in evidence on the faces and body postures of innumerable "shamed" dogs. In my research, what looked to people like their dogs' guilt turned out to be the dogs' deferential, pleading reaction to owners' scolding and punishment: more "please don't hurt me" than "I did a bad thing." That doesn't look so hilarious to me.

See? Humorless. Similarly, my hardline stance against Halloween costumes for dogs (*Don't*)—even if they are dressed as Darth Vader, the Pope, or one of a quartet of a McDonald's Happy Meal—is mirthless. And hey, if I haven't told you, making your dog balance a treat on her nose while you prepare the camera kinda sucks, too.

My colleagues in veterinary behavior are all similarly dour. Their unsmiling assessments of your *Dog Loves Baby!* video— wherein an impressively stoic dog's eyes widen and body freezes as a toddler grabs his fur (until they begin to try to lick/nibble the child off); their condemnation of your "sweet" photo of your child pulling your dog's head into a clumsy embrace—are merciless.

What is wrong with us? Can't we see the love that the humans perpetuating this inanity feel?

I am surprised at my humorlessness because I feel reliable and plentiful joy in being with and thinking about dogs. I'm always laughing around dogs. When I walk into a room with my dogs in it, I can feel the wrinkles of my brow unfurl, my shoulders unhunch, the muscles of my jaw unclench. Seeing a dog approaching me up ahead on a path makes me smile involuntarily and broadly.

There is terrific humor in a life with dogs. It is simply not of the humiliation variety. That kind of humor robs dogs of their dignity. "[A] fair measure of a civilized society is how its institutions behave in the space between what it may have the power to do and what it should do," a dissenting justice in the mail-theft case wrote. We *can* dress the dog as Yoda, or Frodo, or a basting turkey, but we shouldn't. The philosopher Lori Gruen characterizes dignity-robbing acts as those in which "animals are forced to be something other than what they are" and "when they are made to be ridiculous, presented as laughable spectacles." She was almost certainly not smiling when she wrote that. But I have seen her smiling in describing the antics of the dogs she knows, and I am smiling now, thinking of this morning's outing along the sidewalks of the city with one of my dogs, in which he gently but firmly guided me to the doorways of all the pet-food stores on our route.

The joy of dogs is that they free us of our own undignified existence—our self-consciousness and inhibitions; our self-imposed hindrances to pleasure; our unwillingness to be embarrassed, exposed, or vulnerable. I laugh as a dog greets me with fervent licks to my face, in celebration of the level of enthusiasm dogs can feel. What have I felt so enthusiastic about in my life? We cover up and mock the smells of our bodies, but a dog's nose will boldly aim right between my legs, and will sit up with seeming surprise at the air noisily and smellily escaping from their own rumps. I am gleeful at the dog who is excited into zoomy running;* at the small dog cautiously or boldly aiming her nose upward into a large dog; at my dogs' keen attention to words rhyming with "walk," "treat," "nose-work," "okay," and "cat"; at dog tails wagging in synch; at reluctant tolerance of an overfriendly puppy's approach; at rolling in snow; at dogs searching, chasing, finding, retrieving, discovering, digging, gnawing things.

---

* The highly enjoyable "zoomies" has been described by dog experts as a frenetic, careening run in which hindquarters sometimes get ahead of the frontquarters, that "may cause first-time dog owners to suspect that their dog has momentarily lost its [*sic*] mind."

The joy is prompted by their being *who they are*—perfect instances of "dogs," sometimes; and precise instances of who that individual dog is, alltimes.

Though we now can draw a highly intelligible picture of who the dog is, there is still much about our way of dealing with them that ignores or subverts that picture. We have inherited our habits with dogs, and it's high time that we re-examine them.

Look at places where dogs aren't—in zoos, for instance. It would feel outrageous to find a dog in a zoo. This is not because dogs are not sufficiently exotic: there are plenty of non-exotic animals in zoos, especially ubiquitous animals (cockroaches, ants, snakes) there to be admired from behind the safety of glass. Instead, the outrage of the idea is rooted in its simple inapplicability: dogs are *among us*; they are our family, our friends. They are on the sofa next to me right now. And, moreover, they belong among us, there on the sofa—not isolated from people and in cages.*

But where is your friend right now, as I write this and you read it? Perhaps near you, on your own sofa. But the lifestyle of most owners makes another prediction: alone. Contemporary ownership enforces isolation of dogs. In writing about the condition of zoo animals, biologist Heini Hediger expressed concern for the animals' "isolation through captivity." Dog

---

* Nineteenth-century zoos did contain dogs: among the monkeys and large cats in the Bristol Zoological Garden were "exotic" dogs—Saint Bernards, Labradors, and Esquimaux (husky or Malamute). Up until 1950, two decades after the breed's recognition by the AKC, you could still find huskies at a zoo. And dogs have snuck into zoos in other roles: as surrogate family (1841: a chimpanzee was given a puppy after having lost his mate; 1843: a female pointer was deployed to suckle a motherless leopard cub) and therapy animals (a spaniel paired with a panther; a Border collie to keep a lion company). Today in the San Diego Zoo, dogs hang out with cheetahs to model friendly behavior for the cats.

owners risk the inverse: creating captivity through isolation. Dogs are left alone for the greatest portion of their lives; given their dependency on us, their interactions with other dogs and people is highly regulated—and entirely outside their control. Left alone in a crate,* the dog is further restricted in their sensory and physical experience until that magic moment when you walk in the door. They are becoming captive to being ours.

It's unbecoming of the species: dogs are, certainly, more than appendages to us. Like Lori Gruen, philosopher Martha Nussbaum makes the claim that animals have intrinsic dignity. Should we find ourselves in interaction with an animal, she suggests, we should act to enable that animal to flourish—at whatever "sort of thing" it is—dog, elephant, cow, rabbit, horse, slug. Derailing an animal's life, through acts of cruelty, negligence, or death, is clearly wrong. But more interestingly, so are those acts that thwart their capabilities—a dog's capacity to "be a dog."

Even more than acts of dog shaming or dog costume-donning, a person's unwillingness to attend to, and be curious about, who dogs really are, denies them dignity.

As a scientist in search of orderliness and process, my heart leapt at the list of elements that Nussbaum enumerates as necessary for a dignified existence. They are all things we can do for dogs. Enabling their life, bodily health and integrity, and general pursuits for mental and emotional well-being, she begins. Easy: we all feed our dogs, care for them when they are ill, try to treat them nicely, and give them toys. But also, she says: stimulation of the senses, free movement, exposure to

---

* Crating is currently popular as part of a training regime (done with the best intentions, recommended by trainers I respect and admire) to keep dogs comfortable and also non-misbehaving during their hours of solitude. It's still a confinement that limits what the dog can experience, however good those intentions are.

varieties of things—"a rich plurality of life activities." Translated for dogs, I read that as: daily sights and sniffs; ability to run around, to meet new things or a variety of well-loved old things; chances to try something new and challenging. She continues: the possibility of being attached to others; to play.

For dogs: a social life of people and of other dogs; not just time with you, but time on the floor with you, playing or wrestling or touching. Nussbaum: to be in the natural world; to have some control over one's environment. For dogs: to regularly be able to go outside, to smell the grass, to roll in dirt, to splash in water; and to be given choices—as the simple fact of being able to choose improves well-being.

Perhaps not coincidentally, these are the things—the sniffing, licking, running, bonding, playing—that I already find joyful about dogs. When, in two minutes, I rise from this chair, and my dog lifts his head, licks his nose, and dismounts from the sofa in a great stretch of his body toward me, his eyes alert to see what we're about to be doing together, he is completely dignified. And I am lent a measure of dignity by him. *Hilarious!*

Tail of the Dog

Rare is the dog owner I meet who does not have a fond place in their heart for their dog. Whether a source of income, a hunting companion, or, most often, a familial companion and friend, we love our dogs. This is fantastic news not just for dogs, but for our own species. Every time we adopt a new dog, we show our willingness to extend our circle to include them. Every day with that dog, we aim to treat them well: a seventy-billion-dollar pet industry business attests to our aim to get "only the best" for our dogs. We scour pet stores for the best dog food; we provide them with treats and toys; we arrange our lives to allow them to be walked throughout the day. We save a bit of dinner for them. We are at our best when we loop them into the circle of Special Animals we've drawn around ourselves. Our naming of dogs, talking to dogs, and willingness to get on the floor and play with dogs are the happiest results of our granting them personhood, in the broadest sense. On our worst days, we turn to a dog to receive a scratch of the scruff or allow them to lick us with affection.

At the same time, we are inconstant with dogs. Our language reveals our changeable attitude: outside of a literal description of a female dog, *bitch* is decidedly negative. *Doggerel* is childish, unskilled—the clumsy puppy of poetry; the *doghouse* is the place you get sent when you've been bad; *dog-tired* and *sick as a dog* aren't states to be desired; to *hound* someone is harassment (and *harass*, too, comes from the call of "hare" used to egg a hunting dog on game). *Dog days* and a *dog's life* are joyless. *Hangdog* alludes to the medieval practice of publicly hanging dogs accused of committing crimes. Even *dog* is not usually a compliment, when tossed at another person.* Hidden inside *adulation* is the Latin *adulari*, "to fawn over someone like a dog wagging its tail."

As we've seen, when we examine them, many of our entirely normalized behaviors toward dogs turn out to be surprising. We breed dogs into illness; scorn—and attempt to expunge—dogs' reproductive urges; punish dogs; mutilate dogs; abandon dogs. We seem to want them to be human, but then in many ways we treat dogs as though they are definitely not.

What they are is *ours*. Dogs are ours. They are also fast becoming captive to being ours. The dog's tale is that they are appended to us: our own tail, following us; inextricably tied to us. What are our responsibilities to this faithful companion?

---

* With some exceptions: from the late seventeenth century, "you old dog" could also mean "you cheery, hearty person." Twentieth-century hip-hop jargon added another layer: thus we have Sean Connery telling Rob Brown, "You're the man now, dawg" in *Finding Forrester*, mainstreaming a friendly, "buddy"-like use.

There is ample good intention and enthusiasm for dogs today, which I take as auspicious: our hearts are already with the dogs. Take a hard look at the ways we live with dogs now, and where our ideas for living with dogs come from, though, and we see that we've become societally complacent that because dogs are "indulged," the spoiled child of domestic animals, they must have terrific lives.

I suggest we not let our agenda for dogs be set by the accidents of history. In many ways, how we see dogs has been dictated by industries based on profit or questionable motives. It's high time we ask anew how we should live with this species that we have appended to ourselves. There may not be a natural state apart from us for dogs.* Set one "free"—open your door and release the hounds—and they will look for a way to attach themselves to humans, intimately or at a safe distance. They do not, Jack London's imagination notwithstanding, return to being wolves. So the question is, instead, given the dog's current conscription to humans, can we do it better for them?

We can. We can take another look at the state we've wound up in with dogs. For the nonce, we still own dogs; we are owners; they are owned. Moreover, given the species' dependence on humans, one could argue that they *need* to be maintained as owned property, insofar as we need to continue to have responsibility for their care. But property that acknowledges that they are *living* right under our noses. We have helped make dogs who they are; we can neither exempt ourselves nor ignore their animalness.

The animalness of dogs is what got us interested in them

---

* Nor is it clear that a "natural" state is ideal for any animal: some have argued that a wild animal's life is essentially brutish and short.

in the first place: how fabulous to have an animal in the house, with their mysterious thoughts, adventures, and perception— who also gazes your way, smiles at you, and listens to your recap of your day unwaveringly. And yet it is the animalness that, today, we seem to most want to get out of them. To get rid of their sex, their smell—their very biology. A tension arises when we realize we don't know everything about dogs, that we cannot predict or control all of their behavior. That they have motivations we don't like, experiences we don't oversee, needs we can't imagine.

What if, instead, we took their contribution to our family— made up of often radically different members—seriously? If we embraced rather than resisted our differences? That we even enlarge our family to include another species is a textbook example of our capacity for empathy. There are thousands of shelter workers who rise each day tasked with rescuing dogs from the street and abuse; with placing them into good homes. How they maintain their sanity and good-spiritedness is beyond me: they are buoyed, no doubt, by the pure love from the dogs, but they also demonstrate with each dog how much we will endure to help others.

I think this is the way forward for dogs. One of our species' strengths is our simple willingness to help others. So let's help dogs be dogs—try to see them for who they are, so we can help them do what they are trying to do. Allow a dog to sniff that thing, roll in that other thing, have your company, be engaged and social and occupied. How we—we individually and we societally—treat dogs matters. Considering that which is ideal and happiest for them acknowledges the marvel of that hyphen connecting them to us.

Our mutual gaze—the hyphen in the dog-human bond— has changed us as a species, and changes us as individuals.

Indeed, looking at dogs has changed the very way I see the world. Even after Pumpernickel's death, I found myself angling toward certain broad-trunked trees; walking along hedgerows or finding pleasure at signposts or building corners—because these were *her* interests. Finnegan has given me eyes for giant rain-swollen puddles in the park; I am no longer inured to the crashes of garage doors or sudden backfiring cars in the city, because Upton startles at each one. My time with dogs has permanently changed my perception, my habits, the way I move through space.

Who we are with dogs is who we are as people. Every cruelty, embrace, neglect, indulgence, shows us the measure of ourselves when no one is watching. Who would we become as a species if we try to see them anew, for their sake? We'd be an animal I would be glad to know.

Acknowledgments

Thanks, specifically, to the following people for their thoughts, knowledge, and their time on one or more matter of dogly relevance:

"The Perfect Name": Stanley Brandes, Bob Fagen, Jesse Scheidlower, Richard Zacks

"Owning Dogs": David Favre, Stephen Zawistowski

"Things People Say to Their Dogs": Keith Olbermann and all owners who completed the questionnaire

"The Trouble with Breeds": Bronwen Dickey, Brynn White—librarian extraordinaire at the AKC Library, Stephen Zawistowski, the veterinarians and staff at the University of Florida College of Veterinary Medicine's Maddie's Shelter Medicine Program

"Dog Stuff": Katherine Grier (and her well-thumbed book), Daniel Hurewitz, Brynn White

"The Dog in the Mirror": Dan Charnas (you dawg)

"Against Sex": Amy Attas, Thierry Bedossa, Cynda Crawford and others at Maddie's Shelter Medicine Program, Anne-Lil Kvam, Cindy Otto, Stephen Zawistowski

"Humorless": Honor Jones at the *New York Times*, Kirsten Van Vlandren at the Colonial Theater

"Tail of the Dog": Ammon Shea

Thank you, more generally, to nearly a decade of students in Canine Cognition, and over a decade of researchers at the Horowitz Dog Cognition Lab, for continuing conversations about dogs; to the ever-willing owners and cooperative and charming dogs who participate in our studies; and to April Benson, for her generous support of the Lab.

The New York Society Library, Barnard College, and Roe Jan Library provided quiet places to work and productive air to breathe, for which I am thankful.

Thanks to Becca Franks and Jeff Sebo, who have stimulated my thinking about a number of issues in this book; to Wendy Walters, for her essays; to Valeria Luiselli and Jesús Rodriguez-Velasco, for ideas about medieval manuscripts that inspired my thinking about marginalia; to Julie Tate for her thorough fact-checking of "Against Sex," "The Trouble with Breeds," and "Owning Dogs"; and to Elizabeth and Jay, who instilled in me a love of animals, a love of thinking clearly, and a love of questioning the perceived wisdom. For their friendship and conversations about books, thanks to Meakin Armstrong, Betsy Carter, Catherine Chung, Alison Curry, Daniel Hurewitz, Elizabeth Kadetsky, Maira Kalman, Sally Koslow, Aryn Kyle, Susan Orlean, Aaron Retica, Timea Szell, Jennifer Vanderbes, and Bill Vourvoulias.

I owe everyone at Scribner great thanks for continuing to follow me follow my dogs: especially Susan Moldow, Nan Graham, and Roz Lippel. And especially-especially, I am privileged and grateful to continue to have Colin Harrison as reader and editor, and Sarah Goldberg as critical art eye. Jaya Miceli, Kara Watson, Ashley Gilliam, Brian Belfiglio, Abigail Novak, thanks for helping this book come to life—and thanks to Christian Purdy for helping it fly.

If there's got to be a camera pointing at me, I'm always glad that Vegar Abelsnes is behind it. I appreciate his constancy: his photos of me with Finnegan are a record of our life together: beginning in 2008, with *Inside of a Dog* (Finn: age 1), continuing through 2012, 2015, and now, 2019 (Finn: age 11)—even if it is Edsel who made the jacket.

Thanks to Kris Dahl at ICM for many freewheeling, brainstorming conversations, and her steadfast advocacy.

Thanks to Ammon and Ogden, for looking at, walking with, and talking about dogs with me. And again to Ammon, for the generosity of his enthusiasm about each new topic. To Damon, for thinking out loud with me. And again to Ogden, for lending me the drawing on this page.

You can't know how much I thank you, Finnegan and Upton—and the countless other dogs who have met my gaze. I'm so glad to know you all.

Sources

THE PERFECT NAME

8 *a beetle* Anelipsistus americanus: All Latin name examples were found in John Wright's wonderful 2014 *The Naming of the Shrew: A Curious History of Latin Names.*

8 *indri, canary:* Etymologies from the *Oxford English Dictionary.*

9 *"troublesome effects" of actual differences between individual animals:* Martin, P., and H. C. Kraemer. 1987. Individual differences in behaviour and their statistical consequences. *Animal Behaviour, 35,* 1366–1375.

10 *"I had no idea that it would have been more appropriate . . . to assign each of the chimpanzees a number":* Goodall, 1998, cited in E. S. Benson. 2016. Naming the ethological subject. *Science in Context, 29,* 107–128.

10 *on the problems of individual animal identification:* Kenward, R. 2000. *A Manual for Wildlife Radio Tagging.*

11 *on Druzhok:* Pavlov, I. 1893. Vivisection, via D. P. Todes. 2001. *Pavlov's Physiology Factory: Experiment, Interpretation, Laboratory Enterprise.*

11 *no little friend:* Pavlov, I. 1927. *Conditioned Reflexes.*

11 *In contemporary neuroscience labs studying primates:* Sharp, L. April 25, 2017. "The animal commons in experimental laboratory science." Talk delivered at the Human-Animal Studies University seminar, Columbia University.

12 *By six months of age, human infants can recognize speech sounds:* Bortfeld, H., J. L. Morgan, R. M. Golinkoff, and K. Rathbun. 2005. Mommy and me: Familiar names help launch babies into speech-stream segmentation. *Psychological Science, 164,* 298–304.

12 *named cow milk yield and respect:* Bertenshaw, C., and P. Rowlinson. 2009. Exploring stock managers' perceptions of the human-animal relationship on dairy farms and an association with milk production. *Anthrozoös, 22,* 59–69; D. Valenze. 2009. *Milk: A Local and Global History.*

13 *Vienna dog names:* Schmidjell, T., F. Range, L. Huber, and Z. Virányi. 2012. Do owners have a Clever Hans effect on dogs? Results of a pointing study. *Frontiers in Psychology, 3,* 558.

13   *German dog names:* Bräuer, J., J. Call, and M. Tomasello. 2004. Visual perspective taking in dogs (Canis familiaris) in the presence of barriers. *Applied Animal Behaviour Science, 88,* 299–317.

13   *English dog names:* Piotti, P., and J. Kaminski. 2016. Do dogs provide information helpfully? *PLOS One, 11,* e0159797.

13   *New York City dog names:* Horowitz, A., J. Hecht, and A. Dedrick. 2013. Smelling more or less: Investigating the olfactory experience of the domestic dog. *Learning and Motivation, 44,* 207–217.

14   *Racing greyhound names:* Arluke, A., and C. R. Sanders. 1996. *Regarding Animals,* pp. 12–13.

15   *Baatombu naming practices:* Schottman, W. 1993. Proverbial dog names of the Baatombu: A strategic alternative to silence. *Language in Society, 22,* 539.

16   *Top dog names in my neck of the woods:* New York City Department of Health. "Dog names in New York City." http://a816-dohbesp.nyc.gov /IndicatorPublic/dognames/. Retrieved August 18, 2018.

17   *"Spigot," "Bubbler," etc.:* Xenophon. "On Hunting." http://bit.ly/2vT8hx3 & http://bit.ly/2womJOG.

17   *Alexander the Great named his dog:* O'Brien, J. M. 1994. *Alexander the Great: The Invisible Enemy.*

17   *names of Actaeon's dogs:* Mayor, A. "Names of dogs in ancient Greece." http://www.wondersandmarvels.com/2012/07/names-of-dogs-in-ancient -greece-3.html.

17   *Recommended names for hunting dogs of the Middle Ages:* Walker-Meikle, K. 2013. *Medieval Dogs.*

17   *a dog's name "should hold, as it were, implicitly in itself all the elements for a conversation with (the dog) on its character":* May 6, 1871. "The Naming of Dogs." *The Spectator.*

18   *a man named Carl claimed "the name of Rock":* August 19, 1876. *Chicago Field.*

18   *"euphonious and well-sounding words":* October 6, 1888. Notes and Queries, 269. http://bit.ly/2wlMNXY.

18   *AKC naming rules:* http://www.akc.org/register/naming-of-dog/. Retrieved August 8, 2017.

18   *In American English, most di- and trisyllabic names have an emphasis on the first syllable:* Jesse Scheidlower, personal communication, August 29, 2017.

19   *Pekingese stud book names: The American Kennel Gazette and Stud Book,* vol. 34. http://bit.ly/2vpp3oD. Retrieved August 8, 2017.

19   *1706 book on hunting hounds:* October 6, 1888. Notes and Queries. http:// bit.ly/2wlMNXY.

19   *George Washington's dogs:* Grier, K. 2006. *Pets in America: A History,* p. 34.

19   *Nineteenth-century foxhounds:* Trigg, H. C. 1890. *The American Fox-hound.*

19   *Mark Twain's dogs:* Zacks, R. 2016. *Chasing the Last Laugh: Mark Twain's Raucous and Redemptive Round-the-World Comedy Tour.*

19 *Nineteenth-century children's magazines:* 1879–1880. *Harper's Young People*, 20 volumes.

19 *Peter Kelley, Rum Punch, and Billy Sykes living on the South Side:* October 28, 1896. "Fashions in dogs' names." *Austin Daily Statesman*, p. 6.

19 *pedigree English setters names:* 1878. *National American Kennel Club Stud Book*, vol. 1.

19 *Human nicknames used for pets:* Grier 2006, p. 237.

19 *Hartsdale Pet Cemetery first pet:* https://www.hartsdalepetcrematory.com/about-us/our-history/.

20 *Hartsdale gravestone names:* Brandes, S. 2009. The meaning of American pet cemetery gravestones. *Ethnology, 48*, 99–118.

21 *William Safire's call for dog names:* December 22, 1985. "On Language: Name that dog." *New York Times* magazine.

24 *Tlingit naming practices:* Bob Fagen, personal communication, July 2, 2017; see also G. T. Emmons. 1991. *The Tlingit Indians*.

25 *Taiwanese naming practices.* Chen, L. N. H. 2017. Pet-naming practices in Taiwan. *Names, 65*, 167–177.

25 *forums on baby names:* See, e.g., Lauren Collins' Twitter, August 2, 2017, following her *New Yorker* article on naming children.

OWNING DOGS

34 *"After all is said and done, a dog is a dog":* Henderson v. Henderson. 2016 SKQB 282 (CanLII). https://www.canlii.org/en/sk/skqb/doc/2016/2016skqb282/2016skqb282.html.

34 *"Go out and buy another dog":* McLain, T. T. 2009. Detailed discussion: Knick-knack, paddy-whack, give the dog a home?: Custody determination of companion animals upon guardian divorce. *Michigan State University College of Law*. https://www.animallaw.info.

34 *dogs are "assignable property":* Kindregan, C. P., Jr. 2013. Pets in divorce: Family conflict over animal custody. *American Journal of Family Law, 26*, 4, 227–232.

34 *chocolate Lab as "chattel":* July 25, 2002. C.R.S., Plaintiff, v. T.K.S., Defendant. Supreme Court, New York County.

34 *"a visitation schedule for a table or a lamp":* July 5, 2002. Desanctis v. Pritchard, Appellee. Superior Court of Pennsylvania, 803 A.2d 230.

34 *dog furnishings:* Shearin, A. L., and E. A. Ostrander. 2010. Canine morphology: Hunting for genes and tracking mutations. *PLOS Biol, 8*, e1000310.

35 *Dogs Grace . . . and Roxy:* December 31, 2015. Enders v. Baker. Appellate Court of Illinois.

35 *Should a judge grant one party ownership of "the family butter knives":* 2016. Henderson v. Henderson (Canada). https://www.canlii.org.

35 *Custody case for Joey:* November 29, 2013. Travis v. Murray. Supreme Court, New York County.

36   *ownership of a dog was determined by which one could get the dog to come when called:* Walker-Meikle 2013, p. 29.

36   *the proper disposition of an unnamed Boston bull terrier dog:* May 15, 1944. John W. Akers v. Stella Sellers. Appellate Court of Indiana.

36   *Tennessee Dobie-retriever custody case:* Hamilton, J. T. 2005. Dog custody case attracts nationwide interest. In W. L. Montell, ed., *Tales from Tennessee Lawyers*, pp. 180–181.

37   *Dogs are family:* 2015. The Harris Poll. http://www.theharrispoll.com /health-and-life/Pets-are-Members-of-the-Family.html.

38   *bioethicist Bernard Rollin:* August 12, 2015. "When is it ethical to euthanize your pet?" The Conversation. http://theconversation.com /when-is-it-ethical-to-euthanize-your-pet-44806.

40   *the next line of Genesis:* Scully, M. 2003. *Dominion: The Power of Man, the Suffering of Animals, and the Call to Mercy*, p. 44.

40   *Old Testament:* Proverbs 12:10 and Hosea 2:18, respectively, via K. Thomas. 1996. *Man and the Natural World: Changing Attitudes in England 1500–1800*, p. 24.

41   *domestication was seen as good for animals:* Thomas 1996, p. 20.

41   *Etymology of dominance: Oxford American Dictionary.*

41   *law "was established for men's sake":* Wise, S. M. 2003. The evolution of animal law since 1950. In D. J. Salem and A. N. Rowan, eds. *The State of the Animals*, vol. II, pp. 99–105.

41   *Roman origins of legal system:* Wise 2003; also "The common law and civil law traditions." School of Law, UC Berkeley. https://www.law .berkeley.edu/library/robbins/CommonLawCivilLawTraditions.html.

41   *Descartes and Kant views:* Francione, G. L. 2004. Animals—Property or persons? In C. R. Sunstein and M. C. Nussbaum, eds. *Animal Rights: Current Debates and New Directions*, pp. 108–142. Also see Kant, *Anthropology*, from a pragmatic point of view.

42   *Darwin on continuity:* Darwin, C. (1871) 2004. *The Descent of Man*. London: Penguin.

42   *a moral status "no different from that of inanimate objects":* Francione 2014, p. 110.

42   *owners as "social deviants":* Taylor, N., and T. Signal, eds. 2011. *Human-Animal Studies: Theorizing Animals: Re-thinking Humanimal Relations.*

43   *owners as suspicious themselves:* Ritvo, H. 1989. *The Animal Estate: The English and Other Creatures in Victorian England*, pp. 175–176.

43   *"The day may come, when the rest of the animal creation may acquire those rights":* Bentham, J. 1823. *An Introduction to the Principles of Morals and Legislation.* Chapter XVII, section 1, paragraph IV, and footnote 122.

44   *only the "wanton infliction" of pain, "with no reasonable purpose" is unlawful—but not the infliction of pain at all:* "Animal cruelty." *Catholic Encyclopedia.* http://www.catholic.org/encyclopedia/view.php?id=812.

44 *The human-centeredness in the law:* Favre, D., and V. Tsang. 1993. The development of anti-cruelty laws during the 1800s. *Detroit College of Law Review, 1,* 1–36.

44 *New York in the nineteenth century:* See, e.g., Dickens, C. 1842. *American Notes*; Liboiron, M. 2012. History of consumption and waste in the U.S., 1800–1850. In Zimring, C. A., and W. L. Rathje, eds. *Encyclopedia of Consumption and Waste: The Social Science of Garbage*, pp. 356–358; Miller, B. 2000. *Fat of the Land: Garbage of New York—The Last Two Hundred Years.*

45 *dogs had no "socially recognized value":* Favre, D. 2010. Living property: A new status for animals within the legal system. *Marquette Law Review, 93,* 1021.

45 *Henry Bergh and the evolution of the laws:* Favre and Tsang 1993.

45 *the spirit of the law made advances:* Favre 2010.

46 *Virginia property status:* 2008. Virginia Code Ann. § 3.2-6585, from Favre 2010.

46 *New York State anti-cruelty laws:* State of New York Department of Agriculture and Markets. Article 26 of the Agriculture and Markets Law relating to Cruelty to Animals § 353, 353-a.

46 *report of fight of Thursday and Dan:* July 26, 1889. *Cincinnati Enquirer,* p. 2.

46 *"The indiscriminate poisoning of dogs is not permitted in Baltimore":* June 3, 1890. "City dogs that may be captured." *Baltimore Sun.*

48 *"How hard do you hit the dog?":* Monks of New Skete. 2002. *How to Be Your Dog's Best Friend,* p. 75.

48 *Only "an evil state of mind" shows malice:* March 16, 1990. Regalado v. United States. District of Columbia Court of Appeals.

49 *FBI and cruelty cases:* https://www.fbi.gov/news/stories/-tracking-animal-cruelty. Retrieved January 4, 2018.

49 *humans' abiding interest in being able to "control, direct, or consume things":* Favre, D. 2000. Equitable self-ownership for animals. *Duke Law Journal, 50,* 473–502.

49 *"Add a Bike, Pet or Golf Clubs to Your Trip":* Amtrak pop-up during online ticketing. https://www.amtrak.com/ibcontent/ancillary_intro text. Confirmed January 9, 2018.

49 *"odorless, harmless":* https://assistive.amtrak.com/h5/assistive/r/www.amtrak.com/onboard/carry-on-pets.html. Retrieved January 9, 2018.

49 *enforcement of Animal Welfare Act:* Brulliard, K. October 18, 2018. "USDA's enforcement of animal welfare laws plummeted in 2018, agency figures show." *Washington Post.*

49 *"Preventing Animal Cruelty and Torture Act":* https://www.congress.gov/116/bills/hr724/BILLS-116hr724ih.pdf.

50 *dog winterizing:* Brody, J. E. December 19, 2017. "How to 'winterize' your dog." *New York Times.*

50 *dog parking at Ikea:* https://www.apartmenttherapy.com/dog-parking -at-ikea-175781.

50 *use your Labradoodle for a loan:* Francione 2014, pp. 116–117.

50 *Bateson inquiry:* Bateson, P. 2010. Independent inquiry into dog breed-ing.

50 *animals as capital in Egypt:* Mikhail, A. January 30, 2017. Human-Animal Studies seminar, Columbia University.

51 *standards of welfare for breeders:* New York State General Business Law. Article 35-D. "Sale of dogs and cats." https://www.agriculture.ny.gov /AI/AILaws/Art-35D-Sale-of-Dogs-and-Cats.pdf.

51 *"fair market value":* McLain 2009.

51 *animals used for research, product testing, etc.:* Francione 2014, p. 109.

51 *rats, mice, and birds are not considered "animals":* Animal Welfare Act. "The term 'animal' . . . excludes (1) birds, rats of the genus Rattus, and mice of the genus Mus, bred for use in research." https://www.nal.usda .gov/awic/animal-welfare-act. Retrieved January 9, 2018.

52 *a nontrivial number were dogs:* United States Department of Agriculture. 2016. Animal and Plant Health Inspection Service. Annual Report Animal Usage by Fiscal Year. In 2016 that number was 60,979.

52 *Claude Bernard:* Zwart, H. 2008. What is a dog? Animal experiments and animal novels. In *Understanding Nature: Case Studies in Comparative Epistemology.*

52 *brown dog:* Thornton, A. 2012. Portrait of a man and his dog: The Brown Dog affair. https://blogs.ucl.ac.uk/researchers-in-museums/2012/10/22 /portrait-of-a-man-and-his-dog-the-brown-dog-affair/.

53 *Barbra Streisand cloned dog:* Stevens, M. February 28, 2018. "Barbra Streisand cloned her dog. For $50,000, you can clone yours." *New York Times.*

55 *"It costs money to protect animal interests":* Francione, G. L., and A. E. Charlton. "The case against pets." *Aeon.* https://aeon.co/essays /why-keeping-a-pet-is-fundamentally-unethical.

55 *"nearly all of our animal use can be justified* only *by habit":* Francione 2004, p. 115.

56 *we are not even that good at determining what dogs and other animals want now:* See, e.g., Franks, B. 2019. "What do animals want?" *Animal Welfare Science, 28,* 1–10.

56 *habeas corpus for Tommy:* Walsh, B. December 2, 2013. "Do chimps have human rights? This lawsuit says yes." *Time.* Also see https://www.non humanrights.org/blog/lawsuit-filed-today-on-behalf-of-chimpanzee -seeking-legal-personhood/.

57 *entities "of any nature whatsoever" can be persons:* https://www.lawinsider .com/clause/person.

57 *Being a person means you have certain interests that are significant:* Franci-one 2004, p. 131.

57 *"things" were the property of "persons," and lacking any rights:* Wise 2003.

57 *At no time have only humans been persons:* Wise, S. M. February 24–25, 2017. "Nonhuman animals as legal persons." Talk delivered at "I am not an animal!: The signature cry of our species" symposium, Emory University. Video at http://www.earthintransition.org/2017/05/non human-animals-legal-persons/.

57 *"No rights exist as between man and beast":* Cicero, M. T. De finibus, 3.67.

57 *the historical application of habeas corpus:* S. M. Wise. 2007. The entitlement of chimpanzees to the common law writs of habeas corpus and de homine replegiando, *Golden Gate University Law Review*, 37, 257.

57 *a chimp named Cecilia:* "The first 20 days of Cecilia." http://www.projet ogap.org.br/en/noticia/the-first-20-days-of-cecilia/. See also "Chimpanzee recognized as legal person." https://www.nonhumanrights.org/blog /nonhuman-rights-project-praises-argentine-courts-recognition-of -captive-chimpanzees-legal-personhood-and-rights/.

57 *"While it may be arguable that a chimpanzee is not a 'person,' there is no doubt that it is not merely a thing":* May 8, 2018. Opinion on Motion No. 2018-268. In the Matter of Nonhuman Rights Project, Inc., on Behalf of Tommy, Appellant, v. Patrick C. Lavery, &c., et al., Respondents and In the Matter of Nonhuman Rights Project, Inc., on Behalf of Kiko, Appellant, v. Carmen Presti et al., Respondents. State of New York Court of Appeals.

58 *"each successive extension of rights to some new entity has been, theretofore, a bit unthinkable":* Stone, C. D. 1972. Should trees have standing?– Towards legal rights for natural objects. *Southern California Law Review*, 45, 450–501.

58 *the Ganges and a tributary, the Yamuna, in India, became legal persons:* Roy, E. A. March 16, 2017. New Zealand river granted same legal rights as human being. TheGuardian.com; Safi, M. March 21, 2017. Ganges and Yamuna rivers granted same legal rights as human beings. TheGuardian.com.

58 *conceptual division of objects as property or legal persons:* Favre 2000.

60 *domestic animals as citizens:* Donaldson, S., and W. Kymlicka. 2011. *Zoopolis: A Political Theory of Animal Rights.*

61 *considering "well-being" of a dog:* Alaska: Amendment to AS 25.24.160, Chapter 24 on Divorce and Dissolution of Marriage. See https://www .animallaw.info/statute/ak-divorce-§-2524160-judgment; for Illinois see http://www.ilga.gov/legislation/ilcs/ilcs5.asp?ActID=2086.

62 *the duty is owed to individual dogs, not to the state:* Favre 2000, p. 494.

62 *some states have provisions for "sanitary conditions":* See, e.g., Michigan Penal Code § 750.50(1), via Favre 2000.

62 *full dogness:* This list inspired in part by Nussbaum, M. C. 2004. Beyond "compassion and humanity": Justice for nonhuman animals. In Sunstein and Nussbaum, eds., pp. 299–320.

63 *"appetite for garbage, sexual promiscuity":* Serpell, J. 2017. From paragon to pariah: Cross-cultural perspectives on attitudes to dogs. In his *The Domestic Dog: Its Evolution, Behavior, and Interactions with People*, p. 310.

THINGS PEOPLE SAY TO THEIR DOGS

67 *Stephen Colbert:* http://www.cc.com/video-clips/m3omdi/the-colbert -report-malcolm-gladwell.

68 *"Coom biddy":* Thomas 1996, pp. 95–97.

69 *"Well, well!" he says to the dog, Jip:* Lofting, H. (1920) 1948. *The Story of Doctor Dolittle*, p. 150.

70 *dog's "mommy" or "daddy":* Arluke and Sanders 1996, pp. 67ff.

70 *same patterns of brain activity when looking at photos of their dogs:* Stoeckel, L. E., L. S. Palley, R. L. Gollub, et al. 2014. Patterns of brain activation when mothers view their own child and dog: An fMRI study. *PLOS ONE, 9,* e107205.

71 *more variation in a pitch:* Ben-Aderet, T., M. Gallego-Abenza, D. Reby, and N. Mathevon. 2017. Dog-directed speech: Why do we use it and do dogs pay attention to it? *Proceedings of the Royal Society B, 284.*

71 *Instead, we tend to repeat words:* See, e.g., Jeannin, S., C. Gilbert, and G. Leboucher. 2017. Effect of interaction type on the characteristics of pet-directed speech in female dog owners. *Animal Cognition, 20,* 499–509.

71 *we hyperarticulate our vowels:* Burnham, D., C. Kitamura, and U. Vollmer-Conna. 2002. What's new, pussycat? On talking to babies and animals. *Science, 296,* 1435.

71 *hyperarticulation to foreigners learning English as a second language:* Uther, M., M. A. Knoll, D. Burnham. 2007. Do you speak E-N-G-L-I-S-H? A comparison of foreigner- and infant-directed speech. *Speech Communication, 49,* 2–7.

72 *Yurok Indians:* Serpell 2017, p. 303.

75 *women repeat words more:* Prato-Previde, E., G. Fallani, and P. Valsecchi. 2006. Gender differences in owners interacting with pet dogs: An observational study. *Ethology, 112,* 64–73.

78 *Gimme paw! Gimme paw!:* Shared with me via Twitter.

79 *engaging them as if they might respond:* As noted by Beck and Katcher 1983 (in Arluke and Sanders 1996) in their observations of owner-veterinarian interactions.

82 *Bye bye Max, see you tomorrow, little guy:* Robins, D. M., C. R. Sanders, and S. E. Cahill. 1991. Dogs and their people: Pet-facilitated interaction in a public setting. *Journal of Contemporary Ethnography, 20,* 3–25.

82 *"Mommy's so mean tonight":* Tannen, D. 2007. Talking the dog: Framing pets as interactional resources in family discourse. In D. Tannen, S. Kendall, and C. Gordon, eds. *Family Talk: Discourse and Identity in Four American Families*, pp. 49–70.

82   *"human fantasy" of dog communication:* Garber, M. 1996. *Dog Love.*

82   *"We like our pets' silence":* Fudge, E. 2008. *Pets (Art of Living),* p. 52.

83   *Luath:* Magnum, T. 2002. Dog years, human fears. In Nigel Rothfels, ed. *Representing Animals,* pp. 35–47.

83   *"I hate to walk alone—":* December 1827. *Blackwood's Edinburgh* magazine, pp. 731–733.

83   *whistleblowers:* See, e.g., Stables, G. 1893. *Sable and White: The Autobiography of a Show Dog,* via Ritvo 2007.

83   *"best slumber party ever":* https://www.instagram.com/p/BPxjyQdADq9 /?hl=en&taken-by=chloetheminifrenchie.

83   *Instagram dogs:* Newman, A. July 13, 2017. "This Instagram dog wants to sell you a lint roller." *New York Times.*

84   *people with power or authority tend to translate their charges' speech:* Arluke and Sanders 1996, p. 62.

84   *veterinary exam "talk":* Arluke and Sanders 1996, p. 67.

84   *"I am sensing a smell that's not mine":* Jeannin et al. 2017.

84   *the dog is the center:* Goffman 1981, in Tannen 2007.

85   *"inner speech":* See, e.g., Alderson-Day, B., and C. Fernyhough. 2015. Inner speech: Development, cognitive functions, phenomenology, and neurobiology. *Psychological Bulletin, 141,* 931–965.

86   *"Of course you should talk to your dogs madam":* From D. McCaig's introduction to Hearne, V. 2007. *Adam's Task: Calling Animals by Name,* p. xi.

86   I love you: 2002. "Did you know . . ." *Canadian Veterinary Journal, 43,* 344.

86   *Even the simple sound of our voice:* Tannen also talks about talk as *sound.*

THE TROUBLE WITH BREEDS

87   *Clumber spaniel breed standard* (Note: breed standards can also be found on the American Kennel Club website and are widely available online): The Clumber Spaniel Club of America website: https://www.clumbers .org/index.php/clumbers/breed-standard/official-akc-standard. Retrieved February 23, 2019.

88   *"Bunny-tailed Scottish Shepterrier" etc.:* From Territorio de Zaguates.

89   *"understand and care for your dog like never before"; "Knowing your dog's ancestry":* Embark and Wisdom Panel, respectively.

90   *Sloughi breed standard:* https://www.akc.org/dog-breeds/sloughi/. Retrieved February 23, 2019.

91   *Well over fifty million dogs:* Ghirlanda, S., A. Acerbi, H. Herzog, and J. A. Serpell. 2013. Fashion vs. function in cultural evolution: The case of dog breed popularity. *PLOS ONE, 8,* e74770.

91   *"Cross bred" setters:* 1878. *National American Kennel Club Stud Book,* vol. 1.

92   *purebred dogs were meant to have fixed characteristics:* Serpell, J. A., and D. L. Duffy. 2014. Dog breeds and their behavior. In A. Horowitz, ed. *Domestic Dog Cognition and Behavior,* pp. 31–57.

92 *foxhounds run one hundred miles a week:* Kalof 2007.

92 *foxhound breeding:* Ritvo 1989.

93 *pit bulls crossed with terriers:* Dickey, B. 2016. *Pit Bull: The Battle over an American Icon*, p. 33.

93 *"What is beauty good for?":* July 1927. *AKC Gazette.*

93 *Welsh springer spaniel breed standard:* Welsh Springer Spaniel Club of America website: https://www.wssca.com/html/welshStandard.html. Retrieved February 23, 2019.

93 *Max von Stephanitz and Horand:* Stephanitz, V. 1923. "The German Shepherd dog in word and picture." http://bit.ly/2ypKweZ.

93 *German shepherd breed standard:* http://www.akc.org/dog-breeds/german -shepherd-dog/.

94 *Newcastle upon Tyne show:* Pemberton, N., and M. Worboys. June 2009. "The surprising history of Victorian dog shows." *BBC History* magazine.

94 *horse breeding:* Ritvo, H. 1986. Pride and pedigree: The evolution of the victorian dog fancy. *Victorian Studies, 29,* 227–253.

94 *winners at Newcastle:* Lane, C. H. 1902. *Dog Shows and Doggy People*; Sampson, J., and M. M. Binns. 2006. The Kennel Club and the early history of dog shows and breed clubs. In E. A. Ostrander, U. Giger, and K. Lindblad-Toh, eds. *The Dog and Its Genome*, pp. 19–30.

94 *"the choice of points is wholly arbitrary":* Ritvo 1989, p. 105.

94 *"Where there was a name, there was a breed":* Ritvo 1989, p. 107.

95 *bulldog's "good broken up face,"* . . . *"broad, slanting and deep" shoulders:* Ritvo 1989, p. 112; see also Maj. J. M. Taylor. (1874–1891) 1892. Bench Show and Field Trial records and standards of dogs in America and valuable statistics.

95 *"left little room for brains":* Ritvo 1989, p. 114; breed standard: "skull . . . quite flat and rather broad, with fine tapering muzzle of fair length . . . the greyhound type is very objectionable, as there is no brain room in the skull."

95 *Gordon setter standard:* c. 1884. The Malcolm Standard for judging Gordon Setters, p. 3.

95 *Belmont and Malcolm:* Taylor 1892.

96 *cocker spaniel, mastiff, English pug:* spaniel and pug: Taylor 1892; mastiff breed standard 1887.

96 *"Dog fashions for 1889":* Ritvo 1989.

96 *Dog show cheating and Kennel Club formation:* Ritvo 1989, pp. 98–102.

97 *exclusion of dogs "with mange":* 1885. Constitution, bylaws and rules and regulations of the American Kennel Club.

97 *early purebreds:* 1878. *National American Kennel Club Stud Book*, vol. 1; 1898, vol. 15. See also AKC's *The Complete Dog Book*, vol. 20.

97 *nearly 350 recognized breeds:* Per Fédération Cynologique Internationale. http://www.fci.be/en/. Retrieved August 6, 2018.

97 *Barnum dog show:* May 18, 1862. *New York Times.*

98 *Goldenmountainberdoodle:* Seen on Kijiji, the Craigslist of Toronto.

98 *XXL pit bulls, cavachon, and cavapoos:* http://www.foxglovecavachon puppies.com/available-puppies/; http://www.xxldesignerpitbulls.com /general-information.html.

98 *$32,000-a-year preschools:* http://www.blackboardawards.com/down loads/Manhattan_PreSchool_Tuition_08.pdf. Retrieved May 3, 2018.

98 *popular dog breeds in NYC neighborhoods:* https://project.wnyc.org/dogs -of-nyc/. Retrieved May 3, 2018.

98 *Shih Tzu breed standard:* http://americanshihtzuclub.org/breed_standard. Retrieved May 3, 2018.

99 *Labrador retriever breed standard:* https://thelabradorclub.com/about-the -breed/breed-standard/. Retrieved May 3, 2018.

99 *uptick in movie dog breed popularity:* Ghirlanda, S., A. Acerbi, and H. Herzog. 2014. Dog movie stars and dog breed popularity: A case study in media influence on choice. *PLOS ONE, 9,* e106565.

100 *Great Pyrenees breed standard:* Great Pyrenees Club of America website: http://gpcaonline.org/jeillustrated.htm. Retrieved February 23, 2019.

100 *Shakespeare's dogs:* Nagarajan, S. 2017. *Shakespeare's King Lear: An Edition with New Insights,* p. 240.

100 *eighteenth-century mongrel breeds:* Buffon, M. May 1769. Natural history of the dog. *Universal Magazine of Knowledge and Pleasure,* pp. 241–246.

101 *breeds "created out of whole cloth":* Ritvo 1989, p. 106.

101 *Afghan hound on Noah's Ark:* Drury, W. D. 1903. British dogs, their points, selection, and show preparation; Dickey 2016.

102 *Afghan hound breed standard:* http://akc.org/dog-breeds/afghan-hound/.

102 *Xoloitzcuintli breed standard:* http://www.akc.org/dog-breeds/xoloitzcu intli/.

102 *the oldest dogs genetically:* Larson, G., E. K. Karlsson, A. Perri, et al. 2012. Rethinking dog domestication by integrating genetics, archaeology, and biogeography. *Proceedings of the National Academy of Sciences USA, 109,* 8878–8883.

102 *Egyptian dog dish:* http://www.metmuseum.org/art/collection/search/545210.

102 *Medieval art:* Such as the Bayeux Tapestry, eleventh century; and Journey of the Magi, 1435.

103 *Jan Van Eyck:* This is the Arnolfini portrait.

103 *Fyt:* In the seventeenth century; many examples of these paintings.

103 *Rembrandt "The Good Samaritan":* http://www.metmuseum.org/toah /works-of-art/41.1.53/.

103 *"Englishe dogges":* Caius, Johannus. 1576. *De Canibus Britannicus,* translated as *Of Englishe dogges.* https://archive.org/details/ofenglishedogges 00caiuuoft. See also Ritvo 1989, pp. 93–94.

104 *Book of Saint Albans:* Walker-Mielke 2013, p. 82.

104 *Linnaeus:* Sampson and Binns 2006.

104 *purpose of dogs:* Ritvo 1989.

104 *Brittany breed standard:* The American Brittany Club website: http://www .theamericanbrittanyclub.org/Breedstand.htm. Retrieved February 23, 2019.

105 *"They wanted purebreds":* Sandøe, P. 2015. Up Close podcast "Hello, pet!: Our love can hurt our animal friends." https://upclose.unimelb.edu.au.

105 *"undoubted purity":* The Malcolm Standard for judging Gordon Setters. c. 1884.

105 *"Many ill-bred 'mutts'":* Grier 2006, p. 44.

105 *phrenology in* Dog Fancier: 1905.

105 *purity in milk:* Cohen, M., and Y. Otomo, eds. 2017. *Making Milk: The Past, Present and Future of Our Primary Food.*

106 *"hybrid vigor":* As described in O. Sacks. 2017. *The River of Consciousness*, p. 9.

106 *"Creatures of pure blood . . ." etc.:* Stephanitz 1923, pp. 50, 383, 279.

106 *Race or Mongrel:* Full quote from Schultz, on describing people of mixed race: "Or it sees a worthless thing, a mongrel, with its character- istics, of which the chief is lack of character" (1908, p. 260). https://babel .hathitrust.org/cgi/pt?id=osu.32435002808020;view=1up;seq=6.

107 *AKC* Gazette *on mixed breeds:* March 1929; May 1931.

107 *Mongrels were "rubbish":* Ritvo 1989, p. 91.

107 *Mongrels as "degenerate," who "contaminate" pure stock:* Anderson, J. Sep- tember 25, 1793. Thoughts on what is called varieties, or different breeds of domestic animals, suggested by reading Dr. Pallas' account of Russian sheep—By the Editor. *The Bee: or Literary Weekly Intelligencer*, Edinburgh.

108 *"Like a true mongrell . . .":* Citation from 1613, *Oxford English Dictionary.*

108 *the infirm, the downcast:* Dickey 2016.

108 *"Nobody now who is anybody":* Ritvo 1989, pp. 92–93.

108 *"The value of a mongrel":* Gordon Stables, cited in Rogers, K. M. 2005. *First Friend: A History of Dogs and Humans*, p. 141.

108 *Kennel Club on "rescue" dogs:* https://www.thekennelclub.org.uk/services /public/findarescue/Default.aspx. Retrieved August 15, 2018.

108 *information guide:* "Information guide: Find a rescue dog." www.thekennel club.org.uk. Retrieved January 3, 2018; "What to consider when get- ting a rescue dog." www.thekennelclub.org.uk/getting-a-dog-or-puppy /are-you-ready-for-a-dog/key-considerations-when-choosing-a-dog /what-to-consider-when-getting-a-rescue-dog/. Retrieved October 4, 2018.

109 *American Staffordshire terrier breed standard:* Staffordshire Terrier Club of America website: http://www.amstaff.org/standard.html. Retrieved February 23, 2019.

111 *dogs differ in trainability, reactivity:* See, e.g., Merkham, L. R., and C. D. L. Wynne. 2014. Behavioral differences among breeds of domestic dogs (Canis lupus familiaris): Current state of the science. *Applied Ani- mal Behaviour Science*, 155, 12–27.

111 breed differences in behavior: Hecht, J., and A. Horowitz. 2015. Introduction to dog behavior. In E. Weiss, H. Mohan-Gibbons, and S. Zawitowski, eds. *Animal Behavior for Shelter Veterinarians and Staff*, pp. 5–30.

112 bold, noble, etc.: http://www.akc.org. Retrieved October 19, 2017.

112 golden retriever breed standard: https://www.grca.org/about-the-breed/akc-breed-standard/.

112 "good with children": http://www.akc.org/dog-breeds/golden-retriever/. Retrieved October 8, 2017.

113 aggressive behavior of breeds: Ott, S. A., E. Schalke, A. M. von Gaertner, and H. Hackbarth. 2008. Is there a difference? Comparison of golden retrievers and dogs affected by breed-specific legislation regarding aggressive behavior. *Journal of Veterinary Behavior*, *3*, 134–140.

113 Afghan hound breed standard: The Afghan Hound Breed Club of America website: https://afghanhoundclubofamerica.org/index.php/information/breed-standard. Retrieved February 23, 2019.

113 Reykjavík, Iceland, ban on dogs: Billock, J. December 16, 2015. "Illegal in Iceland: Quirky Bans From the Land of Fire and Ice." Smithsonian.com.

113 the Spitz: May 24, 1876. "A whited canine sepulchre." *New York Times*.

114 dog bugaboos: Dickey 2016, pp. 112, 117, 130.

114 Cuban bloodhound: January 28, 1840. *Florida Herald*.

114 "a wave of hysteria": Serpell 2017, p. 310.

114 "Terrorists on four legs": June 4, 1989. *The Observer* (London), p. 13.

114 UK created breed-specific legislation: Taylor and Signal 2011.

114 banned dogs: See, e.g., https://petolog.com/articles/banned-dogs.html.

115 forbids any dog over twenty-five pounds: NYCHA pet policy. Revised April 2010.

115 Teddy Roosevelt had a bull terrier: Dickey 2016, p. 13.

115 what Teddy Roosevelt's bull terrier did: May 10, 1907. "Pete bites a visitor." *Washington Post*, p. 1; May 13, 1907. "President's dog licked." *The Tennessean*, p. 5; May 10, 1907. "Pete the bulldog gets a victim." *New York Times*, p. 1; May 11, 1907. "Plebian pup beats White House Pete." *New York Times*, p. 5.

115 history and confusion over pit bulls: Dickey 2016, pp. 157, 270.

116 Montreal breed ban: Dickey, B. October 11, 2016. "We're safer without pit bull bans." *Los Angeles Times*.

116 half of the dogs labeled pit bulls: Olson, K. R., J. K. Levy, B. Norby, et al. 2011. Pit bull–type dog identification in animal shelters. Fourth Annual Maddie's Shelter Medicine Conference.

116 identified "pit bull type": Olson, K. R., J. K. Levy, B. Norby, et al. 2015. Inconsistent identification of pit bull–type dogs by shelter staff. *The Veterinary Journal*, *206*, 197–202.

116 US v. UK identification: Hoffman, C. L., N. Harrison, L. Wolff, and C. Westgarth. 2014. Is that dog a pit bull? A cross-country comparison of perceptions of shelter workers regarding breed identification. *Journal of Applied Animal Welfare Science*, 17, 322–339.

116 *one drop of non-white blood:* Zimmer, C. 2018. *She Has Her Mother's Laugh: The Powers, Perversions, and Potential of Heredity*, p. 198.

117 *90 percent of breed identifications incorrect:* Voith, V. L., E. Ingram, K. Mitsouras, and K. Irizarry. 2009. Comparison of adoption agency breed identification and DNA breed identification of dogs. *Journal of Applied Animal Welfare Science, 12,* 253–262.

117 *unreliable visual identification:* Croy, K. C., J. K. Levy, K. R. Olson, et al. What kind or dog is that? Accuracy of dog breed assessment by canine stakeholders. http://sheltermedicine.vetmed.ufl.edu/library/research-studies/current-studies/dog-breeds/. Retrieved September 16, 2017.

117 *poor agreement with DNA findings:* Voith, V. L., R. Trevejo, S. Dowling-Guyer, et al. 2013. Comparison of visual and DNA breed identification of dogs and inter-observer reliability. *American Journal of Sociological Research, 3,* 17–29.

117 *Scott and Fuller:* Scott, J. P., and J. L. Fuller. 1965. *Genetics and the Social Behavior of the Dog.*

117 *breed bans don't work to reduce dog attacks:* Serpell 2017.

117 *Danish study:* Forkman, B., and I. C. Meyer. 2018. The effect of the Danish dangerous dog act on the level of dog aggressiveness in Denmark. Paper presented at International Society of Applied Ethology meeting, Prince Edward Island, Canada.

118 *research from the UK, Ireland, and Spain:* Creedon, N., and P. S. Ó Súilleabháin. 2017. Dog bite injuries to humans and the use of breed-specific legislation: A comparison of bites from legislated and non-legislated dog breeds. *Irish Veterinary Journal, 70,* 23; Gaines, S. 2017. Campaign to end BSL. *Veterinary Record, 180,* 126; Mora, E., G. M. Fonseca, P. Navarro, A. Castaño, and J. Lucena. 2018. Fatal dog attacks in Spain under a breed-specific legislation: A ten-year retrospective study. *Journal of Veterinary Behavior, 25,* 76–84.

118 *dachshunds:* See, e.g., Duffy, D. L., Y. Hsu, and J. A. Serpell. 2008. Breed differences in canine aggression. *Applied Animal Behaviour Science, 114,* 441–460.

118 *Boykin spaniel breed standard:* Boykin Spaniel Club website: http://theboykinspanielclub.com/2019_Revised_Boykin_Spaniel_Breed_Standard.pdf. Retrieved February 23, 2019.

118 *dog cloning:* For more on this topic, see, e.g., Brogan, J. March 22, 2018. "The real reasons you shouldn't clone your dog." Smithsonian.com; Duncan, D. E. August 7, 2018. "Inside the very big, very controversial business of dog cloning." *Vanity Fair*; Hecht, J. March 6, 2018. "The hidden dogs of dog cloning." Scientific American blog.

119 *German shorthaired pointer breed standard:* German Shorthaired Pointer Club of America website: http://www.gspca.org/Breed/Standard/index .html. Retrieved February 23, 2019.

120 *"the bulldog had a* face": Stephen Zawistowski, phone interview, July 18, 2017.

120 *bulldog appearance:* See Bateson 2010.

121 *we humans like animals that resemble us:* Hecht, J., and A. Horowitz. 2015. Seeing dogs: Human preferences for dog physical attributes. *Anthrozoös, 28,* 153–163.

121 *soft palate resection surgery:* See also BBC One's *Pedigree Dogs Exposed.*

122 *fifth most popular breed:* https://www.akc.org/expert-advice/news/most -popular-dog-breeds-full-ranking-list/. Retrieved October 5, 2018.

122 *"This type of dog is cute!":* Todd, Z. 2016. "Why do people choose certain dogs." http://www.companionanimalpsychology.com/2016/08/why-do -people-choose-certain-dogs.html?platform=hootsuite.

122 *most popular breeds have most genetic diseases:* Ghirlanda et al. 2013.

122 *American Airlines:* https://www.aa.com/i18n/travel-info/special-assis tance/pets.jsp.

123 *inherited disorders:* See, e.g., Hecht and Horowitz 2015; Bateson 2010.

124 *Great Dane size:* Taylor 1892 (note: early Great Danes were also called Ger man mastiffs); https://www.akc.org/dog-breeds/great-dane/. Retrieved August 7, 2018.

124 *"a distinction without a difference":* Bateson 2010, p. 15.

124 *Dalmatian outbreeding:* The breeder was Robert Schaible, and his story can be found here: http://www.dalmatianheritage.com/about/schaible _research.htm. Further information gathered from the breed fancier's website, https://luadalmatians-world.com/enus/dalmatian-articles/cross breeding.

125 *results of inbreeding.* Bateson 2010; see also Asher, L., G. Diesel, J. F. Summers, P. D. McGreevy, L. M. Collins. 2009. Inherited defects in ped igree dogs. Part 1: Disorders related to breed standards. *The Veterinary Journal, 182,* 402–411.

125 *Pedigree Dogs Exposed:* https://www.youtube.com/watch?v=T3QdR GnSGVI.

126 *Irish water spaniel breed standard:* Irish Water Spaniel Club of America website: https://www.iwsca.org/breedstandard.htm. Retrieved Febru ary 23, 2019.

126 *genetic disorders due to conformation to standards:* Asher et al. 2009.

127 *"society would shut them down":* Rollin, B. E., and M. D. H. Rollin. 2008. Dogmaticism and catechisms: Ethics and companion animals. In S. J. Armstrong and R. G. Botzler, eds. *The Animal Ethics Reader,* p. 548.

127 *on puppy mills:* ASCPA. "A closer look at puppy mills." https://www .aspca.org/animal-cruelty/puppy-mills/closer-look-puppy-mills-old.

127   *"puppy-breeding operations . . . treat dogs as livestock":* Grier 2006, p. 352.

127   *pet stores and puppy mills:* See, e.g., https://www.aspca.org/animal-cruelty /puppy-mills;   http://www.humanesociety.org/assets/facts-pet-stores -puppy-mills.pdf.

128   *AKC on puppy mills:* November 12, 2002. High Volume Breeders Committee Report to The American Kennel Club Board of Directors.

128   *"you can't help breeding":* Sandøe 2015.

128   *"future of domesticated animals . . .":* Sandøe, P., B. L. Nielsen, L. G. Christensen, and P. Sørensen. 1999. Staying good while playing god—the ethics of breeding farm animals. *Animal Welfare, 8,* 313–328.

129   *Puppy Heaven pet store:* http://www.puppyheaven.com/gallerycelebrity .html.

129   *AKC has long fought any restriction on commercial breeding:* Grier 2006, p. 270.

129   *"They don't want to get someone else's unwanted dog . . .":* Fortin, J. October 16, 2017. "California tells pet stores their dogs and cats must be rescues." *New York Times.*

130   *Dogue de Bordeaux breed standard:* https://www.akc.org/dog-breeds /dogue-de-bordeaux/. Retrieved February 23, 2019.

131   *an estimated ninety million dogs:* 89.7 million dogs, per American Pet Products survey, 2017–2018. There is debate about the robustness of this figure, and certainly it is not based on a census of individual dog heads.

131   *seven hundred million dogs:* Hughes, J., and D. W. Macdonald. 2013. A review of the interactions between free-roaming domestic dogs and wildlife. *Biological Conservation, 157,* 341–351.

131   *breeds have an average of over thirty-two inherited disorders:* Ghirlanda et al. 2013; Asher et al. 2009.

133   *Neapolitan mastiff breed standard:* United States Neapolitan Mastiff Club website: https://www.neapolitan.org/standard.html. Retrieved February 23, 2019.

133   *dogs who can raise their inner eyebrow are faster to be adopted:* Waller, B. M, K. Peirce, C. C. Caeiro, et al. 2013. Paedomorphic facial expressions give dogs a selective advantage. *PLOS ONE, 8,* e82686.

133   *Australian idea of an ideal dog:* King, T., L. C. Marston, and P. C. Bennett. 2009. Describing the ideal Australian companion dog. *Applied Animal Behaviour Science, 120,* 84–93.

THE SCIENTIFIC PROCESS
AS PRACTICED AT HOME WATCHING
DOGS ON A THURSDAY EVENING

138   *I've gone on to test—and even affirm—some of my favorite hypotheses:* Published as, respectively: "Disambiguating the guilty look: Salient prompts to a familiar dog behaviour" (2009); "Fair is fine but more is better: Limits to inequity aversion in the domestic dog" (2012); "Smelling them-

selves: Dogs investigate their own odours longer when modified in an 'olfactory mirror' test" (2017); see *Being a Dog: Following the Dog into a World of Smell* (2016); "Smelling more or less: Investigating the olfactory experience of the domestic dog" (2013); "Seeing dogs: Human preferences for dog physical attributes" (2015); "Examining dog-human play: The characteristics, affect, and vocalizations of a unique interspecific interaction" (2016).

DOG STUFF

148   *Canine Styles website:* https://www.caninestyles.com/.

149   *Leonardo Delfuoco Croc purse and pawbag:* https://www.today.com /money/luxury-handbags-go-dogs-2D79703332.

149   *Maschio dog cologne:* https://www.dogfashionspa.com/maschio-dog -cologne.

149   *dog nail polish and bathrobe:* https://www.dogfashionspa.com/dog-nail -polish-dog-nail-file-dog-nail-care.

150   *wealthy women played a sizeable role as breeders:* Grier 2006, p. 302.

150   *dogs have a "possessory interest in . . . a bone":* Cribbet, J. E., and C. W. Johnson. 1989. *Principles of the Law of Property* 4, 3rd ed., cited in Favre 2010.

151   *nineteenth-century pet stores:* Grier 2006, pp. 308–311.

151   *"cashing in":* Craftsman Dog Goods catalog, c. 1930.

151   *pet shops selling dog accoutrements:* As early as 1887: http://newspapers .com.

151   *pet-store names:* Grier 2006, p. 335; also *New York Daily Herald*, 1876; *Philadelphia Inquirer*, 1903.

151   *nineteenth-century pet store as smelly and noisy:* June 28, 1888. "Pretty things to pet." *Pittsburgh Press*, p. 1; also children: Grier 2006, p. 341.

151   *pet-store trade magazines:* Grier 2006, pp. 305, 349.

152   *"they also became consumers":* Grier 2006, pp. 304, 350, 352, 353, 398; also *Anaconda Standard* (Anaconda, Montana), October 25, 1892; *Brooklyn Daily Eagle*, October 24, 1889.

153   *earliest surviving imagery of dogs include collars and leashes:* http://www. sciencemag.org/news/2017/11/these-may-be-world-s-first-images-dogs -and-they-re-wearing-leashes.

153   *wall-relief art:* Johns, C. 2008. *Dogs: History, Myth, Art.*

153   *ancient Egyptian mummified dogs:* From 510 to 230 BCE. "Soulful creatures." Brooklyn Museum. 2018; https://www.brooklynmuseum.org /exhibitions/soulful_creatures_animal_mummies.

153   *Mesopotamian statue of a dog:* Pickeral, T. 2008. *The Dog: 5000 Years of the Dog in Art.*

153   *Egyptian collars:* Phillips, D. 1948. *Ancient Egyptian Animals*, p. 28.

153   *decorated collars:* Pickeral 2008, p. 30.

153   *spiked collars:* Kalof 2007; Grier 2006.

154 *"Who Dog Be You":* Grier 2006, p. 398.

155 *"A dog's collar should be suited to his breed":* Q-W Dog Remedies and Supplies, 1922.

155 *sizing needed for popular breeds:* Catalogue of Dog Furnishings. Walter B. Stevens & Son, Inc., 1920s.

155 *Blackout collar:* Abercrombie & Fitch catalog, 1942.

155 *choke collar: The Dog Breakers' Guide*, vol. 2, no. 10, 1878.

155 *Happidog muzzle:* Catalogue of Dog Furnishings. Walter B. Stevens & Son, Inc., 1920s.

156 *Henry VIII:* Walker-Meikle 2013, pp. 59, 64.

157 *"the dog house a dog would buy for himself":* Q-W Dog Remedies and Supplies, 1922, p. 46.

157 *chaise lounge:* Catalogue of Dog Furnishings. Walter B. Stevens & Son, Inc., 1920s.

157 *bunk bed:* Abercrombie & Fitch catalog, 1937.

158 Vogue *covers: Vogue* 1915; January 15, 1922.

158 *dog in tutu:* Q-W Dog Remedies and Supplies, 1922, p. 29.

158 *knitting patterns:* Grier 2006, p. 404.

159 *free display dog:* Craftsman Dog Goods catalog, c. 1930.

159 *brick exterior of High Ball pet shop:* Seen in photo in Grier 2006, p. 344.

160 *Plucking & Grooming Service:* Abercrombie & Fitch catalog, 1942.

160 *"Exercise for both master and dog":* Abercrombie & Fitch catalog, 1942.

160 *chocolate-scented toys:* Catalogue of Dog Furnishings. Walter B. Stevens & Son, Inc., 1920s.

161 *tooth forceps and tail shield:* Abercrombie & Fitch catalog, 1937, p. 14.

161 *bulldog spreader:* March 16, 1907. The American Stock Keeper (Boston).

162 *auto-stop, dog goggles:* Q-W Dog Remedies and Supplies, 1922.

163 *Middle Ages dog diet:* Walker-Meikle 2013, pp. 37, 44.

163 *"Good sound biscuit for dogs and hogs":* October 18, 1819. *The Times* (London).

164 *"dogs' food":* See, e.g., September 22, 1829, *Morning Post*, p. 1.

164 *biscuits were to be soaked:* February 5, 1825. *Jackson's Oxford Journal*.

164 *James Spratt:* Grier 2006, p. 367.

164 *multibillion-dollar annual industry:* American Pet Products Association. 2017.

164 *other fledgling biscuit brands:* See, e.g., March 16, 1907. American Stock Keeper (Boston), vol. 36, no. 11.

165 *"A guide to the choice of the correct biscuit":* 1911. The Kennel (UK).

165 *competing dog food companies:* 1911. The Kennel (UK); Grier 2006; Abercrombie & Fitch catalog, 1937.

165 *dog "crackers":* Abercrombie & Fitch catalog, 1937.

166 *dog food diets:* See, e.g., March 24, 1897, *New York Times*, p. 8; Dog biscuits—e.g., Champion Dog biscuits—made the same appeal. See, e.g., March 11, 1925, *Indiana* (PA) *Progress*.

166   *reducing the "strong odor" of dogs:* Spratt's charcoal ovals.

166   *Maltoid Milk Bones:* November 15, 1910. *Hartford Courant*, p. 6.

166   *special food for puppies:* Spratt's catalog. 1876, p. 103.

166   *convenience:* Grier 2006.

166   *granulated dog food:* January 28, 1887. *Nottinghamshire Guardian*, p. 1.

166   *Rin-Tin-Tin's food:* December 1, 1926. *Belvidere Daily Republican*, p. 5.

167   *Lassie's food:* April 14, 1949. *Chicago Tribune*, part 3, p. 12.

167   *middlings:* See, e.g., Fifty-sixth annual report of the Secretary of the State Board of Agriculture of the State of Michigan, 1917.

167   *slaughterhouse slurry:* Grier 2006.

168   *Wysong decision:* Wysong Corporation v. APN, Inc.; Big Heart Pet Brands and J. M. Smucker Company; Hill's Pet Nutrition, Inc.; Mars Petcare U.S., Inc.; Nestlé Purina Petcare Company; Wal-Mart Stores, Inc., Defendants-Appellees. United States Court of Appeals for the Sixth Circuit. May 2, 2018.

168   *"dogs are not always able to distinguish between what is good for them":* Spratt's pamphlet.

168   *"why bother with a lot of fuss and muss":* "How to care for your new dog." Purina Dog Care pamphlet.

168   *pampering the dog with "dainties":* The common sense of dog doctoring. Spratt's Patent Limited. 1886.

168   *"Under no circumstances of health does any dog require other food":* The common sense of dog doctoring. Spratt's Patent Limited. 1886, p. 111.

169   *"starve an exceptionally obstinate dog":* Spratt's pamphlet.

169   *"Unlawful to use for human beings":* Q-W Dog Remedies and Supplies, 1922.

170   *proper house manners:* Abercrombie & Fitch catalog, 1937.

170   *To teach a dog to stay in the yard:* "How to care for your new dog." Purina Dog Care pamphlet.

THE DOG IN THE MIRROR

173   *Derrida's cat:* Derrida, J. 2008. "The animal that therefore I am." D. Wills, trans., pp. 4, 50.

175   *"Never say higher or lower":* Gould, S. J. 1996. *Full House: The Spread of Excellence from Plato to Darwin*, p. 137.

175   *"Are humans special among all other animals":* Wasserman, E. A., and T. R. Zentall. 2012. "Introduction." In *Introduction to the Oxford Handbook of Comparative Cognition*, p. 7.

176   *"Here is Plato's man!":* Branham, R. B., and M. O. Goulet-Cazé, eds. 2000. *The Cynics: The Cynic Movement in Antiquity and Its Legacy*, p. 88.

176   *"Now we must redefine tool . . .":* http://www.janegoodall.org.uk/chimpan zees/chimpanzee-central/15-chimpanzees/chimpanzee-central/19-tool making. Retrieved April 12, 2018.

177 *list of distinctive human traits:* I've written a little more about this here: "Are humans unique?" www.psychologytoday.com/us/blog/minds-animals /200907/are-humans-unique.

177 *humans split from chimps and bonobos:* http://www.pbs.org/wgbh/nova /evolution/first-primates-expert-q.html.

177 *primate/canid evolutionary split:* See, e.g., G. E. Lu et al. 2006. Genomic divergences among cattle, dog and human estimated from large-scale alignments of genomic sequences. *BMC Genomics*, 7, 140. See also time tree.org's estimation of divergence between Carnivora and Primates.

178 *dogs making eye contact:* Now widely documented, among the first published works showing dogs' skills at social cognition was Brian Hare, who had been studying chimps. May I send you to *Inside of a Dog* to read about the myriad of other social-cognition experiments done since that impress us all? So I shall.

179 *match a picture of a purebred dog with the dog's person:* Roy, M. M., and N. J. S. Christenfeld. 2004. Do dogs resemble their owners? *Psychological Science*, 15, 361–363; Roy, M. M., and N. J. S. Christenfeld. 2005. Dogs still do resemble their owners. *Psychological Science*, 16, 9; Nakajima, S., M. Yamamoto, and N. Yoshimoto. 2015. Dogs look like their owners: Replications with racially homogenous owner portraits. *Anthrozoös*, 22, 173–181; Payne, C., and K. Jaffe. 2005. Self seeks like: Many humans choose their dog pets following rules used for assortative mating. *Journal of Ethology*, 23, 15–18.

179 *"goofy guy, smiling":* Bhattacharya, S. 2004. Dogs do resemble their owners, finds study. *New Scientist.*

180 *letters of our name & numbers of our birthday:* Jones, J. T., B. W. Pelham, M. C. Mirenberg, and J. J. Hetts. 2002. Name letter preferences are not merely mere exposure: Implicit egotism as self-regulation. *Journal of Experimental Social Psychology*, 38, 170–177.

180 *sit near people resembling us:* Mackinnon, S. P., C. H. Jordan, and A. E. Wilson. 2011. Birds of a feather sit together: Physical similarity predicts seating choice. *Personality and Social Psychology Bulletin,* 37, 879–892.

180 *levels of extraversion and agreeableness match between person and pup:* Turcsán, B., F. Range, Z. Virányi, A. Miklósi, and E. Kubinyi. 2012. Birds of a feather flock together? Perceived personality matching in owner-dog dyads. *Applied Animal Behaviour Science*, 140, 154–160.

181 *low neuroticism, high cortisol variability:* Schöberl, I., M. Wedl, A. Beetz, K. Kotrschal. 2017. Psychobiological factors affecting cortisol variability in human-dog dyads. *PLOS ONE*, 12, e0170707.

181 *Chaplin and Scraps:* https://www.youtube.com/watch?v=txSJDmt4u6Q.

181 *We like person-looking dogs:* Hecht and Horowitz 2015, pp. 153–163.

181 *teddy bears:* Hinde, R. A., and L. A. Barden. 1985. The evolution of the teddy bear. *Animal Behaviour*, 33, 1371–1373.

181 *Mickey Mouse:* Gould, S. J. 1979. Mickey Mouse meets Konrad Lorenz. *Natural History*, *88*, 30–36.

181 *Lorenz on preference for baby-like features:* Lorenz, K. (1950) 1971. Ganzheit und Teil in der tierischen und menschlichen Gemeinschaft. Reprinted in R. Martin, ed., *Studies in Animal and Human Behaviour*, vol. 2, pp. 115–195.

181 *charismatic species:* Kellert, S. R. 1996. *The Value of Life: Biological Diversity and Human Society.*

181 *dogs synchronize with us:* Duranton, C., T. Bedossa, and F. Gaunet. 2017. Interspecific behavioural synchronization: Dogs present locomotor synchrony with humans. *Scientific Report*, *7*, 12384.

182 *"amplify and enlarge aspects of ourselves":* McDonald, H. May 16, 2017. "What animals taught me about being human." *New York Times.*

182 *dogs as "pseudo-humans":* Fudge 2008, p. 2.

182 *"[A]ny suggestion that the pet might be motivated . . .":* Serpell, J. 2003. Anthropomorphism and anthropomorphic selection: Beyond the "cute response." *Society & Animals*, *11*, 83–100.

183 *"there was no doubt that we were men":* Levinas, E. 1997. The name of a dog, or Natural rights. In S. Hand, trans., *Difficult Freedom: Essays on Judaism.*

184 *the first anthropomorphisms:* Horowitz, A. C., and M. Bekoff. 2007. Naturalizing anthropomorphism: Behavioral prompts to our humanizing of animals. *Anthrozoös*, *20*, 23–35.

185 *"spasms of horror and outrage":* Serpell 2017, p. 311.

185 *deaths due to dog attacks:* See, e.g., Langley, R. L. 2009. Human fatalities resulting from dog attacks in the United States, 1979–2005. *Wilderness & Environmental Medicine*, *20*, 19–25; The Center for Disease Control numbers for years since are commensurate.

185 *deaths by salmonella poisoning:* Twenty-nine in 2010, per The Center for Disease Control. https://www.livescience.com/3780-odds-dying .html.

185 *risk of death by falling out of bed:* Per 2014 National Safety Council numbers indicating 38 dog-bite deaths and 1,045 bed-falling deaths. Johnson, R., and L. Gamio. November 17, 2014. "Ebola is the least of your worries." *Washington Post.* The CDC reports that the number of deaths by "fall involving bed" were 13,312 from 1999–2017, about 739 a year. https://wonder.cdc.gov.

187 *to share a space without knowing how the other is sharing it:* This alludes to lines the character Costello says in Coetzee, J. M. 1999. *The Lives of Animals.*

187 *million-plus shelter dogs:* Serpell 2017, p. 310.

188 *tail docking, ear cropping, and bark softening:* See http://www.akc.org /expert-advice/news/issue-analysis-dispelling-myths/. Retrieved August

22, 2018. An incredible document, its claims resoundingly unsupported by evidence and, indeed, discounted by scientific consensus—stating, for instance, that tail docking is not painful because it is "performed shortly after birth, when the puppy's nervous system is not fully developed. As a result, the puppy feels little to no pain, and there are no lasting negative health issues." (On the question of pain, one scientific study of puppies having their tails docked reported that "shrieking" was present in all puppies, with an average of 24 shrieks per puppy during the procedure.) (Noonan, G. J., J. S. Rand, J. K. Blackshaw, and J. Priest. 1996. Behavioural observations of puppies undergoing tail docking. *Applied Animal Behaviour Science, 49,* 335-342.) (On the topic of pain and docking, see also Bennett, P. C., and E. Perini. 2003. Tail docking in dogs: A review of the issues. *Australian Veterinary Journal, 81*, 208–218; Mathews, K. A. 2008. Pain management for the pregnant, lactating and pediatric cat and dog. *Veterinary Clinics of North America Small Animal Practices, 38*, 1291–1308; Patterson-Kane, E. 2017. Canine Tail Docking Independent Report Prepared for the Ministry for Primary Industries: Technical Report; Turner, P. 2010. Tail docking and ear cropping—A reply. *Canadian Veterinary Journal, 51*, 1057–1058; Wansbrough, R. K. 1996. Cosmetic tail docking of dogs. *Australian Veterinay Journal, 74,* 59–63.)

The AKC document's claim that "ear cropping and tail docking (. . .) preserves a dog's ability to perform its historic function" ignores relevant information such as that docking was done to distinguish *non*-working dogs prior to the nineteenth century in England: tails were docked not for "historic" accuracy but to avoid a "tail tax" (Wansbrough 1996).

188   *dogs used in research:* 2016: United States Department of Agriculture, Animal and Plant Health Inspection Service, Annual Report Animal Usage by Fiscal Year; 2017: Favre, personal communication.

189   *dogs used in "experiments, teaching, research, surgery, or tests . . .":* See "Public Search Tool" on https://www.aphis.usda.gov/aphis/ourfocus/animal welfare/sa_awa/awa-inspection-and-annual-reports.

189   *sport of dogs harassing and killing animals:* Kalof 2007; also Dickey 2016.

189   *USDA report on Vick:* http://aldf.org/resources/laws-cases/animal-fight ing-case-study-michael-vick/.

190   *pet dog cages are pink:* A. Podberscek 2009, in Serpell 2017, p. 306.

190   *Video of dog-meat farms:* https://www.usatoday.com/story/sports/winter -olympics-2018/2018/02/12/inside-grim-scene-korean-dog-meat-farm -miles-winter-olympics/328322002/.

DOES MY DOG LOVE ME?

202   *Seligman's learned helplessness experiment:* Overmier, J. B., and M. E. P. Seligman. 1967. Effects of inescapable shock on subsequent escape and

avoidance learning. *Journal of Comparative and Physiological Psychology*, *63*, 28–33.

204 *forced swim/despair test:* McArthur, R., and F. Borsini. 2006. Animal models of depression in drug discovery: A historical perspective. *Pharmacology Biochemistry & Behaviour*, *84*, 436–452.

205 *"rendering or preventing depressive-like states":* Can, A., D. T. Dao, M. Arad, C. E. Terrillion, et al. 2012. The mouse forced swim test. *Journal of Visualized Experiments*, e3638.

205 *Dogs are included to heighten the sense of reality of a scene:* The "reality effect": Barthes, R. 1986. *The Rustle of Language.*

207 *tale of greyhound and baby:* See, e.g., Ibn al-Marzubān. The superiority of dogs over many of those who wear clothes. In A. Mikhail's *The Animal in Ottoman Egypt*, pp. 76–78; S. de Bourbon's De Supersticione: On St. Guinefort; W. R. Spencer's Beth Gêlert; and others.

208 *"a dog looks on his master as a god":* Darwin, C. 1871. *The Descent of Man*, and Selection in relation to sex, vol. 1, p. 66.

208 *the "guilty look":* Horowitz, A. 2009. Disambiguating the "guilty look": Salient prompts to a familiar dog behavior. *Behavioural Processes*, *81*, 447–452; Hecht, J., Á. Miklósi, M. Gácsi. 2012. Behavioural assessment and owner perceptions of behaviours associated with guilt in dogs. *Applied Animal Behaviour Science*, *139*, 134–142.

208 *emotional support dogs:* See, e.g., Crossman, M. K. 2017. Effects of interactions with animals on human psychological distress. *Journal of Clinical Psychology*, *73*, 761–784.

209 *some dogs stop performing a trick:* Range, F., L. Horn, Z. Virányi, and L. Huber. 2008. The absence of reward induces inequity aversion in dogs. *Proceedings of the National Academy of Sciences of the United States of America*, *106*, 340–345.

209 *dogs' pure optimism:* Horowitz, A. 2012. Fair is fine, but more is better: Limits to inequity aversion in the domestic dog. *Social Justice Research*, *25*, 195–212.

210 *they might feel empathetic, but just not to you:* Quervel-Chaumette, M., G. Mainix, F. Range, S. Marshall-Pescini. 2016. Dogs do not show prosocial preferences towards humans. *Frontiers of Psychology, 7,* 1416.

210 *"man himself cannot express love and humility . . .":* Darwin, C. 1872. The expression of the emotions in man and animals, pp. 10–11.

AGAINST SEX

214 *for every one of the hundred dogs you see, eighteen healthy dogs are euthanized:* As discussed later in the chapter, precise euthanasia numbers are notoriously hard to come by. This number is based on the figure of 670,000 dogs killed, from the ASPCA in 2017: https://www.aspca.org/animal-homeless ness/shelter-intake-and-surrender/pet-statistics. Retrieved May 8, 2017.

214 *hundreds of millions:* Another difficult-to-measure number. In 2011 the World Health Organization, concerned with rabies, estimated 200 million: http://www.naiaonline.org/articles/article/the-global-stray-dog-popula tion-crisis-and-humane-relocation#sthash.3xG5GVNv.btP8rtlv.dpbs.

215 *De-sexing is a given:* See, e.g., Bruce Fogle, in Kerasote 2013; Pukka's promise: The quest for longer-lived dogs, p. 345.

215 *"For the urban dog at any rate expectation of sex is slender . . .":* Ackerley, J. R. 1965/1999. *My Dog Tulip,* p. 175.

215 *ovariohysterectomy:* https://www.avma.org/public/PetCare/Pages/spay -neuter.aspx.

216 *"responsible pet owners":* See, e.g., American Veterinarian Medical Association: "responsible pet owners can make a difference." https://www .avma.org/public/PetCare/Pages/spay-neuter.aspx.

217 *compared unfavorably to Michael Vick:* Kerasote 2013, p. 331.

217 *"Spay-neuter" laws:* https://www.avma.org/Advocacy/StateAndLocal /Pages/sr-spay-neuter-laws.aspx. Retrieved July 5, 2017.

218 *The phrase "spay-neuter":* In 1972 "spay or neuter" makes its first appearance in the *New York Times:* Beck, A. M. November 12, 1972. "Packs of stray dogs part of the Brooklyn scene." Before that, there were "spay" and "neuter" classes of cats in cat shows, and occasional "spay or neuter" references in the late '60s.

218 *He urges "all pet owners to SPAY. . .":* August 10, 1967. "Bick's action line." *Cincinnati Enquirer.* For the evolution of de-sexing policy I also drew from the thorough history in Grier 2006.

218 *history of spay-neuter (and shelters):* Grier 2006, pp. 102ff; Stephen Zawistowski. 2008. *Companion Animals in Society.*

218 *"emasculator":* White, G. R. 1914. *Animal Castration: A Book for the Use of Students and Practitioners.*

218 *after World War II:* Stephen Zawistowski, personal communication, July 18, 2017.

218 *first spay-neuter clinics:* May 14, 1972. "Solving the pet explosion." *San Francisco Examiner;* May 12, 1973. "Spay neuter unit to open Friday." *Los Angeles Times.*

218 *the cost of killing the thirteen million strays:* Carden, L. May 30, 1973. "Abandonment: Dog's life, human problem." *Christian Science Monitor,* p. 1.

219 *The Mike Douglas Show:* Lane, M. S., and S. Zawistowski. 2008. *Heritage of Care: The American Society for the Prevention of Cruelty to Animals,* p. 40.

219 *early NYC dog pounds:* July 6, 1877. "Destroying the dogs." *New York Times,* p. 8; Brady, B. 2012. The politics of the pound: Controlling loose dogs in nineteenth-century New York City. *Jefferson Journal of Science and Culture, 2,* 9–25.

220 *Los Angeles spay-neuter laws:* The Los Angeles County Code, Section 10.20.350. https://www.lacounty.gov/residents/animals-pets/spay-neuter.

220 *fine for transgressions*: American Veterinary Medical Association. https://www.avma.org/Advocacy/StateAndLocal/Pages/sr-spay-neuter-laws.aspx.

220 *over one hundred thousand animals a year:* Rowan, A., and T. Kartal. 2018. Dog population & dog sheltering trends in the United States of America. *Animals*, *8*, 68–88.

221 *"Certain types of cancers are eliminated by spaying or neutering":* Los Angeles County Animal Care & Control. http://animalcare.lacounty.gov/spay-and-neuter/. Retrieved August 10, 2018.

221 *New York de-sexing laws:* New York Consolidated Laws, Agriculture and Markets Law AGM § 377-a: Spaying and neutering of dogs and cats.

222 *a de-sexed animal will "live a longer, healthier life":* http://www.animalalliancenyc.org/yourpet/spayneuter.htm. Retrieved August 10, 2018.

222 *"Spaying also prevents unwanted animals from being born":* https://www.nycacc.org/sites/default/files/pdfs/adoptions/DogPassport.pdf. Retrieved February 22, 2019.

222 *laws require that pit bulls be spayed or neutered:* http://blog.dogsbite.org/2010/06/cities-with-successful-pit-bull-laws.html.

223 *number of euthanized animals:* Various sources, e.g., July/August 2008. "Gains in most regions against cat and dog surplus, but no sudden miracles." *Animal People*; Serpell 2017 (citing ASPCA 2014); ASPCA. https://www.aspca.org/animal-homelessness/shelter-intake-and-surrender/pet-statistics. Retrieved May 8, 2017; Stephen Zawistowski, personal communication, July 18, 2017.

223 *2018 report:* Rowan and Kartal 2018.

224 *"overground pet railroad":* Brulliard, K. May 13, 2017. "These rescuers take shelter animals on road trips to help them find new homes." *Washington Post.*

224 *other societal changes have also affected euthanization rates:* Rowan and Kartal 2018.

224 *no effect of opening a subsidized spay-neuter clinic:* Scarlett, J., and N. Johnston. 2012. Impact of a subsidized spay neuter clinic on impoundments and euthanasia in a community shelter and on service and complaint calls to Animal Control. *Journal of Applied Animal Welfare Science*, *1*, 53–69.

225 *"you will do your part":* https://www.avma.org/public/PetCare/Pages/spay-neuter.aspx. Retrieved May 18, 2017.

226 *56 percent of owned dogs being overweight or obese:* For US: https://petobesityprevention.org/2017; see also P. Sandøe, C. Palmer, S. Corr, et al. 2014. Canine and feline obesity: A One Health perspective. *Veterinary Record*, *175*, 610–616.

226 *metabolism of de-sexed dogs slows:* Oberbauer, A. 2017. International Society for Anthrozoology conference, Effective options regarding spay or

neuter of dogs, Davis, California; Belanger, J. M., T. P. Bellumori, D. L. Bannasch, et al. 2017. Correlation of neuter status and expression of heritable disorders. *Canine Genetics and Epidemiology*, *4*, 6; Lund, E. M., P. J. Armstrong, C. A. Kirk, and J. S. Klausner. 2006. Prevalence and risk factors for obesity in adult dogs from private US veterinary practices. *International Journal of Applied Veterinary Medicine*, *4*, 3–5.

226   *"Lake* [sic] *of exercise or overfeeding":* http://www.animalalliancenyc.org /yourpet/spayneuter.htm. Retrieved August 10, 2018.

227   *"around 25 per cent less":* See, e.g., http://newscenter.purina.com/Life SpanStudy.

227   *less likelihood of torn ligaments:* See also Karen Becker, in Kerasote 2013.

227   *illegal* to *de-sex a dog in Norway:* Korneliussen, I. December 29, 2011. "Should dogs be neutered?" *ScienceNordic.*

227   *Norwegian Animal Welfare Act:* https://www.animallaw.info/statute /noway-cruelty-norwegian-animal-welfare-act-2010#s9. Retrieved August 10, 2018.

228   *80 percent of US dogs de-sexed:* Humane Society of the United States, via D. Quenqua. December 2, 2013. "New strides in spaying and neutering." *New York Times.*

228   *Switzerland's Animal Protection Act:* Swiss Federal Food Safety and Veterinary Office. "Dignity of the animal." https://www.blv.admin.ch/blv /en/home/tiere/tierschutz/wuerde-des-tieres.html. Retrieved August 10, 2018.

228   *"Neutering can never be a substitute . . .":* Korneliussen 2011.

228   *rate of dogs de-sexed in underserved communities:* http://www.humanesociety .org/issues/pet_overpopulation/facts/pet_ownership_statistics.html.

229   *"basic biology suggests . . .":* Hart, B. 2017. International Society for Anthrozoology conference. Effective options regarding spay or neuter of dogs. Davis, California.

229   *Various effects of hormones:* Role of estrogen on learning, memory, and mood: Gillies, G. E., and S. McArthur. 2010. Estrogen actions in the brain and the basis for differential action in men and women: A case for sex-specific medicines. *Pharmacological Reviews*, *62*, 155–198; estrogen in growth and development of bone: Väänänen, H. K., and P. L. Härkönen. 1996. Estrogen and bone metabolism. *Maturitas*, *23 Suppl*, S65–69; testosterone on increasing muscle mass: Griggs, R. C., W. Kingston, R. F. Jozefowicz, et al. 1989. Effect of testosterone on muscle mass and muscle protein synthesis. *Journal of Applied Physiology*, *66*, 498–503; progesterone as "neuroprotective": Wei, J., and G. Xiao. 2013. The neuroprotective effects of progesterone on traumatic brain injury: Current status and future prospects. *Acta Pharmacologica Sinica*, *34*, 1485–1490.

229   *dogs at the Penn Vet Working Dog Center:* Cindy Otto, personal communication, July 9, 2018.

229   *uptick in dogs with adrenal dysfunction:* Kerasote 2013, pp. 333–334.

230 *"might trigger metastatic cells"*: Hart 2017. For more on the biology: Zink, C. 2013. Early spay-neuter considerations for the canine athlete: One veterinarian's opinion, http://www.caninesports.com; Sandøe, P., S. Corr, and C. Palmer. 2016. Routine neutering of companion animals. In *Companion Animal Ethics*, pp. 150–168.

230 *rates of diseases post de-sexing:* Hart 2017.

231 *rates of age-related cognitive impairment:* Hart, B. 2001. Effect of gonadectomy on subsequent development of age-related cognitive impairment in dogs. *Journal of the American Veterinary Medical Association*, *219*, 51–56.

231 *reduction in unwanted behaviors post de-sexing:* Hart 2017.

232 *risks of surgery:* Sandøe et al. 2016.

232 *rate of death by anesthesia:* Accounts of the rates of mortality during anesthesia vary by an exponent, probably due to uncontrolled situational differences between studies. But this 1 percent figure is borne out in a number of them, e.g., Bille, C., V. Auvigne, S. Libermann, et al. 2012. Risk of anaesthetic mortality in dogs and cats: An observational cohort study of 3546 cases. *Veterinary Anaesthesia and Analgesia*, *39*, 59–68.

236 *grants for research leading to development of an affordable chemical sterilant:* https://www.michelsonprizeandgrants.org/. Retrieved August 10, 2018.

237 *vasectomy, tubal ligation, and hysterectomy:* Alliance for Contraception for Cats and Dogs. http://www.acc-d.org/research-innovation /non-surgical-approaches; Mowatt, T. June 2011. "The 'pill' for strays: Nonsurgical sterilization: New approaches to overpopulation." The Bark; Quenqua 2013; 2017. International Society for Anthrozoology conference. Effective options regarding spay or neuter of dogs. Davis, California.

237 *their bodies cannot maintain core temperature under anesthesia:* See, e.g., Fox, L. K., M. C. Flegal, and S. M. Kuhlman. 2009. Principles of anesthesia monitoring—body temperature. *Journal of Investigative Surgery*, *21*, 373–374; Clutton, R. E. 2017. Limiting heat loss during surgery in small animals. *Veterinary Record*, *180*.

237 *"a hindrance to population control":* Miller, L., and S. Zawistowski. 2017. Animal shelter medicine: Dancing to a changing tune. *Veterinary Heritage*, *40*, 44–49.

238 *"consulting with veterinarians for information":* https://www.avma.org /KB/Policies/Pages/Dog-And-Cat-Population-Control.aspx. Retrieved August 8, 2017.

240 *"The thought's obvious if you think about someone wanting to spay* you": Kagan, S. May 10, 2017. "How much should we care about animals?" Roundtable, Columbia University.

241 *"look at every animal as an animal":* Sandøe 2015.

243 *"it was recognised that animals can be frustrated . . .":* Sandøe 2015.

243 *Neuticles:* http://www.neuticles.com. Retrieved November 1, 2018.

244 *"He'll be smaller, or not muscular, more girly"*: White, R. August 18, 2013. Cutting edgy. *New York Post.*

244 *"A bitch in estrus is very messy . . ."*: Oberbauer 2017.

244 *gonadectomy of monkeys:* Richards, A. B., R. W. Morris, S. Ward, et al. 2009. Gonadectomy negatively impacts social behavior of adolescent male primates. *Hormones and Behavior*, 56, 140–148.

245 *male dogs preferred by law enforcement:* Cindy Otto, personal communication, August 3, 2017.

245 *spaying female search-and-rescue dogs:* Jones, K. E., K. Dashfield, A. B. Downend, and C. M. Otto. 2004. Search-and-rescue dogs: An overview for veterinarians. *JAVMA*, 225, 854–860.

247 *"not a dog problem, it's a human problem"*: Carden 1973.

247 *a shelter does not truly shelter animals . . . :* Rollin, B. E. 2011. *Putting the Horse before Descartes: My Life's Work on Behalf of Animals*, p. 55.

247 *dog breeds that appear in movies:* Herzog, H. 2014. Biology, culture, and the origins of pet-keeping. *Animal Behavior and Cognition*, 1, 296–308.

248 *how we act toward them is not "morally irrelevant"*: Kagan, S. 2016. What's wrong with speciesism? (Society for Applied Philosophy annual lecture 2015). *Journal of Applied Philosophy*, 33.

HUMORLESS

253 *"I stole mail. This is my punishment"*: Ziel, P. 2005. Eighteenth century public humiliation penalties in twenty-first century America: The "shameful" return of "Scarlet letter" punishments in U.S. v. Gementera. *BYU Journal of Public Law*, 19, 499–522.

254 *a dissenting justice in the mail-theft case:* Judge Hawkins. 2004. United States v. Gementera. U.S. Court of Appeals for the Ninth Circuit, 379 F.3d 596.

255 *dignity-robbing acts:* Gruen, L. 2014. Dignity, captivity, and an ethics of sight. In L. Gruen, ed. *The Ethics of Captivity*, ch. 14.

255 *zoomies:* Lindsay, S. 2005. *Handbook of Applied Dog Behavior and Training*, vol. 3, p. 322.

256 *"isolation through captivity"*: Hediger, H. 1964. *Wild Animals in Captivity: An Outline of the Biology of ZoologicalGardens.*

256 *dogs at the Bristol Zoological Garden and as companions:* Flack, A. January 24, 2012. Dogs in zoos: Marking new territory. https://sniffingthepast .wordpress.com/2012/01/24/dogs-in-zoos-marking-new-territory/.

256 *dogs and cheetahs at the San Diego Zoo:* http://zoo.sandiegozoo.org/ani mals/cheetah.

257 *captivity:* Some of this section draws from my 2014 essay, *Canis familiaris*: Companion and captive. In Gruen 2014, pp. 7–21.

257 *enable that animal to flourish—at whatever "sort of thing" it is:* Nussbaum 2004.

TAIL OF THE DOG

259 *seventy-billion-dollar pet industry business:* 2017. American Pet Products. https://www.americanpetproducts.org/press_industrytrends.asp.

260 *language of dog words:* "Adulation" and "hangdog" come from Barnette, M. 2003. *Dog Days and Dandelions: A Lively Guide to the Animal Meanings behind Everyday Words*; "You old dog" via *Green's Dictionary of Slang*. For more on doggy words see Serpell 2017; see also Pfister, D. S. 2017. Against the droid's "instrument of efficiency," for animalizing technologies in a posthumanist spirit. *Philosophy & Rhetoric*, *50*, 201–227.

261 *the animal's "natural" state:* Horta, O. 2010. Debunking the idyllic view of natural processes: Population dynamics and suffering in the wild. *Télos*, *17*, 73–88.

Index

Alexandra Horowitz is the author of three previous books, *Being a Dog: Following the Dog Into a World of Smell* (2016); *On Looking* (2013); and *Inside of a Dog: What Dogs See, Smell, and Know* (2009), a *New York Times* bestseller. She is Senior Research Fellow and head of the Dog Cognition Lab at Barnard College, Columbia University. She is owned by canines Finnegan and Upton, and tolerated by feline Edsel.

Turn the page to read the first pages of
Alexandra Horowitz's #1 *New York Times* bestseller

INSIDE OF A DOG

WHAT DOGS SEE, SMELL, AND KNOW

and

BEING A DOG

FOLLOWING THE DOG INTO A WORLD OF SMELL

A *Science Friday*, *Forbes*, and *Library Journal*
Best Science Book of the Year

Both available from Scribner in your favorite format

From *Inside of a Dog*

Prelude

First you see the head. Over the crest of the hill appears a muzzle, drooling. It is as yet not visibly attached to anything. A limb jangles into view, followed in unhasty succession by a second, third, and fourth, bearing a hundred and forty pounds of body between them. The wolfhound, three feet at his shoulder and five feet to his tail, spies the long-haired Chihuahua, half a dog high, hidden in the grasses between her owner's feet. The Chihuahua is six pounds, each of them trembling. With one languorous leap, his ears perked high, the wolfhound arrives in front of the Chihuahua. The Chihuahua looks demurely away; the wolfhound bends down to Chihuahua level and nips her side. The Chihuahua looks back at the hound, who raises his rear end up in the air, tail held high, in preparation to attack. Instead of fleeing from this apparent danger, the Chihuahua matches his pose and leaps onto the wolfhound's face, embracing his nose with her tiny paws. They begin to play.

For five minutes these dogs tumble, grab, bite, and lunge at each other. The wolfhound throws himself onto his side and the little dog responds with attacks to his face, belly, and paws. A swipe by the hound sends the Chihuahua scurrying backward, and she timidly sidesteps out of his reach. The hound barks, jumps up, and arrives back on his feet with a thud. At this, the Chihuahua races toward one of those feet and bites it, hard. They are in mid-embrace—the hound with his mouth surrounding the body of the Chihuahua, the Chihuahua kicking back at the hound's face—when an owner snaps a leash on the hound's collar and pulls him upright and away. The Chihuahua rights herself, looks after them, barks once, and trots back to her owner.

These dogs are so incommensurable with each other that they may as well be different species. The ease of play between them always puzzled me. The wolfhound bit, mouthed, and charged at the Chihuahua; yet the little dog responded not with fright but in kind. What explains their ability to play together? Why doesn't the hound see the Chihuahua as prey? Why doesn't the Chihuahua see the wolfhound as predator? The answer turns out to have nothing to do with the Chihuahua's delusion of canine grandeur or the hound's lack of predatory drive. Neither is it simply hardwired instinct taking over.

There are two ways to learn how play works—and what playing dogs are thinking, perceiving, and saying: be born as a dog, or spend a lot of time carefully observing dogs. The former was unavailable to me. Come along as I describe what I've learned by watching.

I am a dog person.

My home has always had a dog in it. My affinity for dogs began with our family dog, Aster, with his blue eyes, lopped tail, and nighttime neighborhood ramblings that often left me up late, wearing pajamas and worry, waiting for his midnight return. I long mourned the death of Heidi, a springer spaniel who ran with excitement—my childhood imagination had her tongue trailing out of the side of her mouth and her long ears blown back with the happy vigor of her run—right under a car's tires on the state highway near our home. As a college student, I gazed with admiration and affection at an adopted chow mix Beckett as she stoically watched me leave for the day.

And now at my feet lies the warm, curly, panting form of Pumpernickel—*Pump*—a mutt who has lived with me for all of her sixteen years and through all of my adulthood. I have begun every one of my days in five states, five years of graduate school, and four jobs with her tail-thumping greeting when she hears me stir in the morning. As anyone who considers himself a dog person will recognize, I cannot imagine my life without this dog.

I am a dog person, a lover of dogs. I am also a scientist.

I study animal behavior. Professionally, I am wary of anthropomorphizing animals, attributing to them the feelings, thoughts, and desires that we use to describe ourselves. In learning how to study the behavior of animals, I was taught and adhered to the scientist's code for describing actions: be objective; do not explain a behavior by appeal to a mental process when explanation by simpler processes will do; a phenomenon that is not publicly observable and confirmable is not the stuff of science. These days, as a professor of animal behavior, comparative cognition, and psychology, I teach from masterful texts that deal in quantifiable fact. They describe everything from hormonal and genetic explanations for the social behavior of animals, to conditioned responses, fixed action patterns, and optimal foraging rates, in the same steady, objective tone.

And yet.

Most of the questions my students have about animals remain quietly unanswered in these texts. At conferences where I have presented my research, other academics inevitably direct the postlecture conversations to their own experiences with their pets. And I still have the same questions I'd always had about my own dog—and no sudden rush of answers. Science, as practiced and reified in texts, rarely addresses our experiences of living with and attempting to understand the minds of our animals.

In my first years of graduate school, when I began studying the science of the mind, with a special interest in the minds of non-human animals, it never occurred to me to study dogs. Dogs seemed so familiar, so understood. There is nothing to be learned from dogs, colleagues claimed: dogs are simple, happy creatures whom we need to train and feed and love, and that is all there is to them. There is no *data* in dogs. That was the conventional wisdom among scientists. My dissertation advisor studied, respectably, baboons: primates are the animals of choice in the field of animal cognition. The assumption is that the likeliest place to find skills and cognition approaching our own is in our primate brethren. That was, and remains, the prevailing view of behavioral scientists. Worse still, dog owners seemed to have already covered the territory of theorizing about the dog mind, and their theories were generated from anecdotes and misapplied anthropomorphisms. The very notion of the mind of a dog was tainted.

And yet.

I spent many recreational hours during my years of graduate school in California in the local dog parks and beaches with Pumpernickel. At the time I was in training as an ethologist, a scientist of animal behavior. I joined two research groups observing highly social creatures: the white rhinoceros at the Wild Animal Park in Escondido, and the bonobos (pygmy chimpanzees) at the Park and the San Diego Zoo. I learned the science of careful observations, data gathering, and statistical analysis. Over time, this way of looking began seeping into those recreational hours at the dog parks. Suddenly the dogs, with their fluent travel between their own social world and that of people, became entirely unfamiliar: I stopped seeing their behavior as simple and understood.

Where I once saw and smiled at play between Pumpernickel and the local bull terrier, I now saw a complex dance requiring mutual cooperation, split-second communications, and assessment of each other's abilities and desires. The slightest turn of a head or the point of a nose now seemed directed, meaningful. I saw dogs whose owners did not understand a single thing their dogs were doing; I saw dogs too clever for their playmates; I saw people misreading canine requests as confusion and delight as aggression. I began bringing a video camera with us and taping our outings at the parks. At home I watched the tapes of dogs playing with dogs, of people ball- and Frisbee-tossing to their dogs—tapes of chasing, fighting, petting, running, barking. With new sensitivity to the possible richness of social interactions in an entirely non-linguistic world, all of these once ordinary activities now seemed to me to be an untapped font of information. When I began watching the videos in extremely slow-motion playback, I saw behaviors I had never seen in years of living with dogs. Examined closely, simple play frolicking between two dogs became a dizzying series of synchronous behaviors, active role swapping, variations on communicative displays, flexible adaptation to others' attention, and rapid movement between highly diverse play acts.

What I was seeing were snapshots of the minds of the dogs, visible in the ways they communicated with each other and tried to communicate with the people around them—and, too, in the way they interpreted other dogs' and people's actions.

I never saw Pumpernickel—or any dog—the same way again. Far from being a killjoy on the delights of interacting with her, though, the spectacles of science gave me a rich new way to look at what she was doing: a new way to understand life as a dog.

Since those first hours of viewing, I have studied dogs at play: playing with other dogs and playing with people. At the time I was unwittingly part of a sea change taking place in science's attitude toward studying dogs. The transformation is not yet complete, but the landscape of dog research is already remarkably different than it was twenty years ago. Where once there was an inappreciable number of studies of dog cognition and behavior, there are now conferences on the dog, research groups devoted to studying the dog, experimental and ethological studies on the dog in the United States and abroad, and dog research results sprinkled through scientific journals. The scientists doing this work have seen what I have seen: the dog is a perfect entry into the study of non-human animals. Dogs have lived with human beings for thousands, maybe hundreds of thousands of years. Through the artificial selection of domestication, they have evolved to be sensitive to just those things that importantly make up our cognition, including, critically, attention to others.

In this book I introduce you to the science of the dog.

Scientists working in laboratories and in the field, studying working dogs and companion dogs, have gathered an impressive amount of information on the biology of dogs—their sensory abilities, their behavior—and on the psychology of dogs—their cognition. Drawing from the accumulated results of hundreds of research programs, we can begin to create a picture of the dog from the inside—of the skill of his nose, what he hears, how his eyes turn to us, and the brain behind it all. The dog cognition work reviewed includes my own but extends far beyond it to summarize all the results from recent research. For some topics on which there is no reliable information yet on dogs, I incorporate studies on other animals that might help us understand a dog's life, too. (For those whose appetite for the original research articles is whetted by the accounts herein, full citations appear at the book's end.)

We do no disservice to dogs by stepping away from the leash and considering them scientifically. Their abilities and point of view merit special attention. And the result is magnificent: far from being distanced by science, we are brought closer to and can marvel at the true nature of the dog. Used rigorously but creatively, the process and results of science can shed new light on discussions that people have daily about what their dog knows, understands, or believes. Through my personal journey, learning to look systemically and scientifically at my own dog's behavior, I came to have a better understanding of, appreciation of, and relationship with her.

I've gotten inside of the dog, and have glimpsed the dog's point of view. You can do the same. If you have a dog in the room with you, what you see in that great, furry pile of dogness is about to change.

From *Being a Dog*

1: Nose of a Dog

Finnegan's is ebony-black, moist, and dappled, two cavernous bass clefs at its front. Upton's is cleft with a visible valley, the whole thing guarded by short whiskers standing at attention.

These are my dogs, and these are my dogs' noses.

Before I became a research scientist studying dog cognition, I didn't think much about the dog nose. It may have been frowned at when poking impolitely at the privates of visitors to my home, or dabbed with peanut butter to encourage the swallowing of a pill. Even then, though, little regard was given to the nose itself—to its form, to its movement, to the impossibly convoluted and complex vault it opens into.

This oversight isn't restricted to dog noses. We rarely study the nose on each other's face. At the nose prominently displayed—indeed, jutting out, leading the way for the rest of the body. Without looking, try to describe your partner's nose, or your mother's. If it's not beakish or buttony, well, *it's just a nose*. Two nostrils dangling from a squashed, fleshy tetrahedron.

I gaze at my son's nose, but mostly at its surface—where the freckles have begun to assemble on his fair skin. But the snout of the dog gets my full attention. Now I look at dogs nose-first. For I am besotted with dogs, and to know a dog is to be interested in what it's like to be a dog. And that all begins with the nose.

What the dog sees and knows comes through his nose, and the information that every dog—the tracking dog, of course, but also the dog lying next to you, snoring, on the couch—has about the world based on smell is unthinkably rich. It is rich in a way we humans once knew about, once acted on, but have since neglected.

By smelling, tapping into this sensory resource that we have but that we largely ignore, the dog has become an informant. Working dogs, trained to tell us what they naturally know, detect the presence of illegal substances and unwanted pests. But the dog also knows about the upcoming weather, the way afternoon smells, and whether you are sick or upset. Every inhaled gulp of air is full of information. It holds the odors of people who have recently passed by, leaving olfactory trails in their wake. It catches pollens and plant notes carried on the breeze. Each noseful captures the traces of animals who have walked, run, cowered, eaten, or died nearby. It traps the electric charge and round humid molecules from distant rainstorms.

This book is an exploration of what the dog's nose knows as has never been done before. What does your dog smell on you, on the ground, or with his nose deep in the fur of another dog? What does he know about you—that you might not know yourself? What is it like to smell the world with that amazing nose leading the dog through his days?

To find out, I tracked the tracking dogs. Over the last years I have watched detection dogs grow up, be trained, and find their quarry, be it drugs, food, or people. With my Dog Cognition Lab at Barnard College, I have researched the pet dog's experience of himself, other dogs, and the smells of the human world in which he lives. I have spoken to scientists who study and model the dog nose, and to trainers and handlers who follow it. It is an examination of all aspects of the dog's olfactory world, and the magnificent organ that leads to it.

But it is also an exploration of the noses on *our* faces. We have untrained ourselves, we humans—unlearned how to smell, over millennia. We are out of the habit of smelling. Why, you may not even have smelled this book yet, though it is but inches from your face. I find people who are smelling, and practice their methods.

Having myself committed a lifetime of not smelling, I let my dogs' behavior counsel me: I have ventured to be a little more like a dog myself. In my book *Inside of a Dog* I began an imaginative leap into what it might be like to be a dog—and here I leap with four feet. I try to take my nose to the places the dog nose goes. And I sniff.

I begin this process by learning more about our own sense of smell. And then I train my nose to better conjure what it might be like to have the mind and nose of a dog.

My inspiration and guides are our family's own dogs, Finnegan and Upton. Both are highly charismatic mutts. My husband

and I met Finnegan's nose through the bars of a crate at a shelter that imports unwanted dogs from the South. He was four months old, had had ringworm and parvovirus, and, though recovering, was skinny and a bit sickly. I should say that I don't go to shelters much, because when I do, I inevitably walk out with a new animal. When I first saw him, in that crate at eye level, he wagged mightily, accepted a finger poked through the bars for licking, poked his nose through reciprocally, and then, as we moved on, sat down patiently. I looked back at him often: he was sitting and . . . waiting. We took him out of the crate to meet him, and he moved between my husband and me, looking at each of us in the face. Weary, he leaned against me. That was that. We took him home.

Finn is now eight years older. He still has the look of that puppy who leaned. While his coat is a glossy black, as though we polish him daily, it is his way of *looking* that most captures him. One gets the feeling that he is always aware of what is happening. His eyes penetrate us. They follow us, they check with us when another animal is misbehaving, they look to us dolefully when we head out the door. Ears back, eyes full, he is hard to leave. He does not look simply with his eyes: his nose examines us. When we return home, he sniffs us, as close as we will let him, in an exploration of where we've gone, what we've eaten, whom we've touched or pet. Never have I returned home, having met a dog on the street, and escaped Finn's examination.

I tend to think of Finn as a "professional dog." He is eminently civilized: without our explicitly teaching him, he fell into line with what we expect from a dog in the house. He swallowed the little culture of our family whole. Upton, by contrast, whom we met three years into his life, is feral by comparison. He had been relinquished to the shelter from which he was initially adopted three years prior. We've seen his first photos: a small-bodied hound, ears too large for his head. Nose a blur. Well, his head and body grew up: he's a large, brindle, hound mix, with full eyes and a corkscrew tail. Whiskers punctuate his snout; his jowls droop. He is a dog's dog, incurably friendly with any dog, and has a gangly, goofy run. There is no photo of Upton in which he looks streamlined, athletic, or svelte. In running, his jowls flap, he tilts, his ears go akimbo. He is generously silly. Alas, he was also not a city dog before we knew him, and he is easily startled by every and any sound—car door, garbage truck, garage door opening, street sign shaking in the wind, jackhammer, a bag flapping in a tree, a person suddenly appearing from around the corner . . . you name it. For this reason, while I have followed both of their noses to whatever sundry and sordid spots they're smelling, it is only Finn who I bring out to do new investigative smelling work. He could half write this book himself.

Take a breath (through the nose, please). We are going on a journey through scents and smelling, with a tour through the improbable science about the olfactory abilities of the dog—and the abilities of our own noses, waiting for us to discover them. By following the dog's lead, we can learn from him about what we are missing—some of which is beyond our ability to sense, and some of which we simply need a guide to see. The world abounds with aromas, but we are spectacleless. The dog can serve as our spectacles.

In so doing, we may also see how to return to that perhaps more primal, so-called animal state of knowledge about ourselves and the world that we have forgotten in a culture wrought of technology and lab tests. To follow animals is to become more attuned to our own existence. To follow dogs is to begin to apprehend the experience of our silent, loyal partners through our days.